PORTIA
ZVAVAHERA

ZVAKAZARURWA

PORTIA ZVAVAHERA
ZVAKAZARURWA

Kettle's Yard, Cambridge
22.10.24–16.02.25
Fruitmarket, Edinburgh
01.03.25–25.05.25

Curated by
Tamar Garb

With thanks to
Stevenson
and David Zwirner

Cover image:
Pane rima rakakomba (1)
(There's too much darkness)
2023 (detail)

Published by

Fruitmarket
45 Market St.
Edinburgh
EH1 1DF
www.fruitmarket.co.uk

and

Kettle's Yard
University of Cambridge
Castle St.
Cambridge
CB3 0AQ
www.kettlesyard.cam.ac.uk

Publication supported by
David Zwirner

ISBN978-1-904561-70-5

Edited by Fiona Bradley

Publication designed
and typeset by
Elizabeth McLean
Assisted by Susan Gladwin

Distributed in the UK, Europe
and the rest of the world by
ACC Art Books
Riverside House, Dock Lane
Melton, Woodbridge
Suffolk, IP12 1PE
accartbooks.com

KETTLE'S YARD

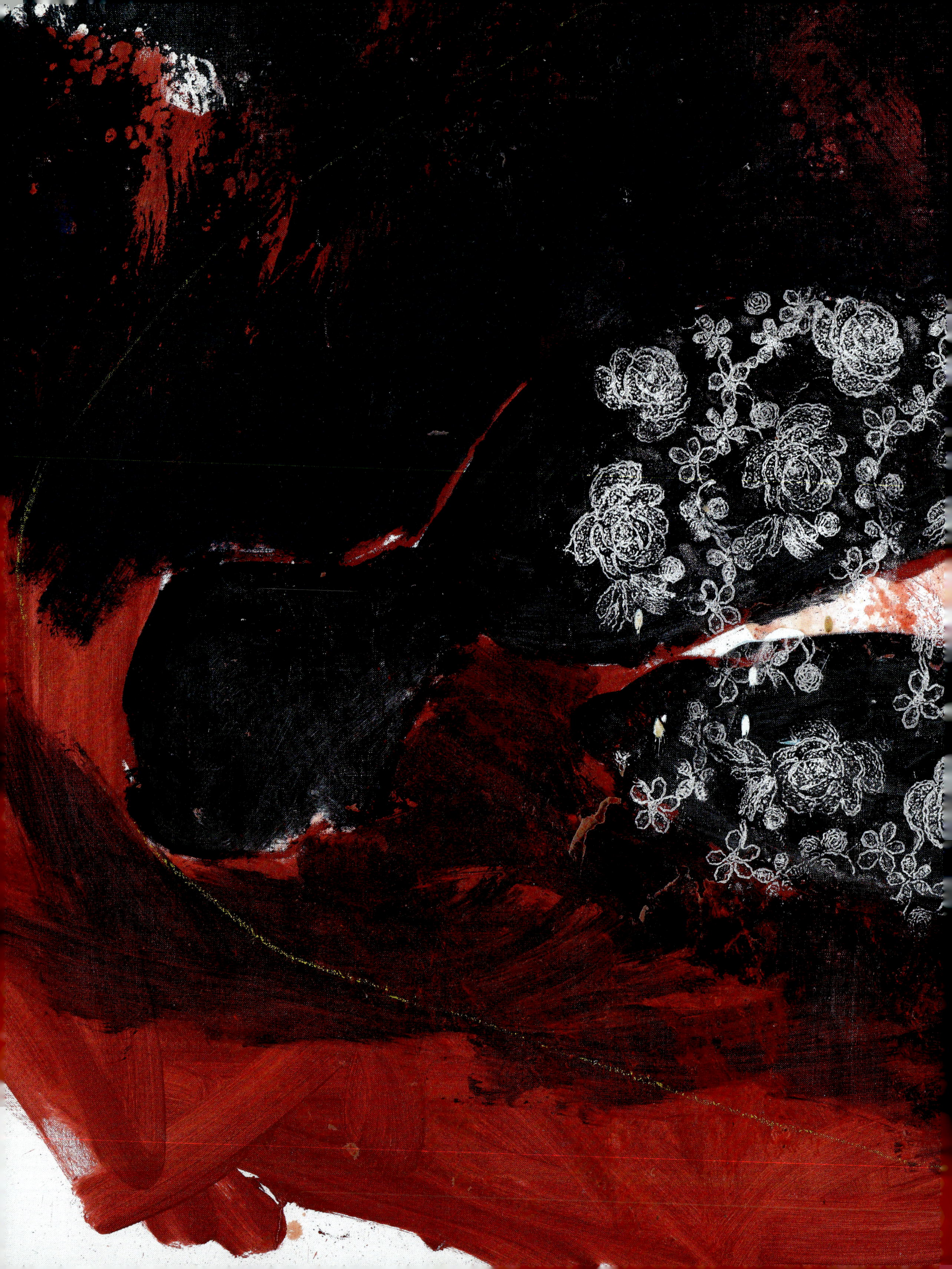

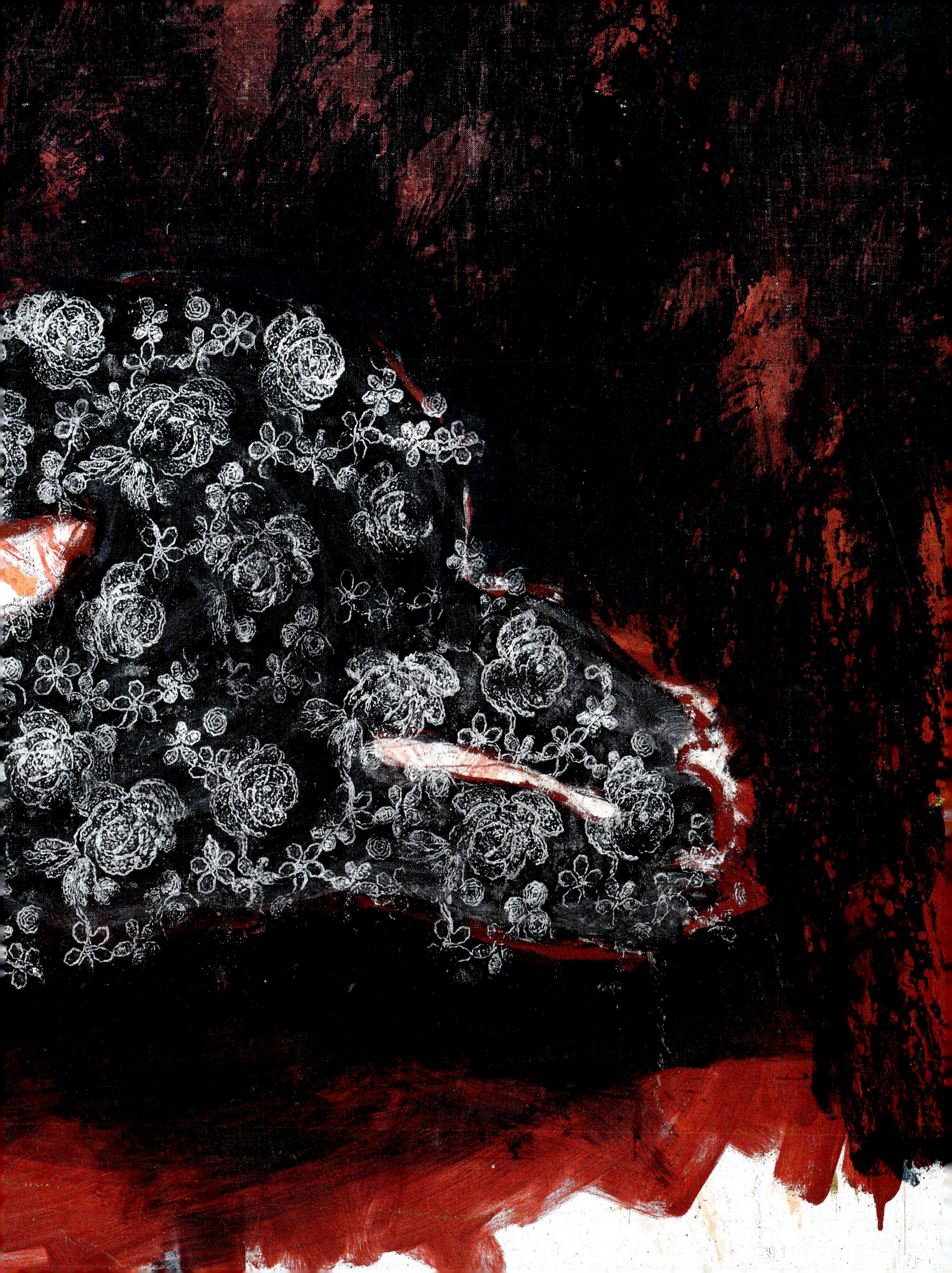

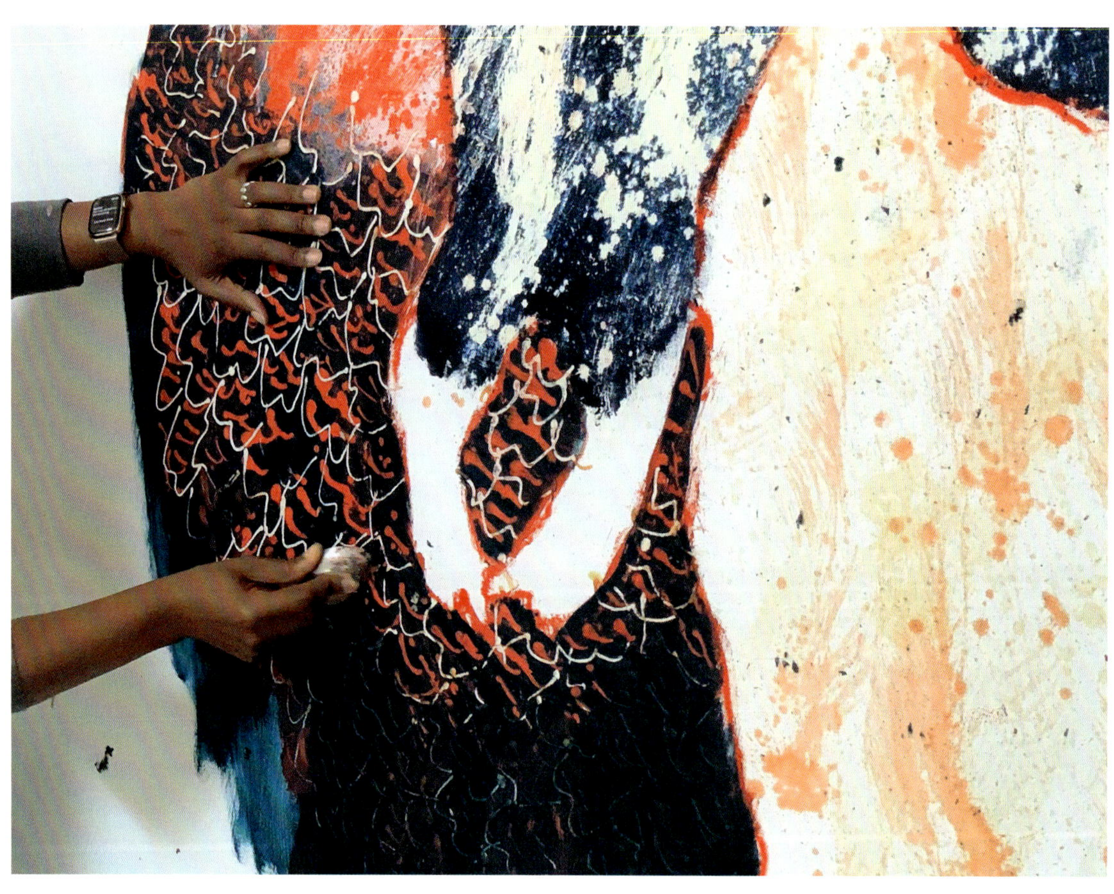

INTRODUCTION

FIONA BRADLEY AND ANDREW NAIRNE

previous:
Hide There
2024 (detail)
Oil-based printing
ink and oil bar on linen

opposite:
Portia Zvavahera
working on
Lifted Away
in the studio,
Harare, 2024

Portia Zvavahera's paintings weave new worlds from her dreams. Her rich, densely patterned, intensely coloured surfaces invite the viewer into a visually seductive personal cosmology featuring figures, creatures, shapes and shadows that first come to her in the night. Her work is autobiographical and essentially figurative, but she taps into that register of representation that we may recognise from our own dreaming – that odd understanding that we are seeing something (our own self, our home, an animal, a friend) that we know, but while it definitely is that thing that we know, it does not necessarily always look like it, or always look the same from one dream to another.

Zvavahera was born in Harare, Zimbabwe in 1985, and still lives there, working from a studio in her home, the paintings grounded in her natural as well as supernatural surroundings. This exhibition, titled *Zvakazarurwa*, is – somewhat incredibly given the international acclaim her work has received in recent years, evidenced in her prominence in the 59th Venice Biennale exhibition, *The Milk of Dreams* in 2022 – her first solo exhibition in public galleries in Europe.

Zvakazarurwa means 'revelations' in Shona, the language in which she thinks and dreams, and is curated by Tamar Garb, a recognised authority on contemporary art from Africa as well as the work of women artists and feminist aesthetics. Garb has followed Zvavahera's practice for some years, and made several visits to her studio in the course of preparing the exhibition, talking with her about her work and selecting together a sequence of paintings that root the most recent in the evolution of her image making since 2012. The earliest works in the exhibition combine images of childbirth and motherhood with repetitive mark making and pattern. They are visceral, even shocking. Their immediacy of affect is continued in works that follow and is developed rather than diluted in the very latest canvases, for example *Hide There* (2024) in which a figure kneels alone, her face obscure, her body covered up in lace. Above her lurk a group of menacing rats, kept away by a feathery wing. We know from conversations with the artist that the figure represents herself, and that the rats are malign forces threatening her and her family that visit her in her dreams and must be fought off through painting. Lace – made by printing from fragments of lace directly on to the surface of the painting – recalls a bride's veil, and is understood by Zvavahera as a protective shield.

Studio view, Harare, 2024

Hide There was made this year and is part of a group of paintings completed by the artist especially for this exhibition. They were taking shape in the studio during Garb's visits, and she – and we – have been able to observe the process of their making: Zvavahera's distinctive combination of painting and print-making techniques, employing ink, oil bar and wax, from which each work is made. Zvavahera works on several paintings at once, developing the imagery from a particular dream over several canvases, and it has been a privilege to see this sequence come into being.

These paintings of 2024 relate to *Pane rima rakakomba (1)* (There's too much darkness, 2023) and respond to the same dream. *Pane rima rakakomba* was shown as part of Zvavahera's exhibition of the same name at Stevenson in Cape Town in South Africa in the summer of 2023 and was the focus of the conversation Garb convened about Zvavahera's work between herself and Sinazo Chiya, Tandazani Dhlakama and Pumla Gobodo-Madikizela that features in this book. It is an extraordinarily rich conversation that draws on each woman's particular experience and knowledge and situates Zvavahera's painting in multiple contemporary and historical Zimbabwean, African and international contexts.

We are enormously grateful to Tamar Garb for convening this vital conversation, for curating the exhibition so superbly in dialogue with the artist and ourselves, and for her insightful essay for this publication. Hers is a sensitive, profoundly knowledgeable, scholarly yet accessible approach, and we thank her for letting us all share in her understanding of Portia Zvavahera's

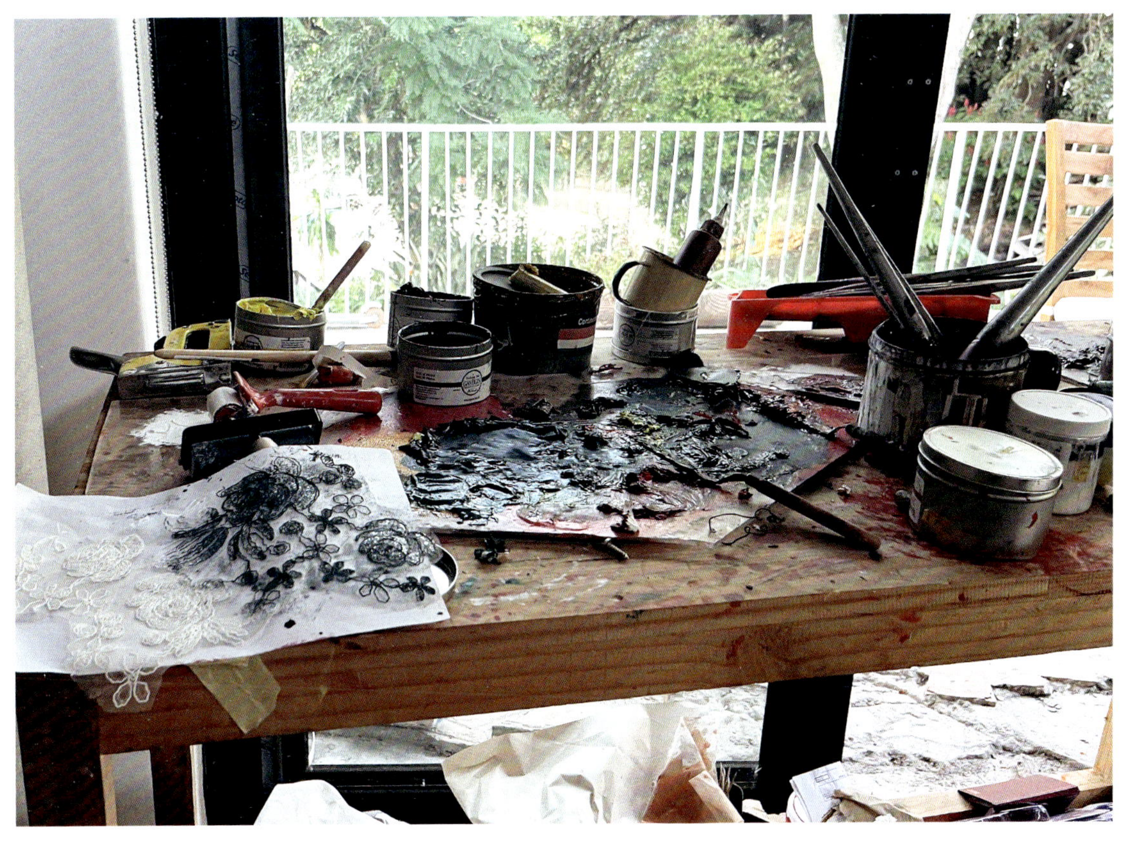

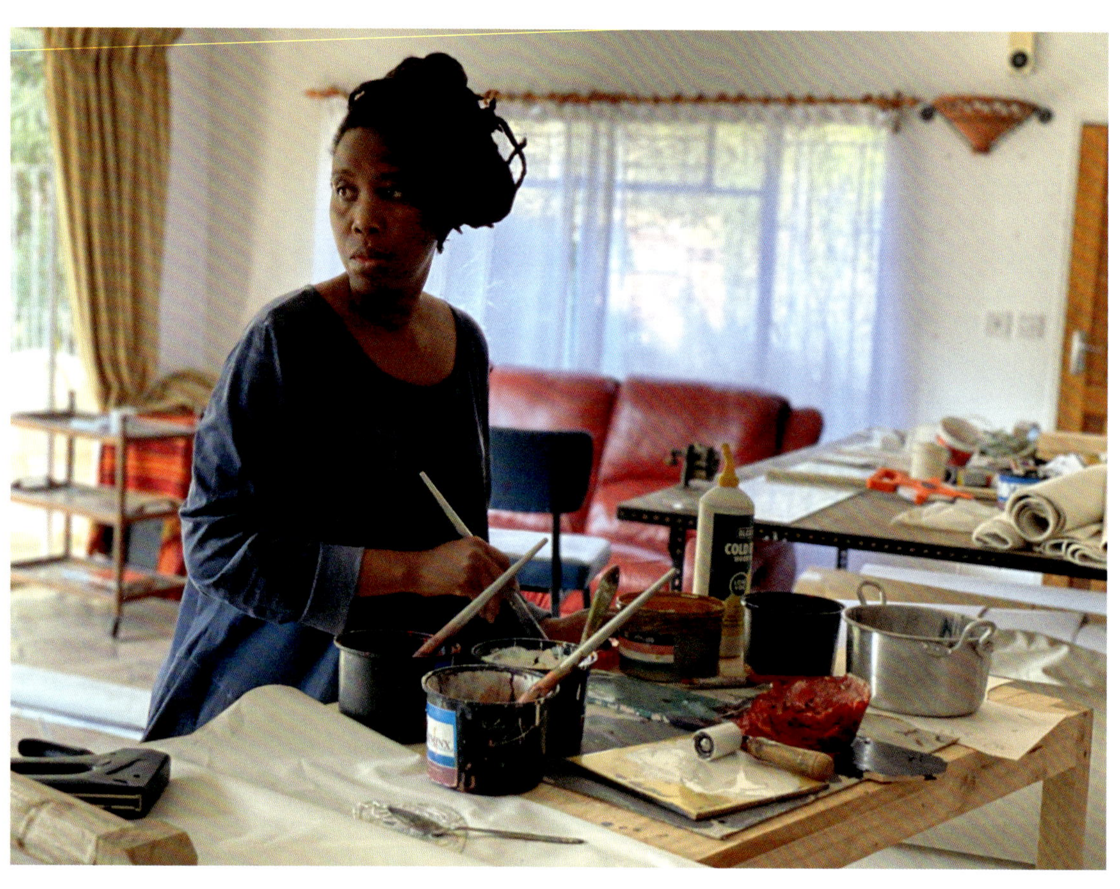

opposite:
Studio view,
Harare

overleaf:
Lifted Away
2024
Oil-based printing
ink and oil bar on linen
214 × 385 cm

work; for enabling the exhibition and this publication to benefit from her recent research as well as her long-standing expertise.

In developing and presenting *Zvakazarurwa* we have relied on the support of a great many people. We thank in particular Michael Stevenson, Sophie Perryer and David Brodie at Stevenson in Cape Town; and David Zwirner, Rodolphe von Hofmannsthal and Eve Baer Reilly at David Zwirner in London. We are grateful to the lenders to the exhibition who have shared their love of Zvavahera's work with us and agreed to part with precious paintings from their collections for the exhibitions in Cambridge and Edinburgh. As always, a new exhibition and publication and the success of our associated public programmes relies on the talent and dedication of our respective teams, while the bold and elegant design of this book is due to the skill of Elizabeth McLean, Deputy Director at Fruitmarket. Thank you to all.

These are difficult times for public galleries, and to make a project of this ambition happen we rely on the financial support we receive from our public funders, Arts Council England and Creative Scotland, and the enlightened generosity of our regular patrons and supporters. They understand the value of what we do and the importance of providing free access to culture, enabling a wide range of audiences to share in the work of the world's best artists. Their continued support enables us to plan and make the forward commitment to artists that ambitious programmes depend on. In addition to their vital support, this exhibition has also received generous help from David Zwirner, and from Mercedes Vilardell. We have been delighted to bring together supporter circles for the exhibition in both Kettle's Yard and Fruitmarket, and we thank them also for their commitment to Zvavahera's work, and to ours.

Above all, we are grateful to Portia Zvavahera. For her astonishingly accomplished, intelligent and beautiful paintings; for her generous spirit and for her willingness to share her singular vision with us all.

Fiona Bradley, Director, Fruitmarket, Edinburgh
Andrew Nairne, Director, Kettle's Yard, Cambridge

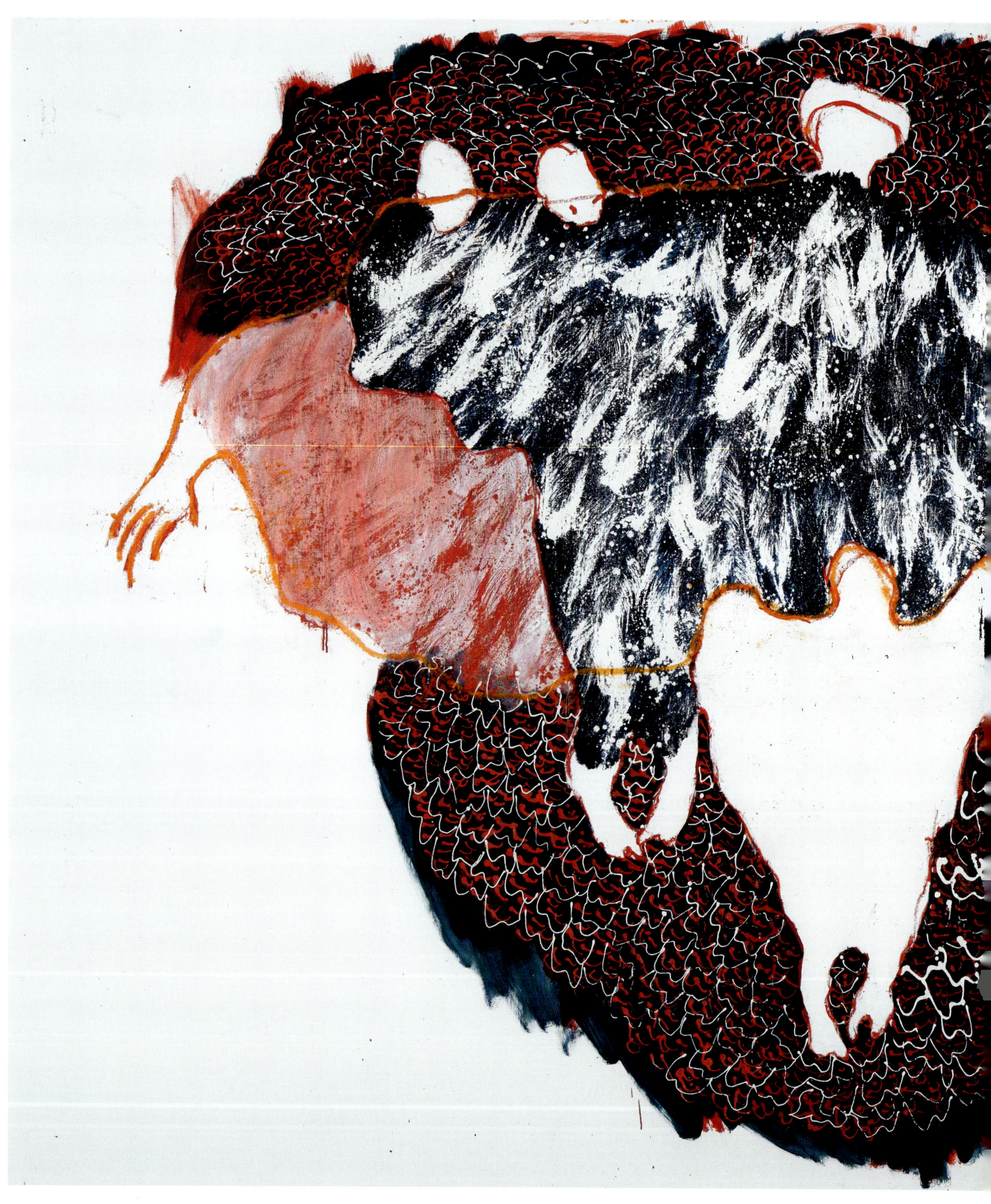

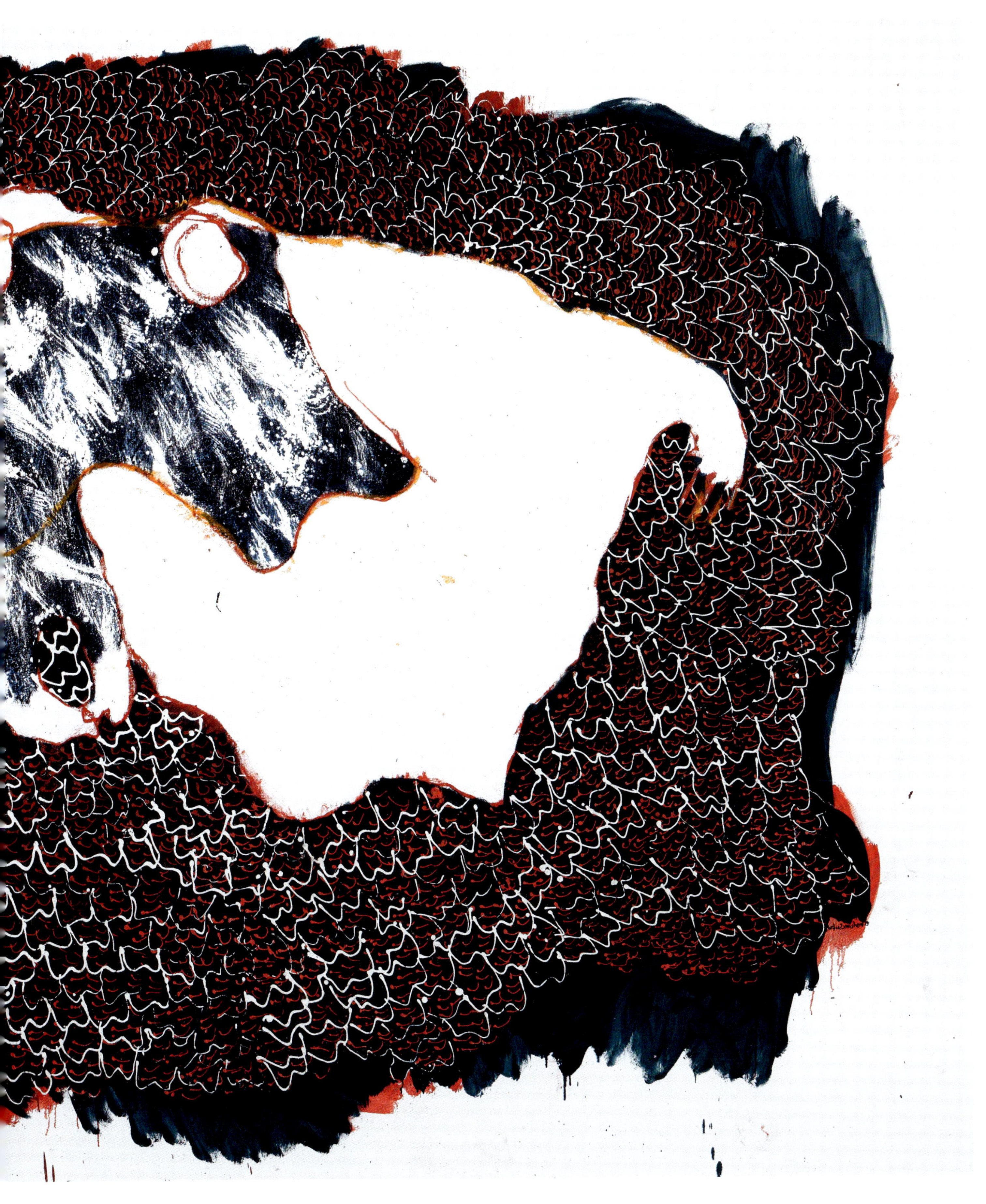

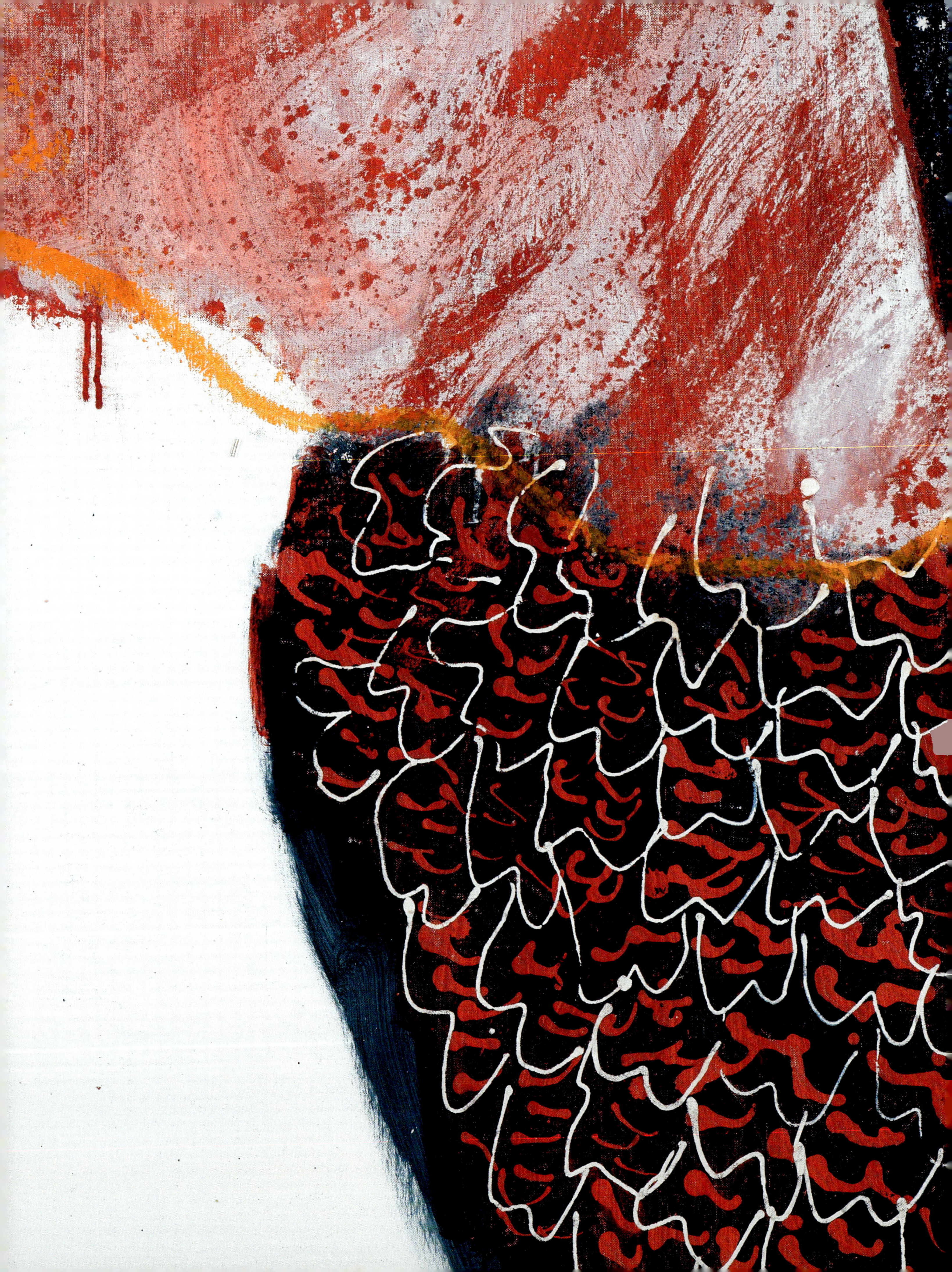

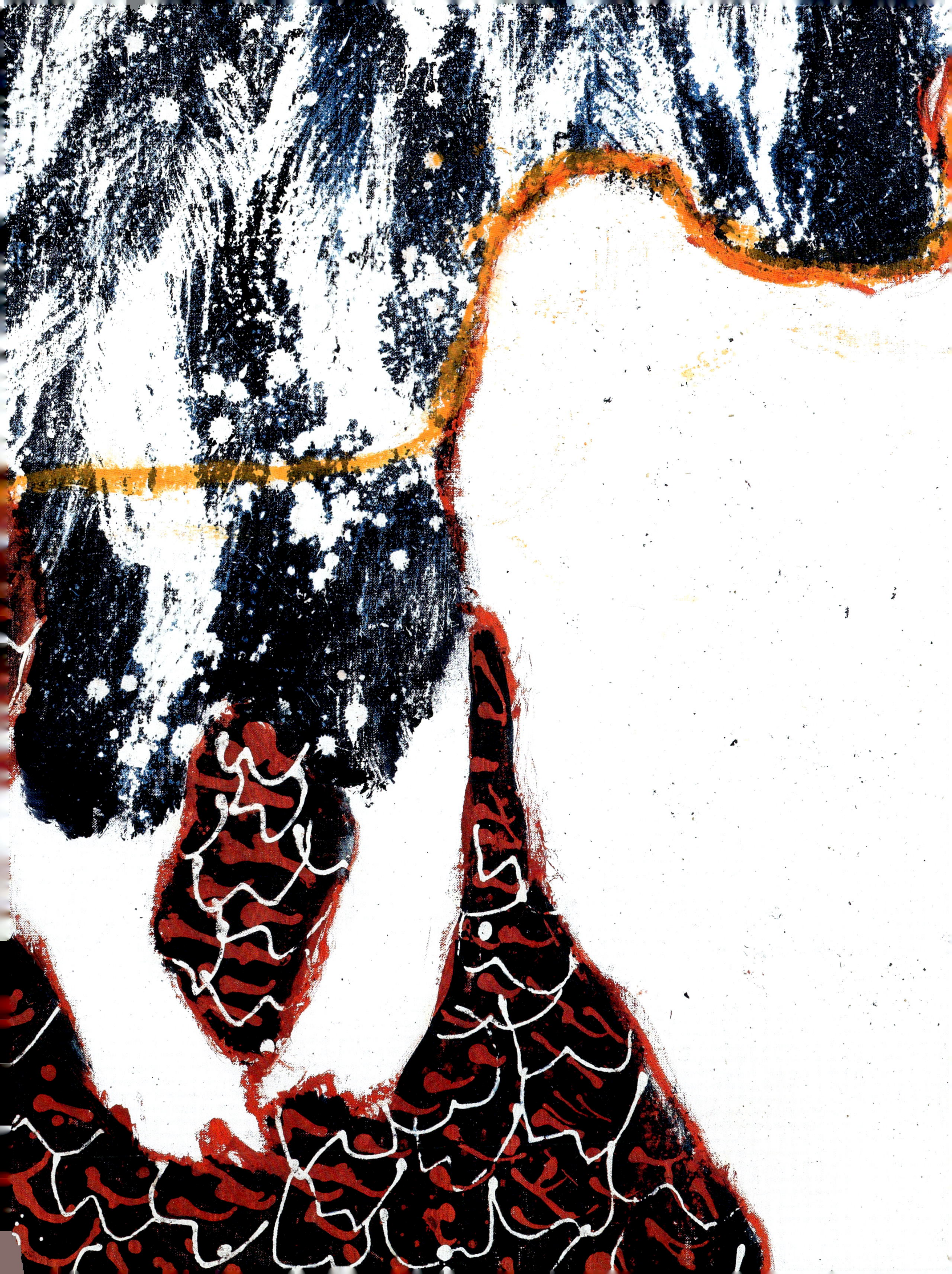

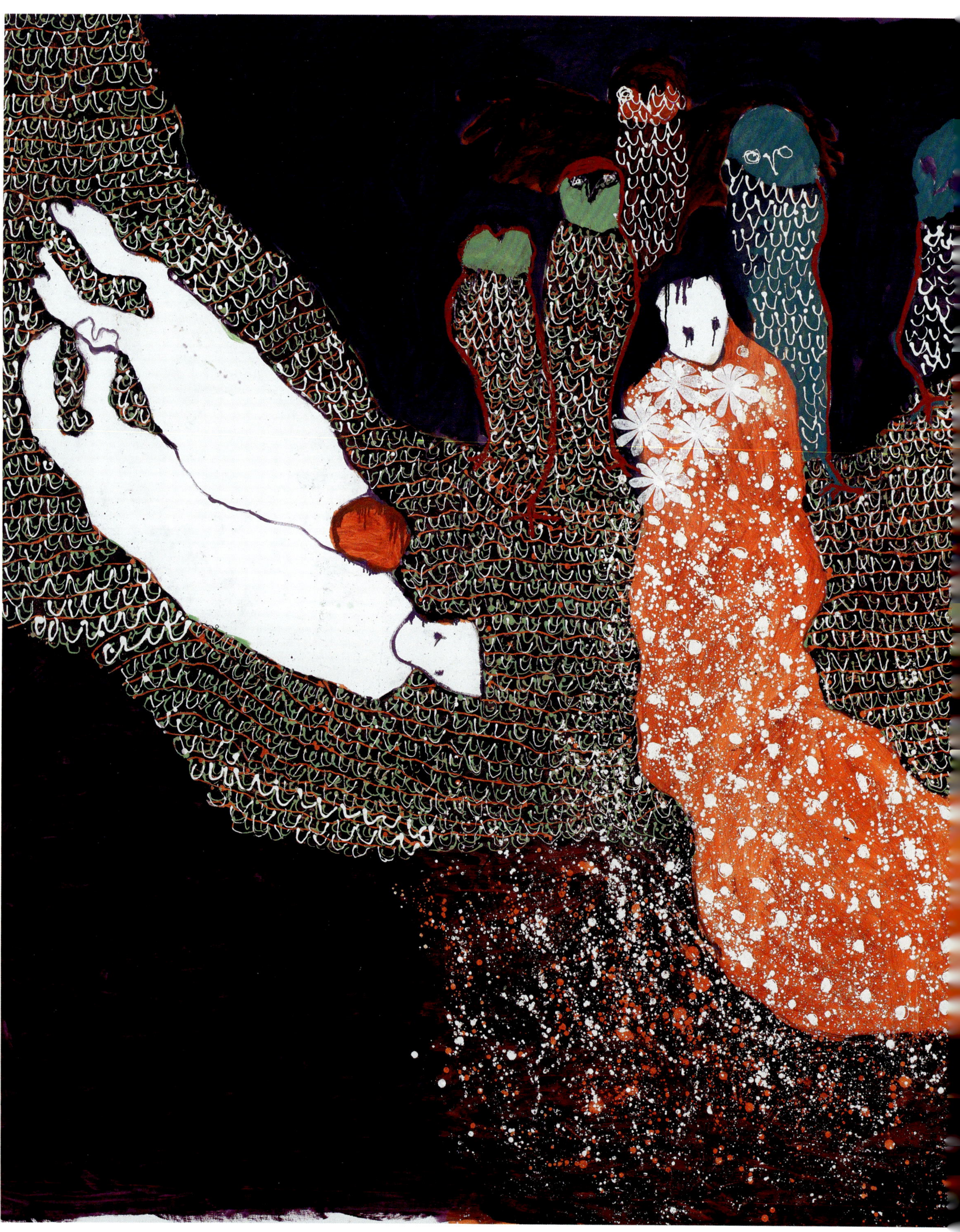

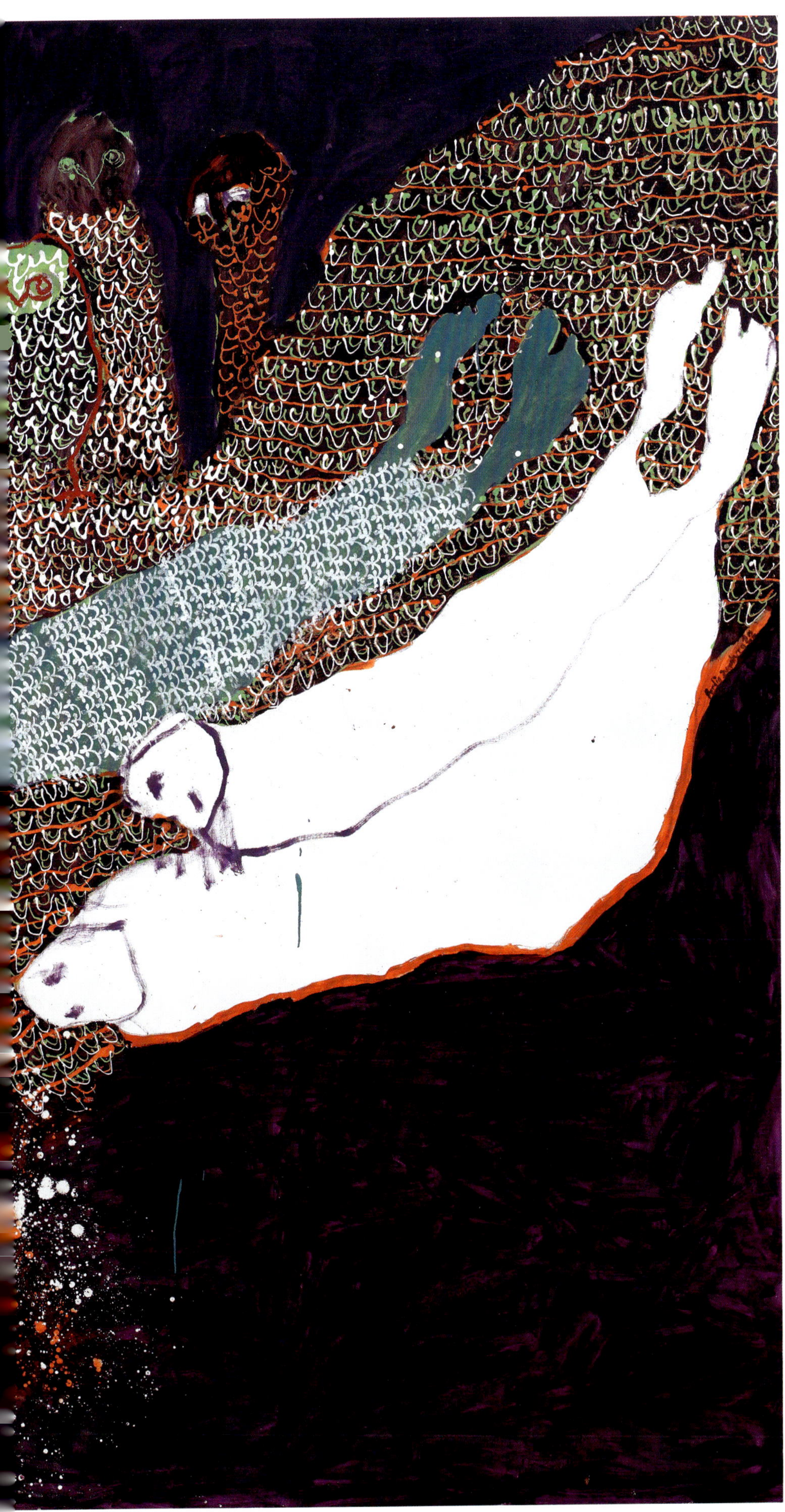

Kudonhedzwa kwevanhu
(Fallen people)
2022
Oil-based printing
ink and oil bar on linen
212.5 × 299.6 cm

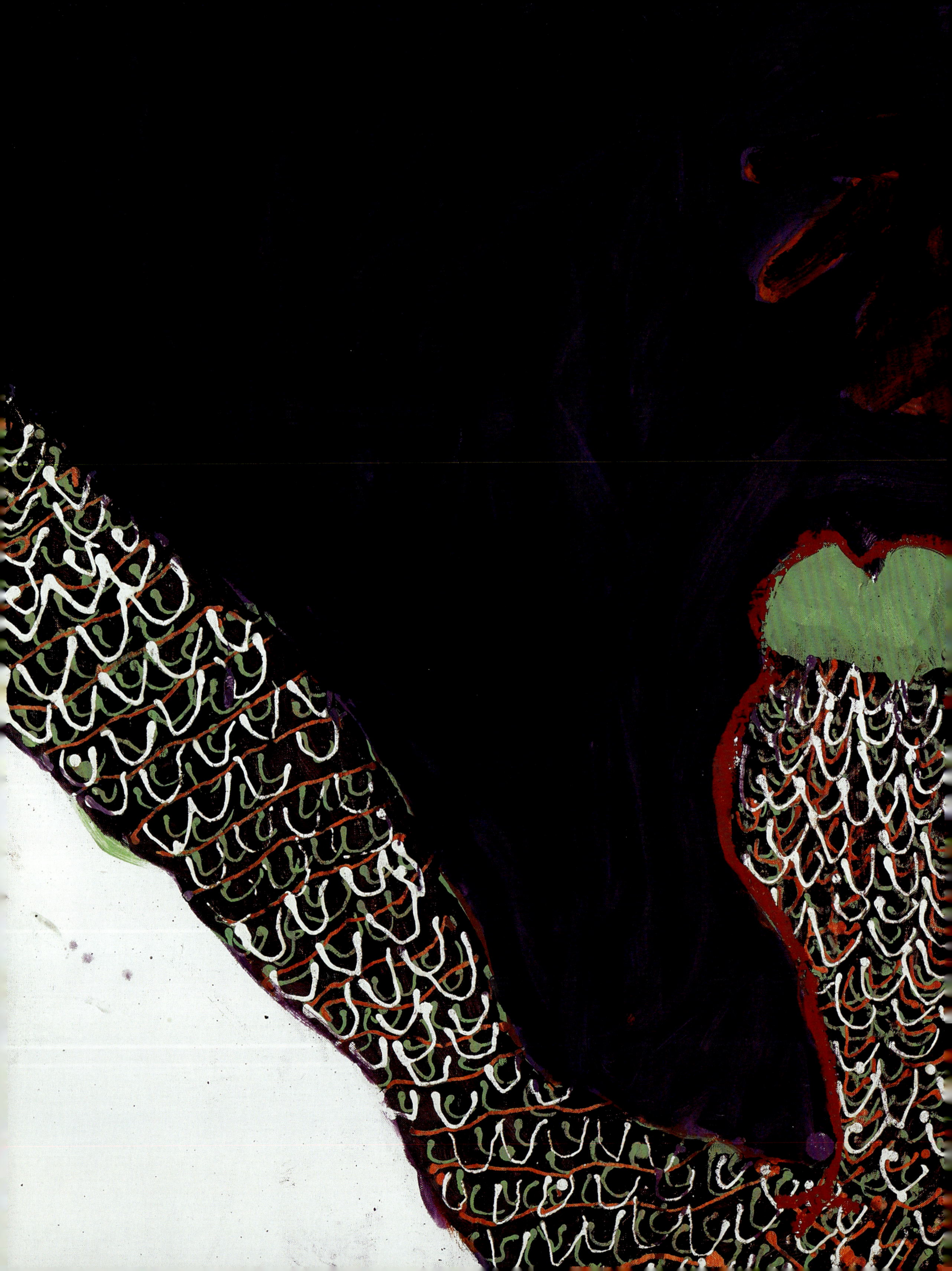

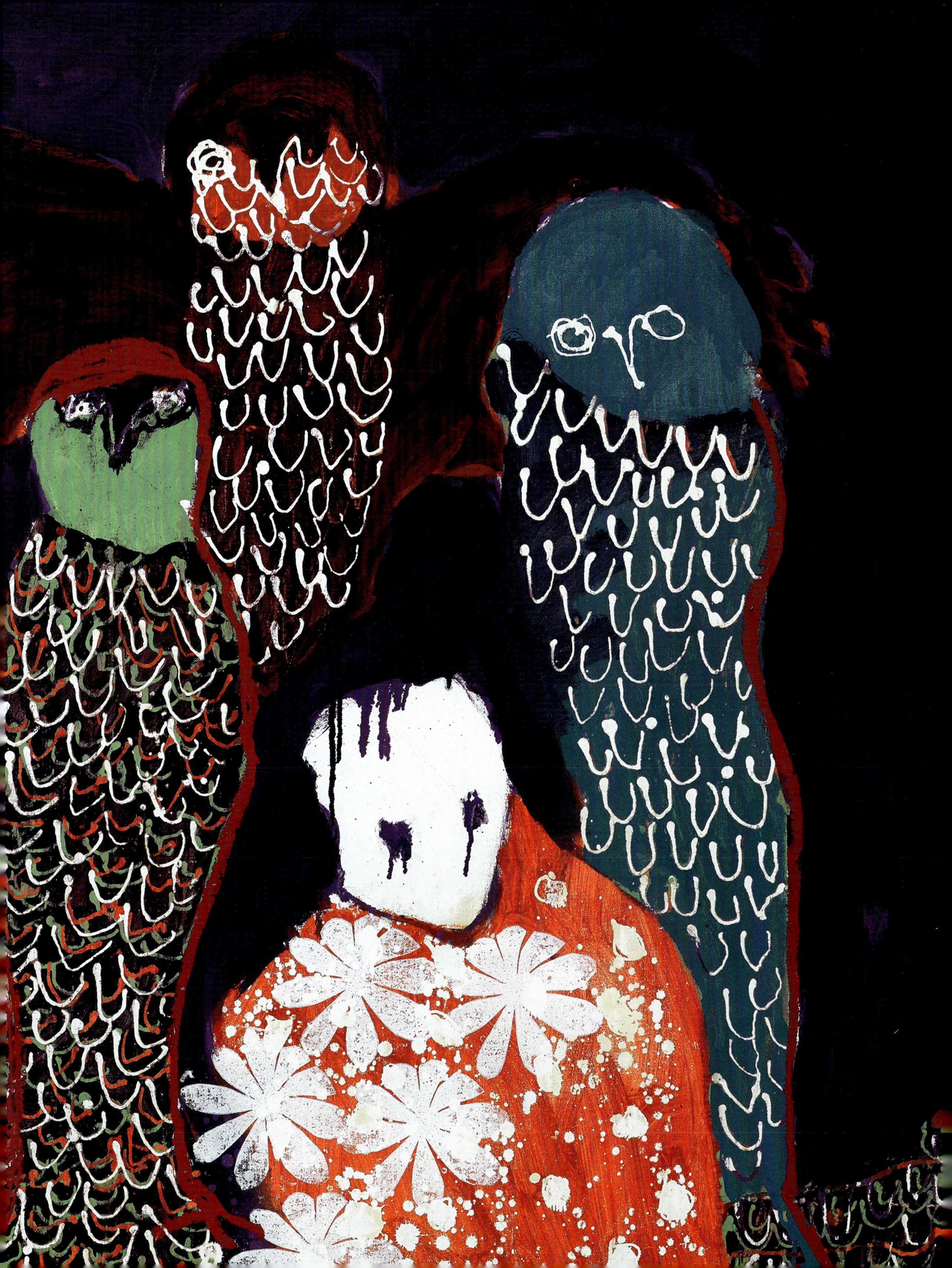

PAINTING/PRINTING AND THE POETICS OF REVELATION

TAMAR GARB

I'm always thinking in Shona. Even as I am speaking right now,
I'm thinking in Shona. The English titles come because people want
to understand what I mean. I dream in Shona and everything is Shona.
Portia Zvavahera in conversation with Sinazo Chiya (2017)[1]

Portia Zvavahera insisted on titling this show in Shona, her mother tongue. Like everything in her work, the result is a slow reveal. For those of us who don't speak the language, it is the musicality and shape of the word *Zvakazarurwa*, its phonetic repetitions and rhythms, its spacing of consonants and vowels, that strikes us first. We must rely on the English translation (Revelations) to move beyond the materiality and resonance of the noun and disclose something of what it means to suggest: from the overt reference to Christian theology and the promise it holds for the faithful, to the intimation that we are living in the plural. We are in the realm of 'revelations', a word that suggests the apocalyptic 'Book of Revelation' but extends and exceeds its specificity, leading us into dense and pluriversal[2] encounters across cultures and contexts, practices and languages, belief systems and ways of life.

Intimating the final book of the Christian Bible, also known as 'The Book of the Apocalypse', in Shona rather than in ancient Greek or translated into English, is to acknowledge the particularity and peculiarity of its point of reception and repurposing. The bible is mediated and materialised in place and time. In the contact zone of erstwhile colonialism and missionary entanglement in southern Africa, where English became the *lingua franca*, the scriptures come face to face with local and ancestral cosmologies. They are re-formed by Shona-speaking actors and agents whose ways of worship, philosophical outlook and relationship to time, cannot be subsumed into an exclusively Western epistemology or worldview.[3] But nor does this suggest the counterpart of an homogenous or autochthonous 'indigeneity'. For Shona-speaking communities, which comprise the vast majority of the current population of Zimbabwe, are themselves historically split into various ethnic groups, once codified and corralled by settlers and missionaries into an artificial unity centring around a common system of writing that was required by ecclesiastical and colonial bureaucracies, and later weaponised by the post-independence government of Robert Mugabe in the interests of an ethno-essentialist construction of identity.[4] Language and politics are always intertwined and while Shona cosmology proffers an alternative vantage point from which to look, it does not provide a ready-made tradition or unified identity that is fixed or stuck in the past. Like all culture it is constantly reforming and reshaping itself in dialogic and disputatious encounter – it is porous, palimpsestic and provisional. To invoke *Zvakazarurwa*, therefore, is not only to be in the space of translation – an abstract and theoretical zone suggesting the relativity and contingency of meaning – but is also to speak from a specific and shifting locus of power, faith, ritual, narrative and experience, which the intertwined practices of painting/printing/praying come to embody and express.

Portia Zvavahera is Harare based and raised. Her rootedness in Shona language and culture goes hand in hand with her exposure, via secular education and the Pentecostal church, to an ethos that is always and already woven from multiple sources and stories. Educated like all Zimbabwean children of her generation in the colonially-derived English school system, with its maths and science, English and history, art classes and home economics, she also learned from her grandmother's and mother's mouths and ways, the lessons and languages of her people. An English-medium schooling co-habits with a vernacular and domestic life that invokes diverse logics and linguistic codes. Shona itself is a language that is steeped in metaphor and analogy, its recourse to proverbs, constructed as bipartite aphorisms, encoding a folk wisdom and epistemology that complements and counters the reasoning and common sense of the West.[5] Here separations between the spirit and physical worlds, perceivable and unperceivable reality, human and non-human animals, sleeping and waking states, are neither rigidly nor securely policed and the metaphysical permeates the material in strange and often mystifying ways. Captured in a typical Shona proverb is a worldview that retains the mystery of life while acknowledging the principle of causality:

kune chauraya zizi harifi nemhepo
(something has caused the death of the owl; it does not die of the wind)

A creature dies. The cause is unknown. But the logic of causation is implicit. The symmetry and poetic balance of the proverb, its use of parallelism and repetition of syllables and sounds, as well as its deceptive simplicity and figural distillation of forces (animal, elemental, temporal) produces a concatenation of concepts: life and death, nature and the supernatural, fact and speculative fiction.

Central to Shona proverbs and folklore is the use of imagery and visual metaphors. Crucial too is the poetics of the dream, conceived as an interface between life on Earth and a life or being beyond. Like Christian parables and fables, the narrative content of dreams and stories provides a pretext for a hidden message or meaning that takes time to be revealed or understood. The manifest content of the dream, in Freudian language, screens its latent or underlying meaning from the dreamer.[6] For Zvavahera, the divine appears in the visions that materialise in the half-conscious state of sleep, when often cryptic and coded communications are literalised in human and non-human form with sometimes terrifying and inexplicable power. The dream, she avows, is the vehicle through which God speaks. But the work of the artist is to contend with a form of communication that is both veiled and abstruse.

Only in the working and reworking of elements of the dream, extracting, filtering, exploring and materialising their parameters, can its potential for prophecy and prophylaxis be gradually and painstakingly uncovered. The revelation is the work/labour of art: it is not known in advance, it is not guaranteed or foreseen and it is only recognised after the fact.

The path from dream to painting is a laborious one. It is not a matter of transcription or illustration. There is no attempt to recreate the story of the dream as a sequential narrative event. Rather, its exploration requires a kind of submission, akin to prayer, which allows the ambiguous imagery and concentrated energy of the dream and its prophetic content to speak.

The process starts with the writing down of the dream and the sketching of its elements and forms in a private and personalised kind of visual diary. This is an attempt to hold on to the dream, to retain and rescue its elements from the darkness and remain within its powerful aura. It's a defence against forgetting. The dream needs to be integrated into waking life as a store or archive of energy, the source of which is unscripted and obscure. Through surrender and immersion, the dream takes shape as form, often abstracted and distilled, always mediated via the learned languages of art. But perhaps it is art that invents the dream rather than the other way round. For the dream is recoverable only in the process of representation, itself neither neutral nor pure. And the line between nocturnal and diurnal imaginings is never fixed or secure.

For Zvavahera, a powerful dream can be the basis of many paintings. Take for example *Pane rima rakakomba (1)* (There's too much darkness, 2023, pp.26–27, 90–1, 93, 94), a monumental work based on a nightmare that the artist had during pregnancy, and whose thematics and energy are explored in a number of recent works. In this dream, rats and other menacing creatures appear to advance on a sleeping woman. They are totems of dread and destruction that have to be contained and neutralised by being captured and conquered in paint. Like almost all animals in Zvavahera's image bank, rats embody threat and danger. In *Pane rima rakakomba (1)*, the long-tailed, purple rodents bear down on the reclining figure, a surrogate for the artist herself. They are shadowy, sketched-in creatures, half-hidden in the patterned expanse, while eerily and ominously present. They are harbingers and carriers of doom. But to offset their threatening advance, Zvavahera includes the cradling figure of a kneeling, winged angel, arm elongated and outstretched to underpin the prostrate and swollen body of the woman. Familiar in shape and attitude (notwithstanding her expressively stretched-out limb), the angel appears culled from late medieval Christian imaginary, suggesting the Duccios and Giottos of the past. So too does the all-over patterned effect of the surface with its repeated leaves and sinuous lines, flattened shapes and abstracted bodies, as in the four supplicating creatures who seem to be united in prayer. These figural types are received and re-made, like the gospels, in new and unprecedented ways.

Subsumed into Zvavahera's decorative schema, which is colour-saturated and intense, these figures appear to be drawn from the emplaced unconscious and inner life of the situated subject/artist whilst also stemming from inherited pictorial and painterly traditions.

The overall effect of the work is achieved through Zvavahera's unique process of making. Her method integrates both painting and printing techniques and proceeds through layering, applying and subtracting materials, painstakingly and methodically over time. The whole composition is first brushed in with strokes of oil-based printing ink or drawn with oil bar crayon onto an outstretched canvas that lies quite loosely on the floor. Only once the design is mapped and laid out is the work raised to the vertical and pinned to a board or wall. After layers of ink are applied in large areas so that they drip and flow with gravity, the canvas is returned to the floor for the application of molten wax, applied with a batik tool called a tjanting, to create a network of marks and stains. These are later revealed through the scraping off and removal of the wax. Using the back of an old metal spoon, Zvavahera pushes and pulls at her surface, rhythmically, laboriously, so that the earlier tones and tints seep through. Sometimes a domestic iron is also used to melt and remove the wax. The method is of veiling and unveiling, covering and disclosing until the unified effect is achieved. In the end, the overall rhythm of a filigreed pattern of marks appears offset by the liquidity of the inky washes whose layered tones are exposed at the edges of the canvas: we see the underlying pink and the overlaid purple of the piece, together creating a warm and expansive environment for the coloured cloaks of the supplicating figures in front.

By the time Zvavahera came to produce this pivotal painting, she had been experimenting with the combination of painting and printing techniques for more than a decade. Earlier works such as *Embraced and Protected in You* (2016, pp.58–59) or *Tavingwa Nezvehusiku* (2018, pp.28–31) include her characteristic bold shapes and sinuous contour lines, but at the same time large areas of the works' surfaces are overlaid with repeated motifs, achieved with cut-out stencils onto which ink is rolled before they are pressed and printed onto the canvas in carefully demarcated zones. The overall effect is of transparent veils

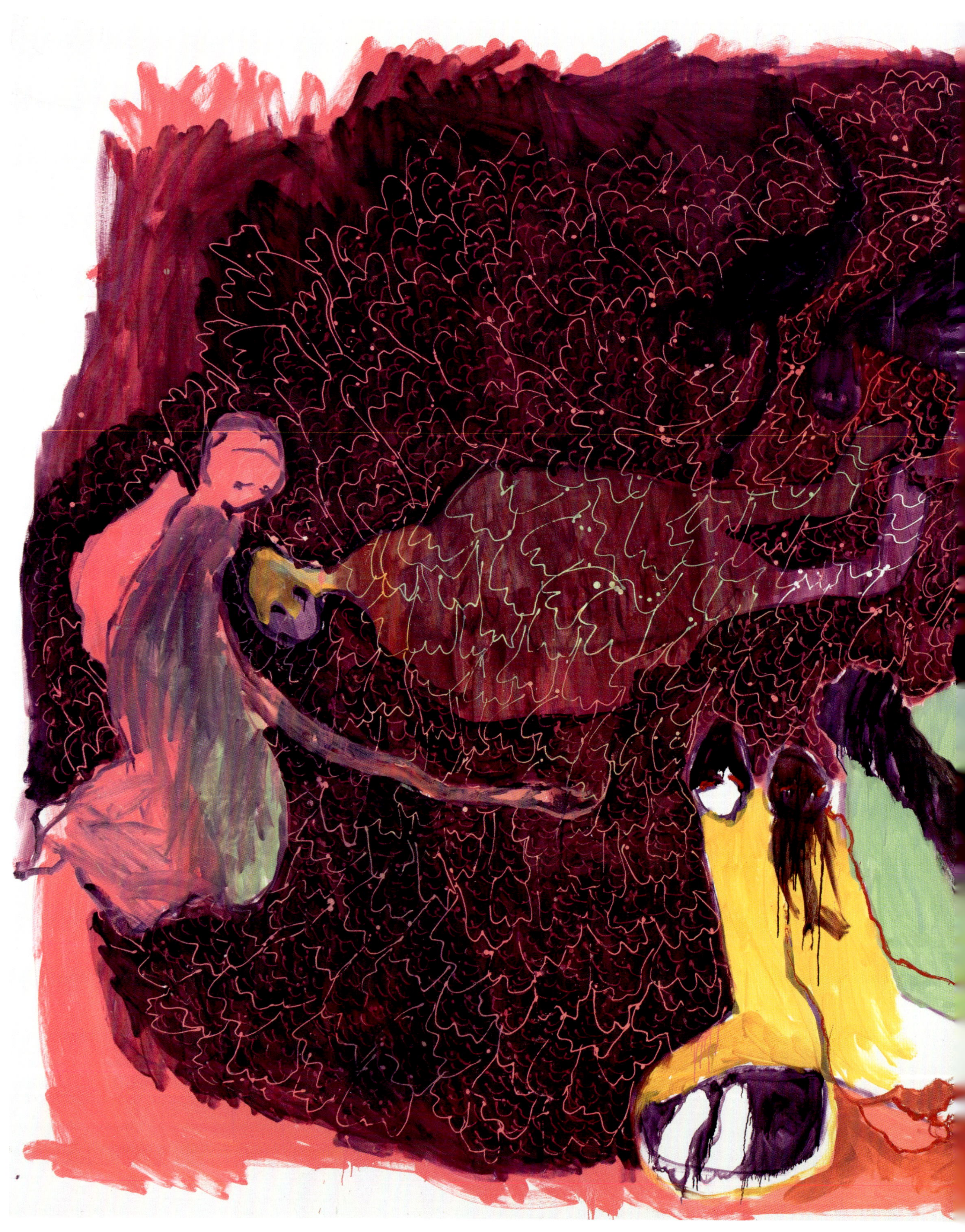

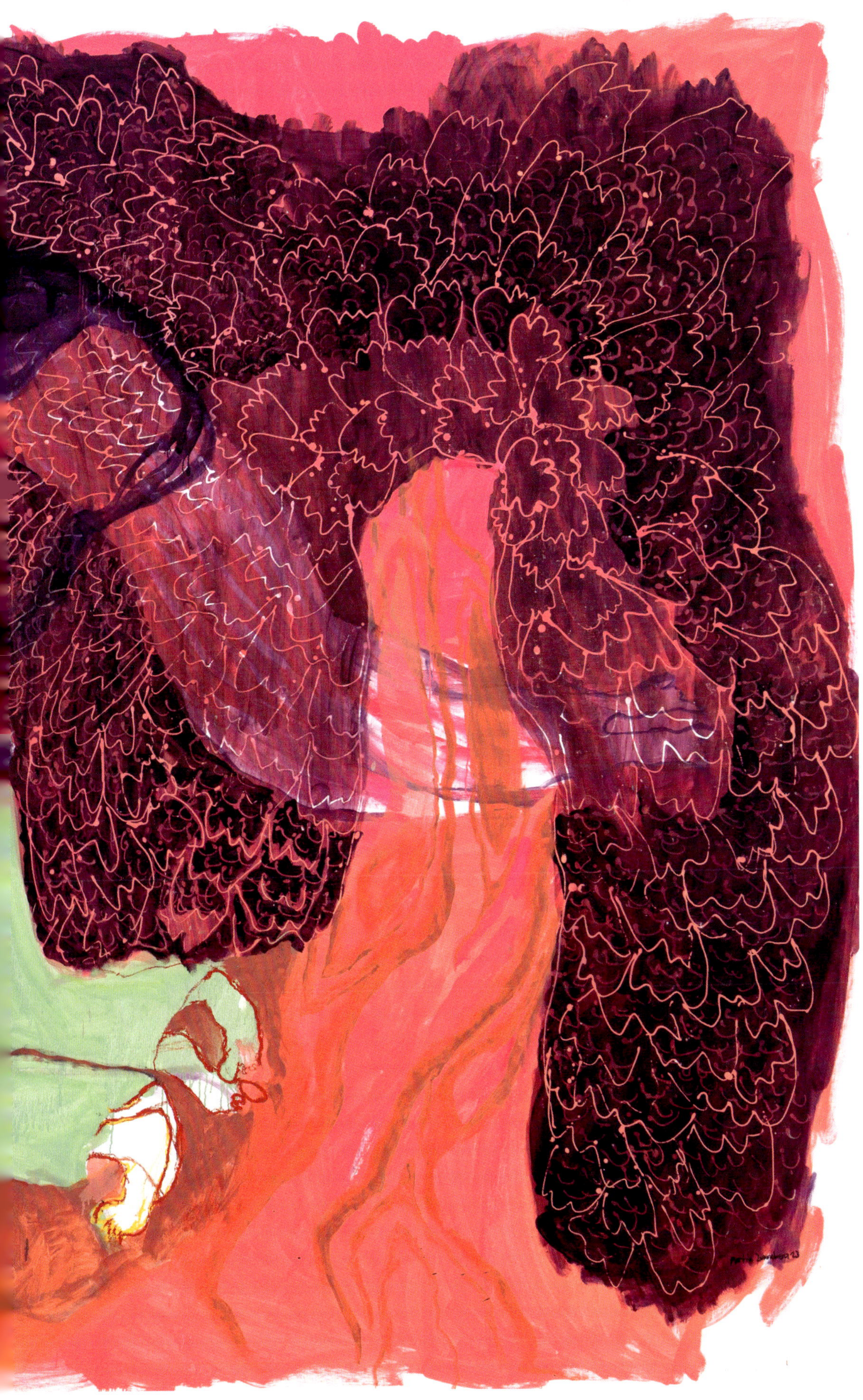

Pane rima rakakomba (1)
(There's too much darkness)
2023
Oil-based printing ink
and oil bar on canvas
222 × 332 cm

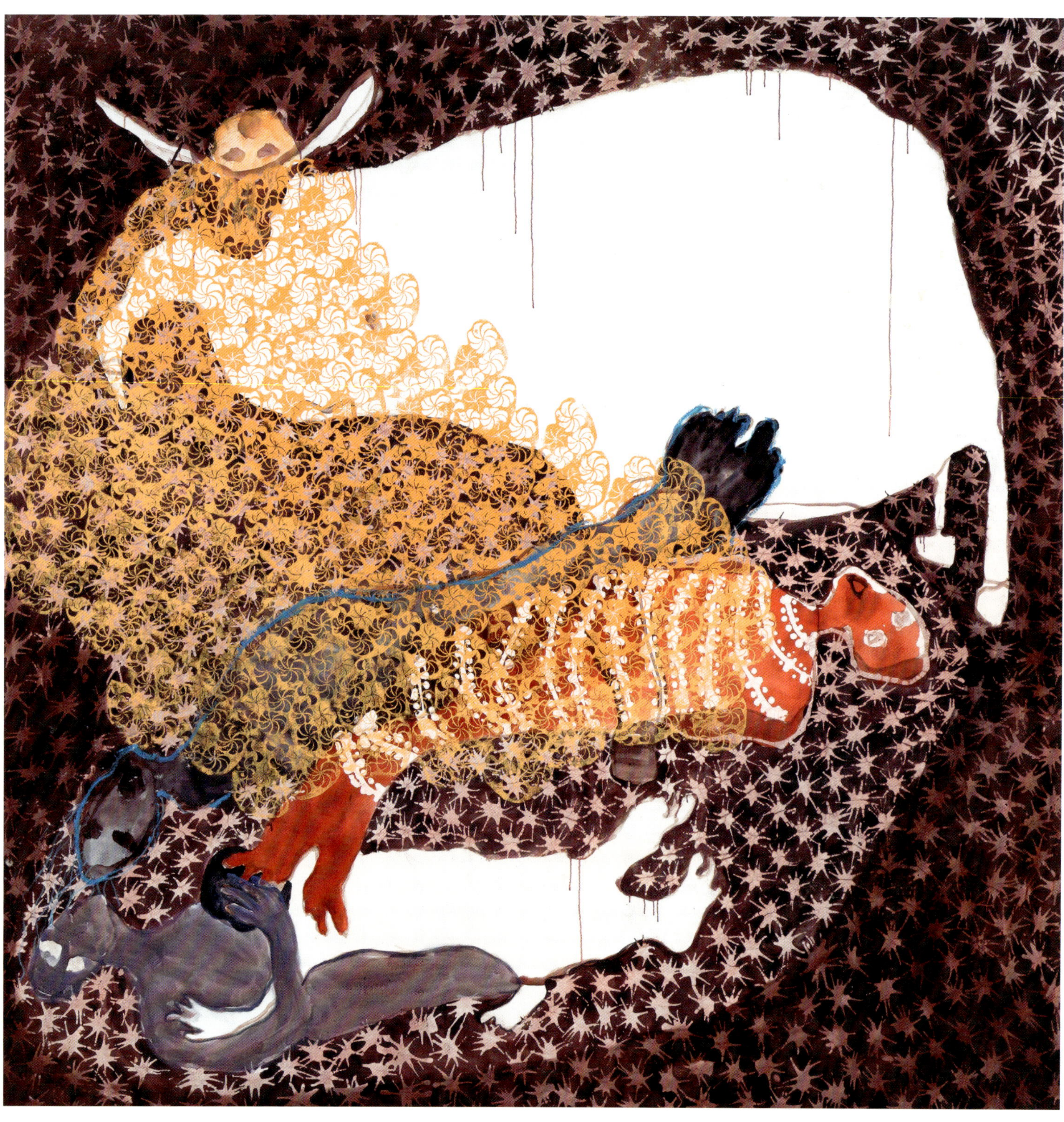

Tavingwa Nezvehusiku
2018
Oil-based printing ink
and oil bar on canvas
198 × 198 cm

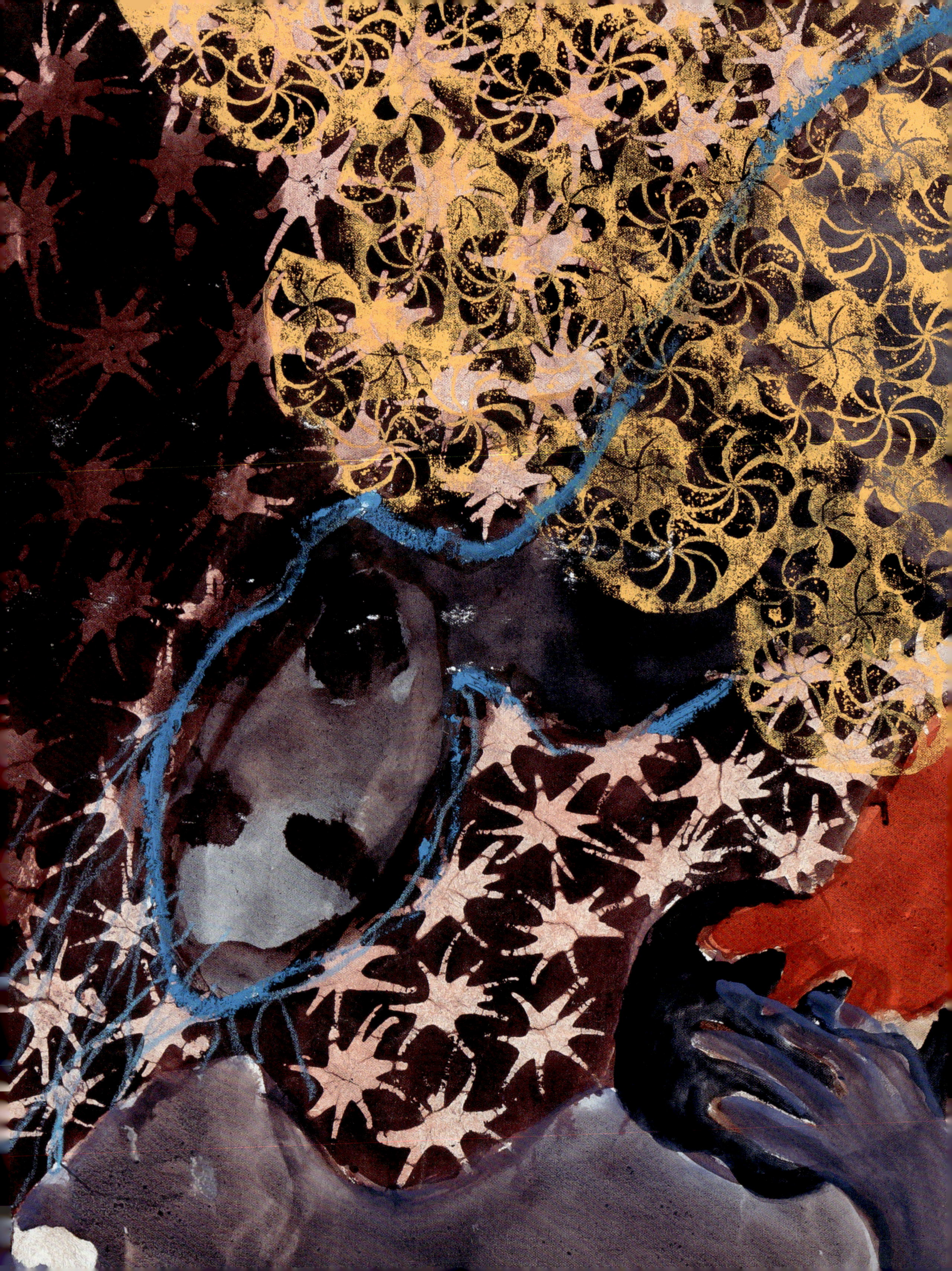

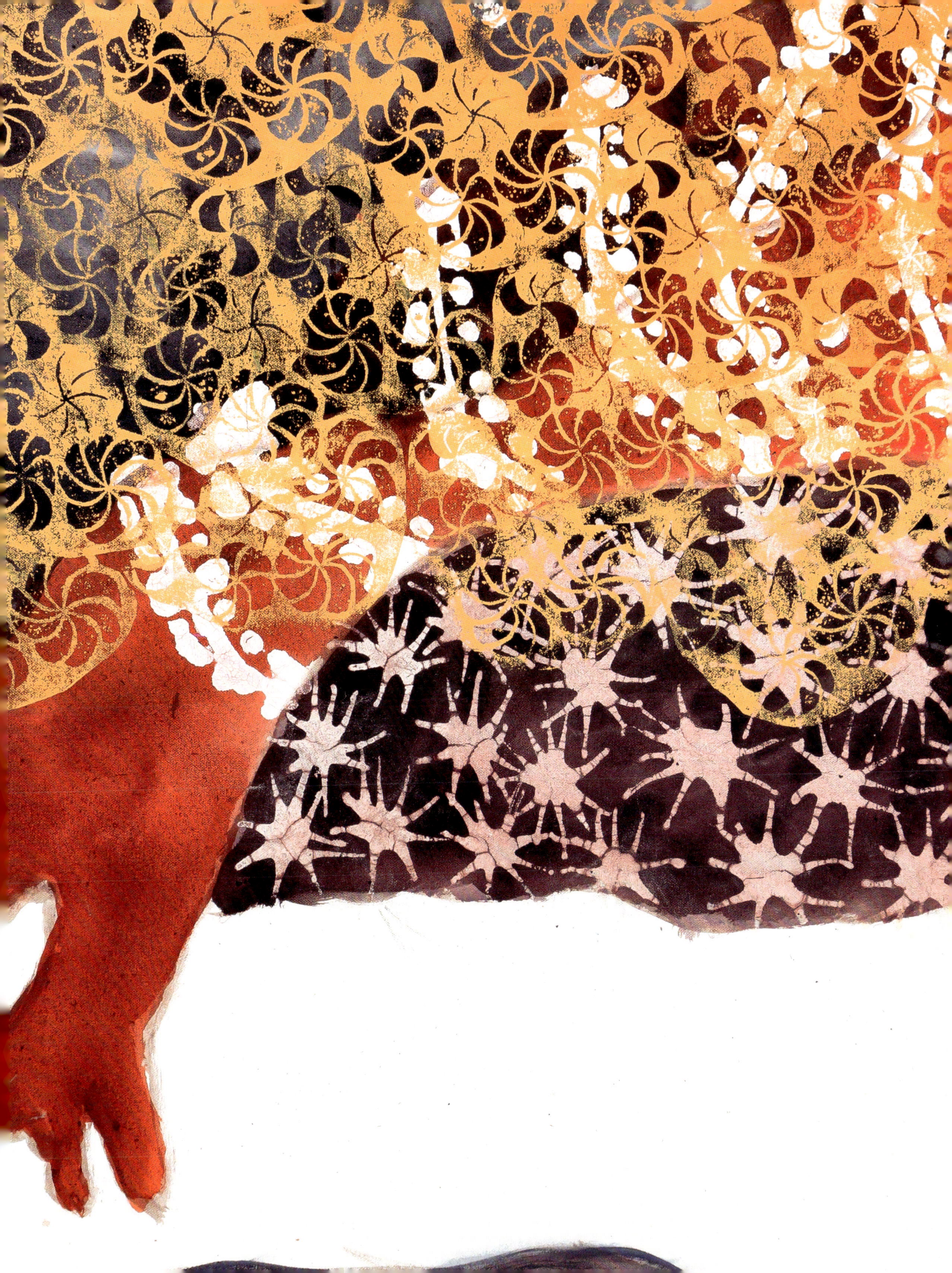

This is Where I Travelled (4)
2020
Oil-based printing
ink and oil bar on canvas
242.5 × 201 cm

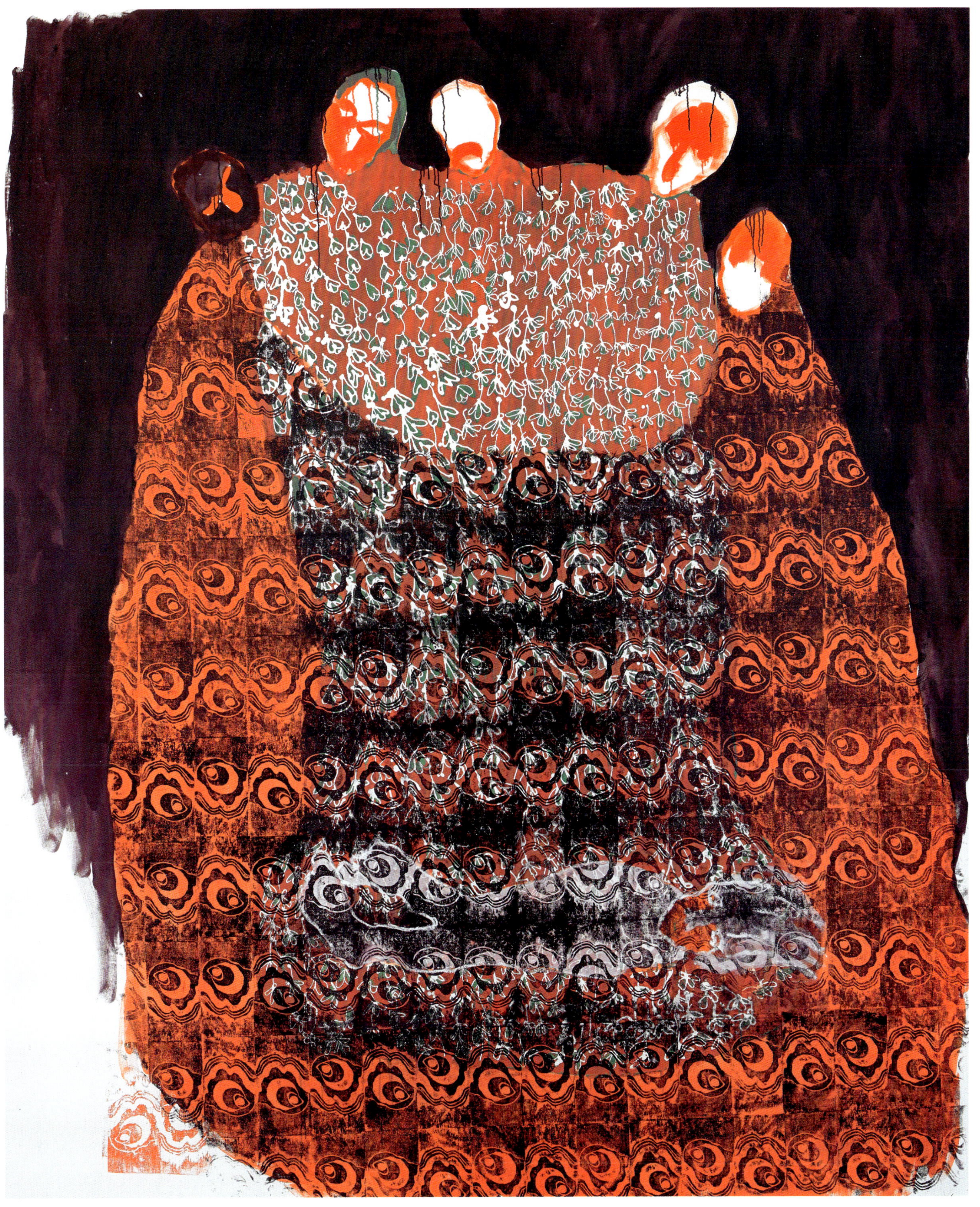

and lace-like layerings that play with the rhythms of disclosure and disguise, sometimes framing the bare expanses of colour in a flurry of floral or star-like shapes, at other times overlaying and disrupting the underlying forms with an intrusion or invasion of pattern. The effect can feel dizzying, almost hallucinogenic at times, but the method is painstaking and time-consuming, proceeding with patience and care as each piece of card or lino is placed on the surface and the play between transparency and opacity, solidity and liquidity, presence and absence is achieved. In earlier works, like *Ndahwarara* (2014, p.37) or *Ndokumbirawo Ishe* (2014, pp.38–39), the printed shapes that suggest fabric designs and colourful textiles were often contained within the outlines of reclining or writhing female figures, signalling local sartorial codes and styles. We see the echoes of African wax print fabric and *chitenges* wrapped and draped on the bodies in customary colours and familiar styles.[7] Drawn from fashion magazines and actual cloths, the regional decorative references are evident and clear.[8] In time, though, these repetitious and recurring motifs (stars, flowers, leaves and lace) spread all over the surface of the canvas, exceeding the dresses and bodies of the figures, to produce an aesthetic that is not so much locked to local fashion as to a visual language that escapes the remit of illustration or functional design. It has a cultural resonance and a place-specific referentiality of course, but it also abstracts and exceeds its customary use in quotidian clothing or brightly coloured cloth.

The embrace of pattern and an all-over painterly surface, expressive distortion and an abstracted, optical energy, is not the hallmark of Zvavahera's work alone.[9] To trace the origins of these qualities in her work is to examine her formation within the context of Harare's contemporary art scene with its long history of navigation between purportedly 'modernist' and 'indigenous' practices – themselves neither separated nor isolated but mutually inflected and formed.[10] As a young artist Zvavahera frequented spaces like Gallery Delta in Harare, where she saw the work of artists such as Helen Lieros (a semi-abstract painter who had founded the gallery with her husband Derek Huggins in 1975), Charles Kamangwana (a figurative artist specialising in stylised scenes of everyday life) and painter/printmaker Chikonzero Chazunguza, who worked with seriality and repetition, and who was to be her teacher at the Harare

Chikonzero Chazunguza
Cityscape 2
2009
Mixed media (acrylics and pastels) on canvas
70 × 90 cm

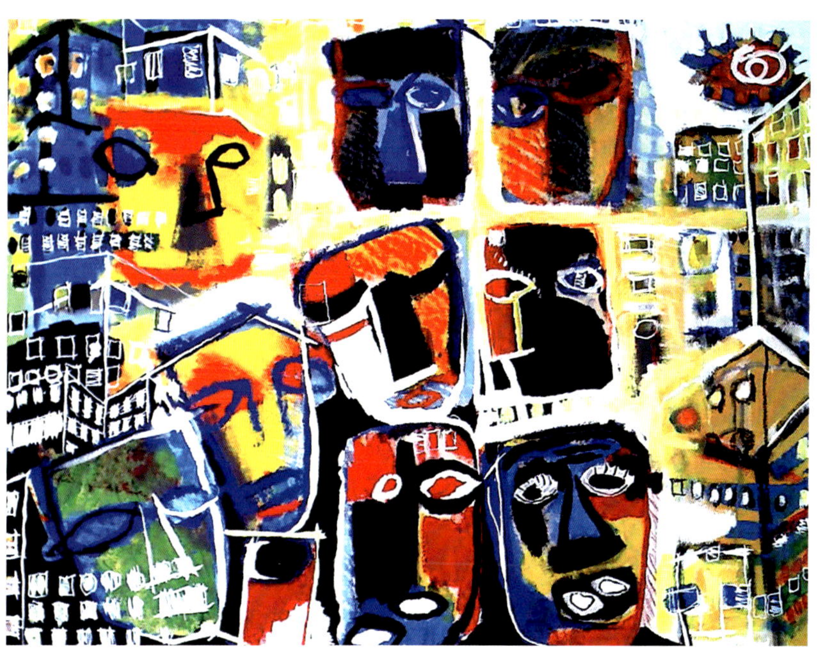

Polytechnic in 2005–2006 where he encouraged her to mix mediums and materials. All of these artists worked knowingly and creatively with form and design, exploring multiple sources and techniques of making while mixing and matching as they pleased. As such they were consummately 'modern' artists, wedded to inventing a pictorial language that could speak to the complexity of their situated sociality and subjectivity while simultaneously engaging with a wider world of which they were very much a part.

From early on Zvavahera was exposed to an experimental and innovative art education that encouraged both resourcefulness and rigour. Following her participation in standard-order high school art classes, where mimetic drawing and skills-based lessons were learned, as well as early exposure to oil paintings housed in the Zimbabwean National Gallery, Zvavahera enrolled

Ndahwarara
2014
Oil-based printing
ink on paper
150.5 × 97 cm

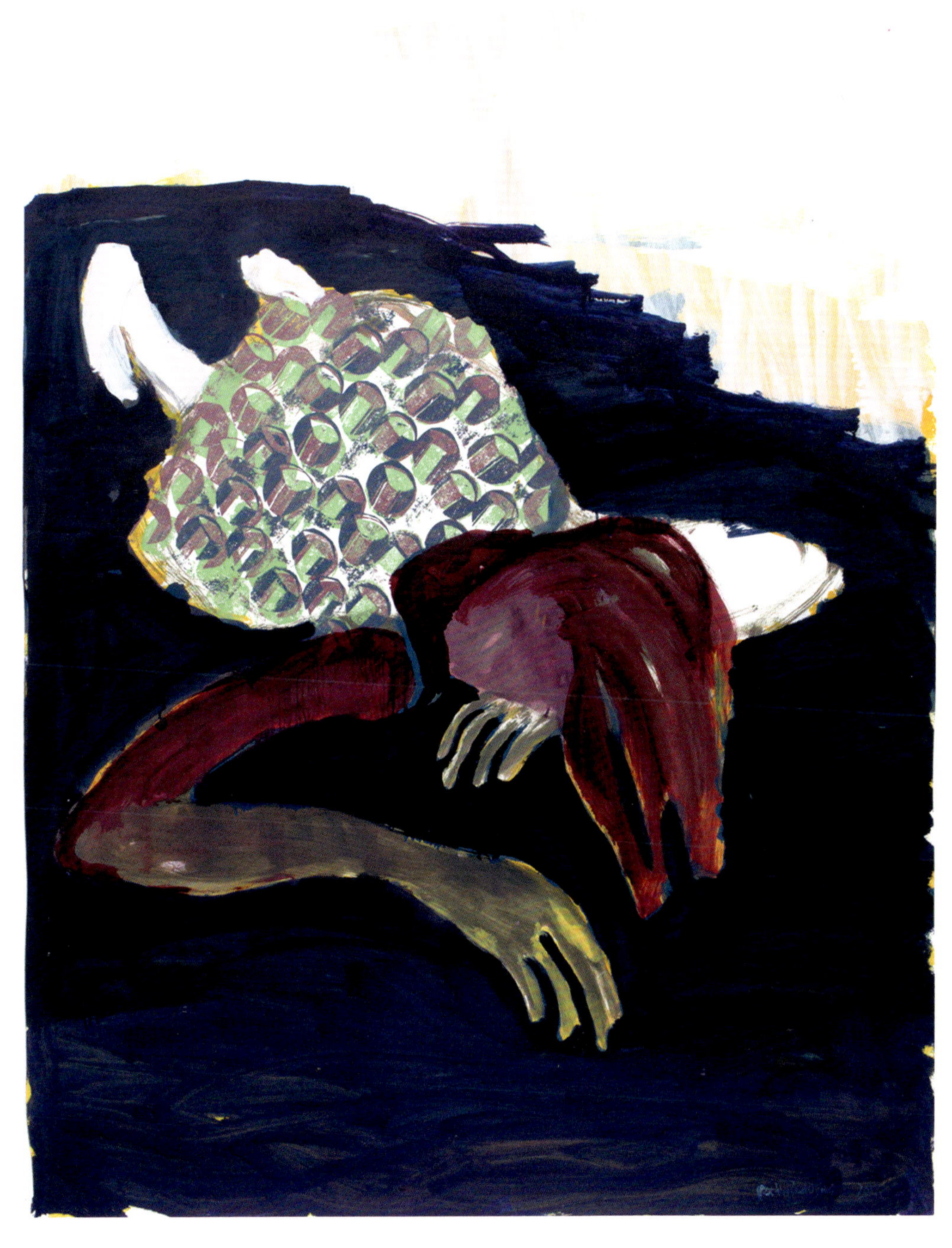

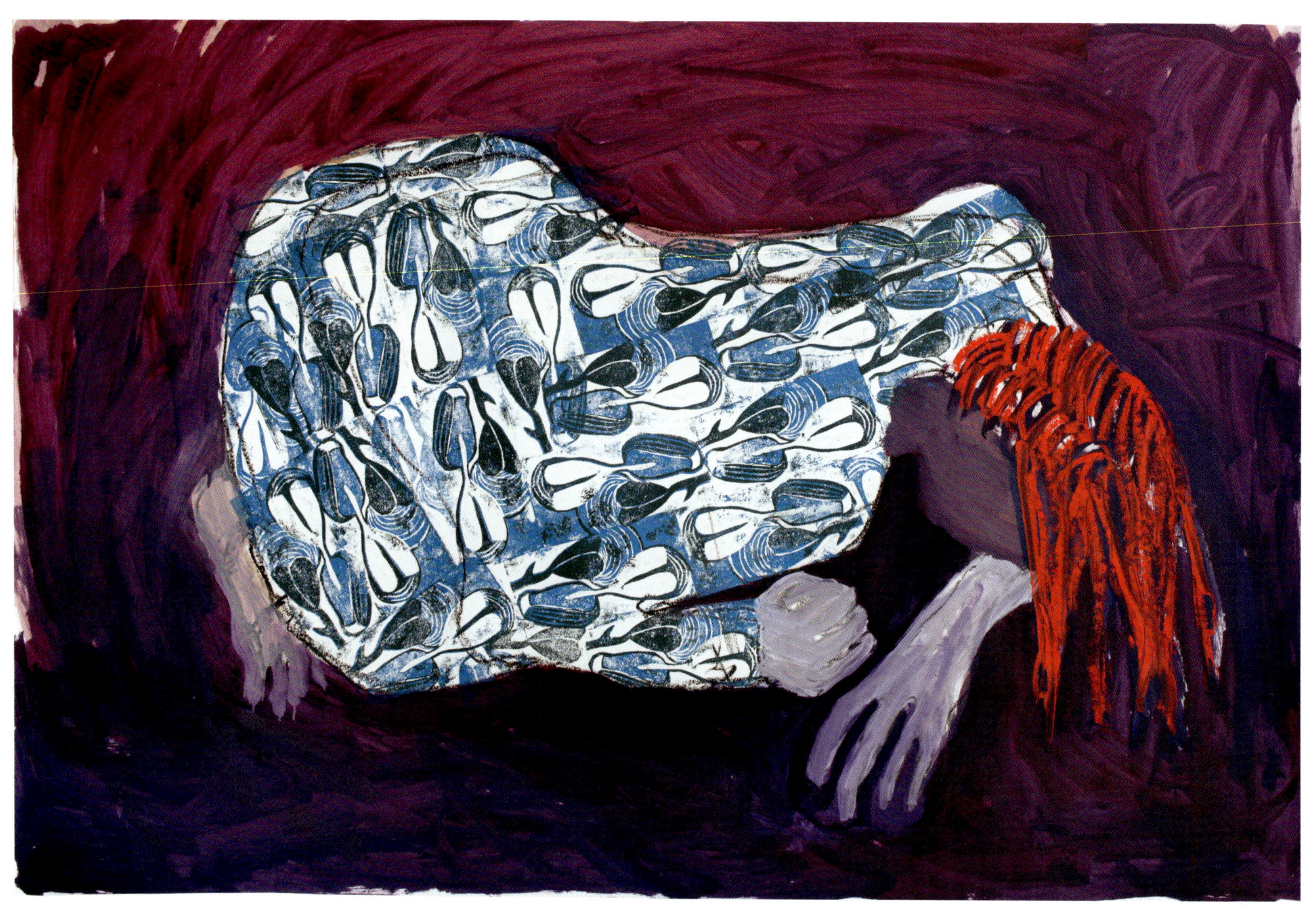

Ndokumbirawo Ishe
2014
Oil-based printing
ink on paper
98 × 150 cm

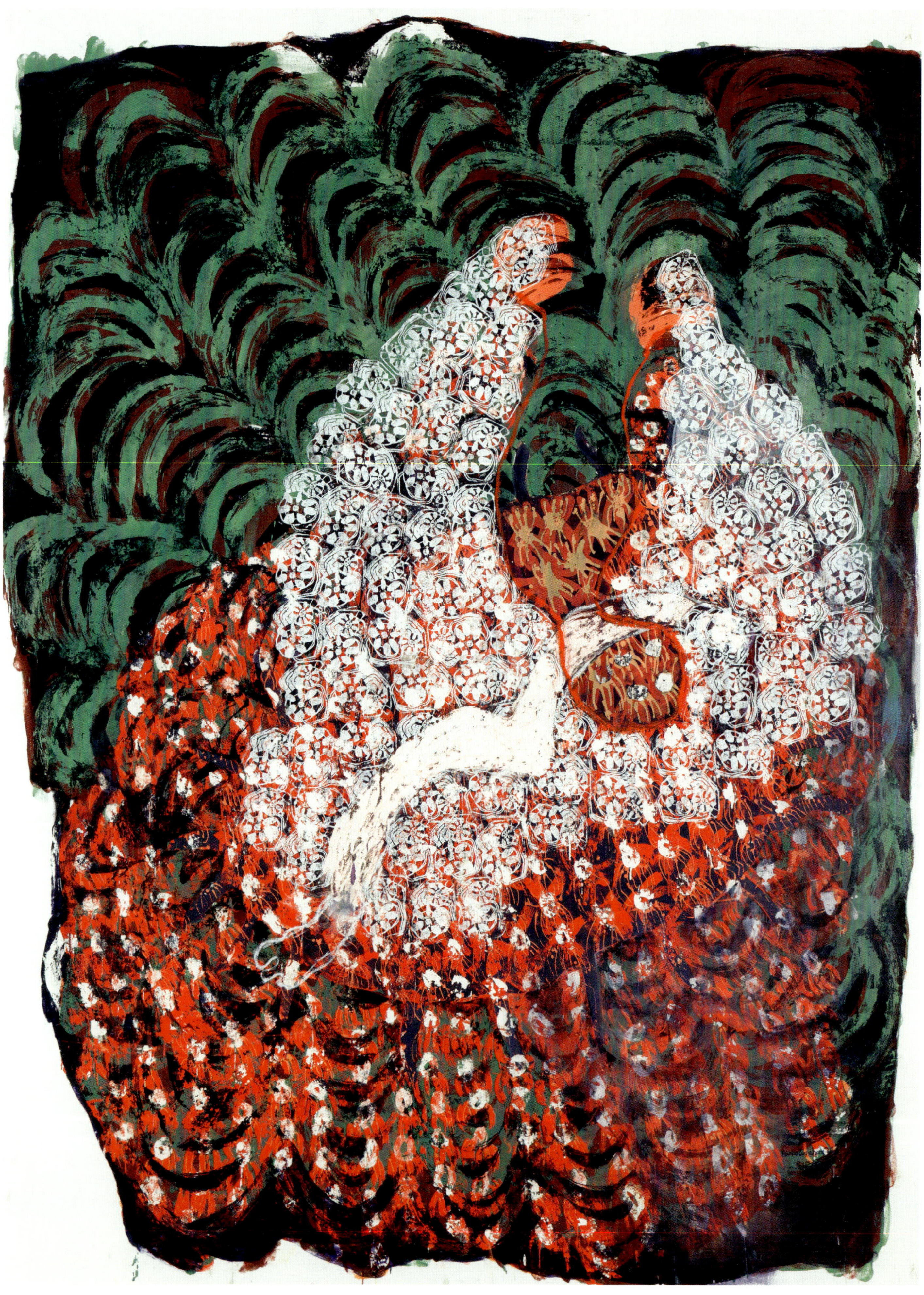

Vachengeti vangu
(My guardian)
2020
Oil-based printing ink
and oil bar on canvas
260 × 193 cm

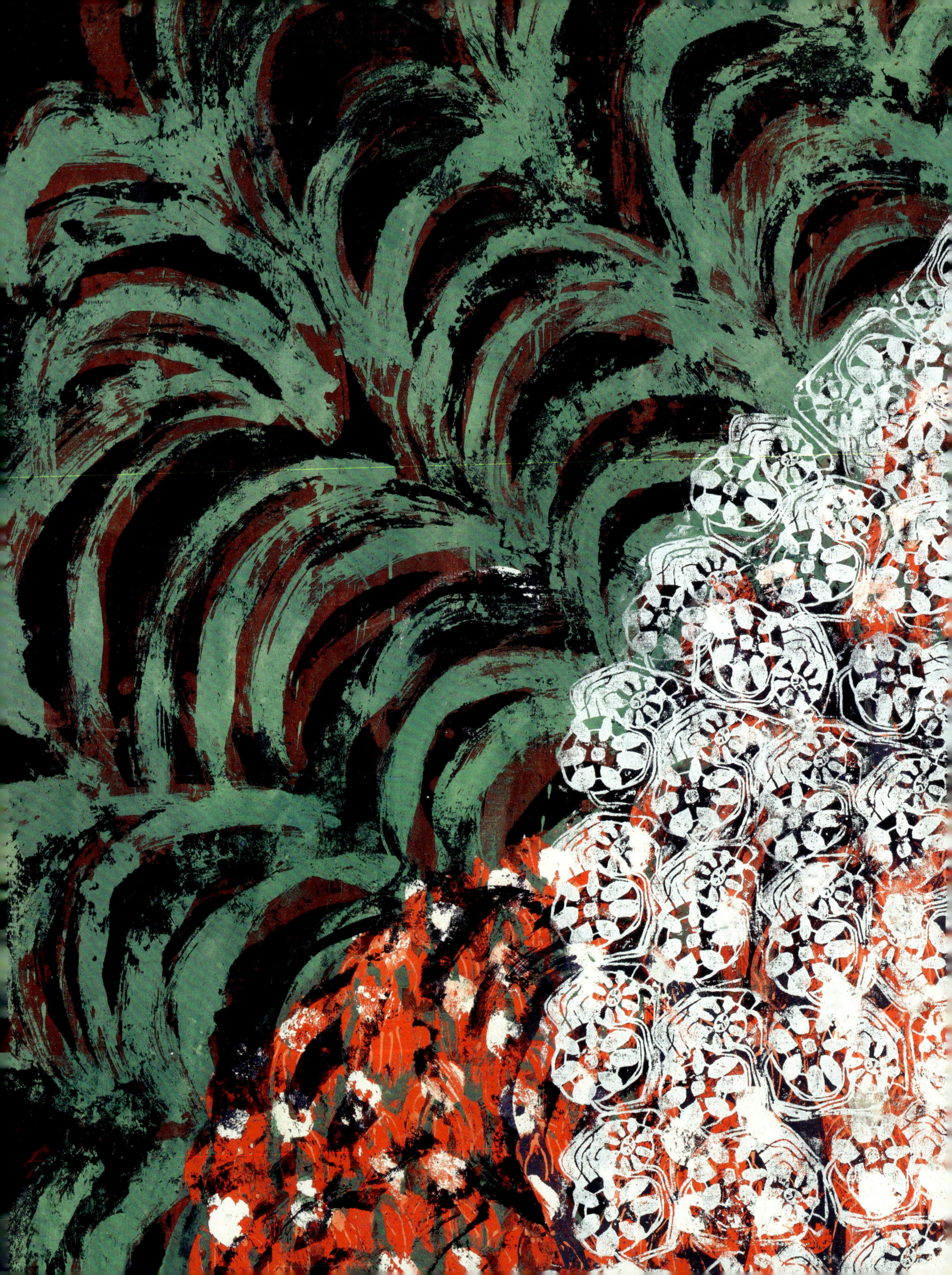

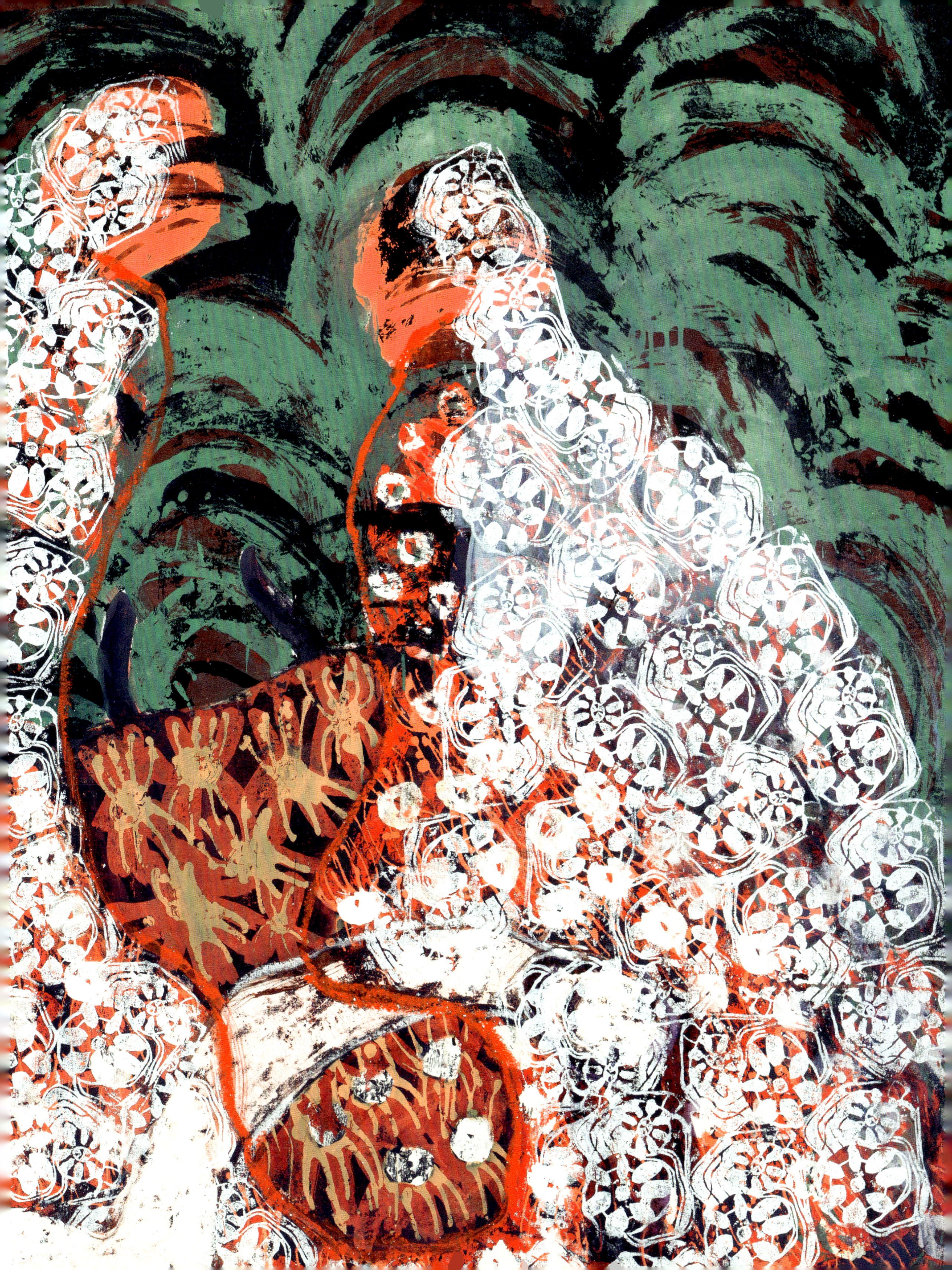

in Harare's BAT Visual Art Studios, based at the gallery, where she (one of only two women students) studied between 2003 and 2004.[11] Established by pioneer museum director and teacher Frank McEwen in the then Rhodes Centenary National Gallery as the Workshop School in the early 1950s, the school's early pedagogic mission skirted a delicate line between the embrace of European formal experimentation and a commitment to what was understood as an African derived and autochthonous creativity and consciousness, which McEwen regarded as 'authentic' and 'pure'.[12] He favoured untutored or self-trained participants in his programme, unaware that some of his protégés hid their mission-based training from him in order to comply with his need for 'unspoiled' and impressionable acolytes. While he acknowledged that there really was no such thing as a separable, unified style that expressed the spirit and skills of the locals, he paradoxically championed a 'most profound, inborn pan-African conception, endemic within the life-blood of the continent as a whole', which was expressed, he believed, through art.[13] While he started out prioritising painting classes, it was eventually the practice of soapstone carving, with its simplifications and stylisations of form, that came to dominate the workshop. McEwen promoted the (now highly contested) idea that this artform – referred to as 'Shona Sculpture' and marketed as such world-wide – represented the 'native' and untainted vision of the Shona people, drawn from the shared myths, memories, symbolism and religion of the ancients, and incarnated in stone carvings into abstracted three-dimensional form.[14] McEwen's stewardship and patronage of soapstone artists resulted in the emergence of a 'school' and a sculptural style characterised by simplified non-naturalistic forms and polished, grain-rich surfaces in which animal/human hybrids and fantasy creatures achieve a refinement and elegance that earned them renown worldwide.[15]

Characteristic of such work was that produced by Sylvester Mubayi, McEwen's favoured artist, whom he regarded as greater than Henry Moore or Eduardo Paolozzi, beating them at their very own game. Mubayi excelled in animal/human composites, seen for example in his *Skeletal Baboon Spirit*, c.1969, a highly stylised and elegant stone sculpture, with its carved out central cavity, polished surface and rhythmic folding of forms. Not surprisingly, McEwen's

Sylvester Mubayi
Skeletal Baboon Spirit
c.1969
Green serpentine
31.5 × 8 × 14.5 cm

taste had been nurtured in Paris and London, where he was acquainted with artists like Pablo Picasso, Ossip Zadkine and Constantin Brancusi, themselves indebted to earlier forms of African sculpture, particularly its recourse to non-naturalistic conceptions of figuration and form.[16] And of course, Mubayi and his contemporaries were themselves acquainted with these artists, whose work was shown at the National Gallery (home of the Workshop School) alongside European oil painting and prints under McEwen's curatorial stewardship. The idea, therefore, that they were excavating an ancient aesthetic in pristine isolation or self-referential introspection is untenable. Far from being locked in a sealed-off tradition of making, stuck in an unchanging past, Zimbabwean artists were refining their skills by engaging with the work of others. Neither entirely 'pure' nor 'derivative', 'traditional' nor 'modern', the entangled histories of Harare (or Salisbury as it was then called) and Paris in the contact zones of modernity, therefore, disrupt these very antinomies, showing how they are mutually constituted and framed.[17]

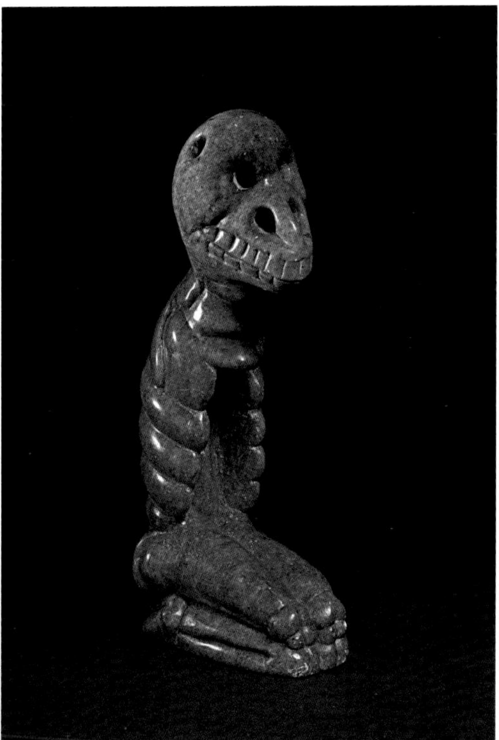

Amongst the artists that rose to prominence under McEwen's patronage was the painter/sculptor Thomas Mukarobgwa (1924–1999), who worked as an attendant at the gallery for much of his career, and whose gestural, painterly compositions

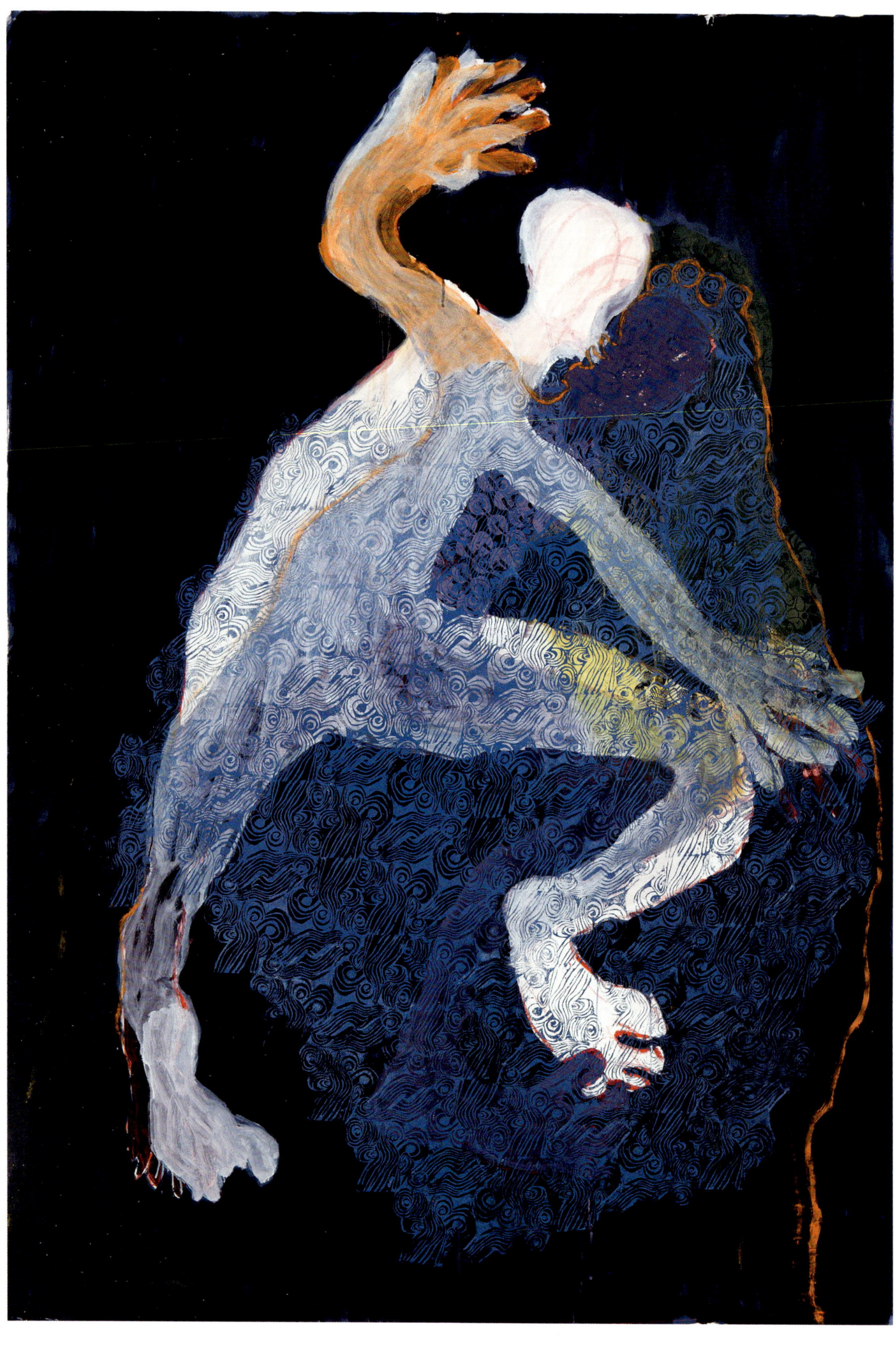

I Want to Stay in Love
2017
Oil-based printing
ink on paper
203 × 140 cm

with their saturated colours and simplified drawing are characteristic of the kind of expressive non-naturalism that was fostered at the Workshop School. Mukarobgwa was devoted, like many modern painters, to the idea of painting as a forum for the externalisation of an inner life and spiritual self-consciousness, and his visionary canvases (often including angels and imaginary creatures) have come to embody an assertion of sentience and selfhood, qualities that were denied Black Africans under colonial rule.[18] His sinuous lines, agitated surfaces, painterly mark-making and shallow, colourful compositions with their all-over texture and patterned effects position him as amongst the founding figures of an African-based modernism that bypasses the binaries of figuration and abstraction.[19] While drawn from 'life', whether observed or imagined, Mukarobgwa's animistic paintings, like *Dying People in the Bush*, 1962, harness oneiric visions and local landscapes into concentrated compositions of painterly and optical profusion. Figures are abstracted and flattened, colours are heightened and rich, brush marks appear visible and varied in the shallow and vibrating intensity of the picture plane that connotes an entire culture and world.

Thomas Mukarobgwa
Dying People in the Bush
1962
Oil on board
59 × 91.9 cm

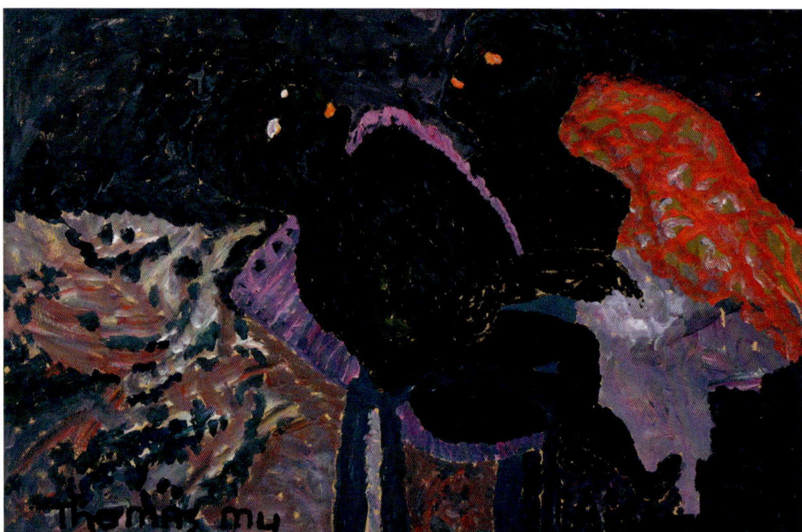

The assertion of an African subjectivity and cosmology, through an embrace of modernist experimentation and self-expression, comes to have a compelling and radical force for subsequent generations of artists and critics. It is not difficult to see Zvavahera and her contemporaries like Misheck Masamvu and Virginia Chihota, all born after the declaration of an independent Zimbabwe in 1980, as heirs to the radical poetics and pictorial innovations epitomised by Mukarogbwa and others. Zvavahera's invention of her own form of expressive and concentrated anti-naturalism, born of her personal amalgamation of sources, visions, techniques and technologies, did not emerge in isolation or overnight. In fact, it was hard won and adapted and developed over time. After leaving the BAT Visual Art Studios, where she had been taught by Charles Kamangwana, in 2005 Zvavahera enrolled as a student at the Harare Polytechnic where she worked under the exacting but imaginative tutelage of its Head of Department of Arts, Chikonzero Chazunguza, a printer/painter/activist whose influence as a teacher was profound. Having studied for seven years in Bulgaria, Chazunguza had been exposed to European academic and avant-garde practices and was schooled in art's global histories and developments. It was this worldly consciousness and cosmopolitanism that he valued and that he wished to reconcile with a commitment (both aesthetic and political) to the fostering of a post-colonial Zimbabwean culture that was locally engaged and informed. Not for him either an insular ethnocentrism or derivative subservience to foreign technologies and forms. Contemporary art provided the space for a mixture of possibilities that held the potential for the development of new and unprecedented languages incorporating multiple points of origin and inspiration. As part of the ambitious curriculum at the polytechnic that he initiated, therefore, students studied art history alongside classes in ceramics, textiles, sculpture, printmaking and painting.[20] At the same time, the use of local materials, found objects and home-grown expertise (from embroidery to doily making to woodcraft and clay work) was valued alongside the harnessing of personal experience and perspectives. Critical self-consciousness was demanded while technical skills were honed through the repetition of exercises and tasks. One of these involved the amalgamation of two mediums in one artwork to produce something both radical and new. It was in response to

Handidi Kuzviona
2016
Oil-based printing
ink on paper
238 × 140 cm

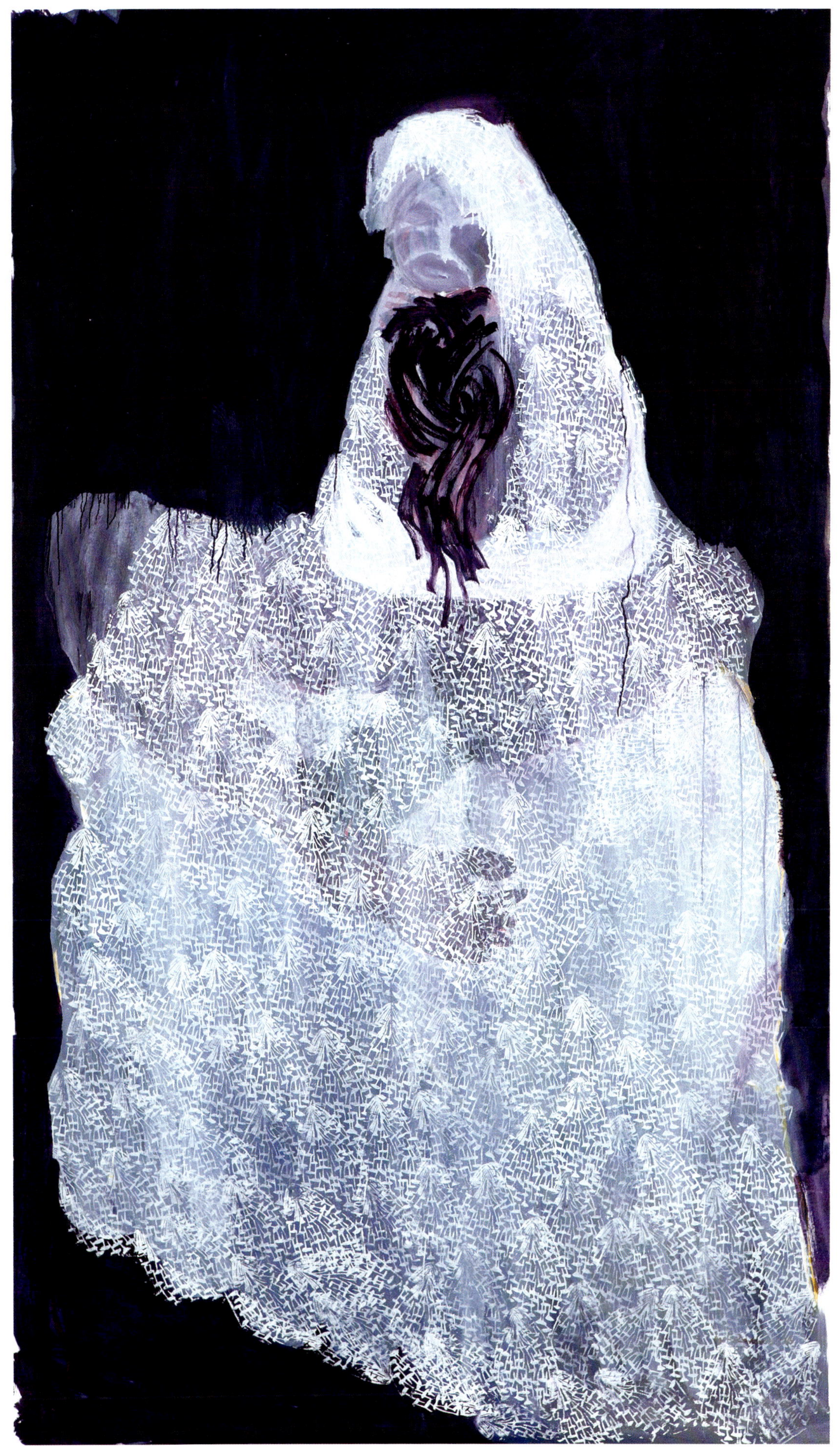

This is Where I Travelled (2)
2020
Oil-based printing
ink and oil-bar on canvas
206.4 × 177.3 cm

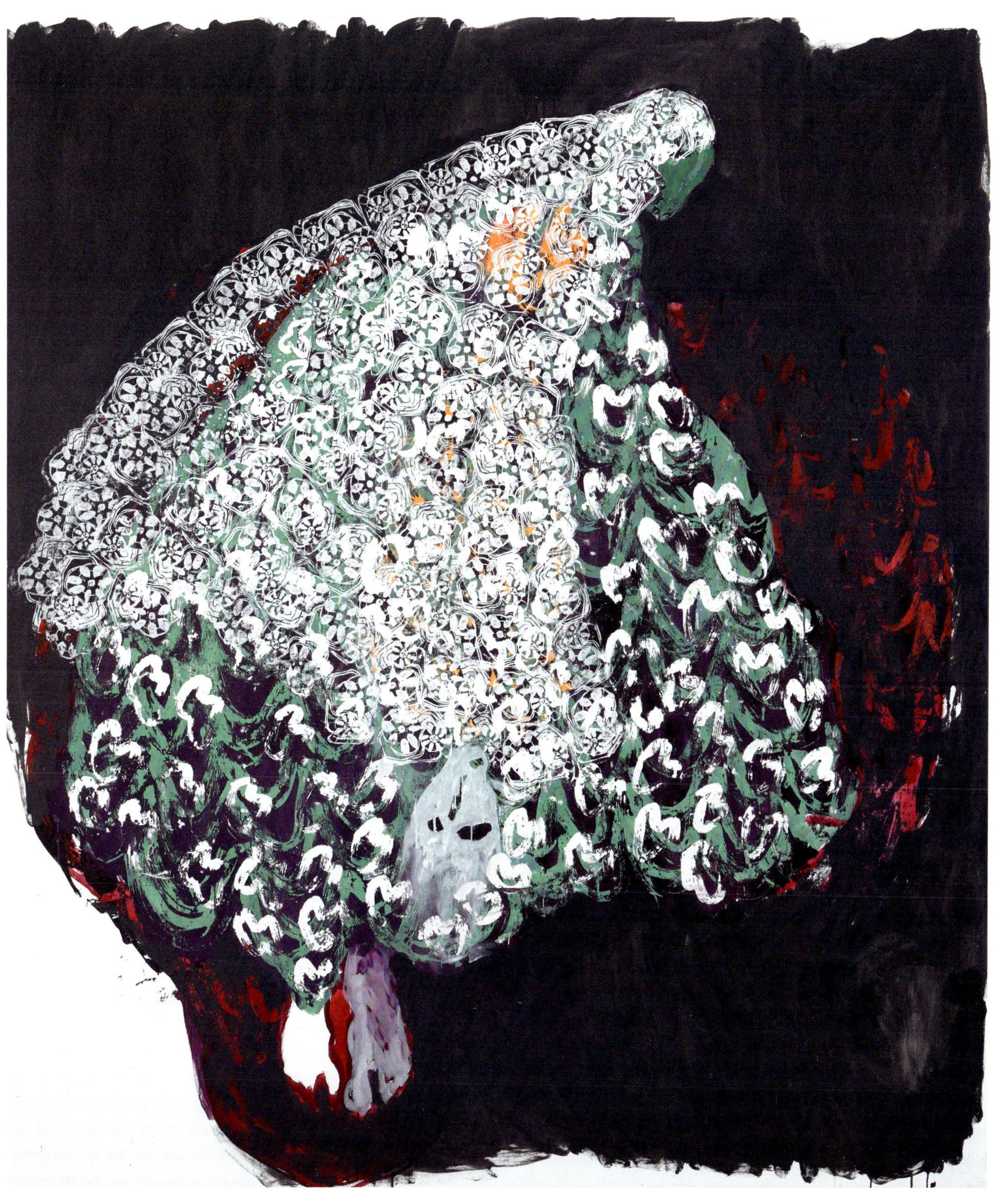

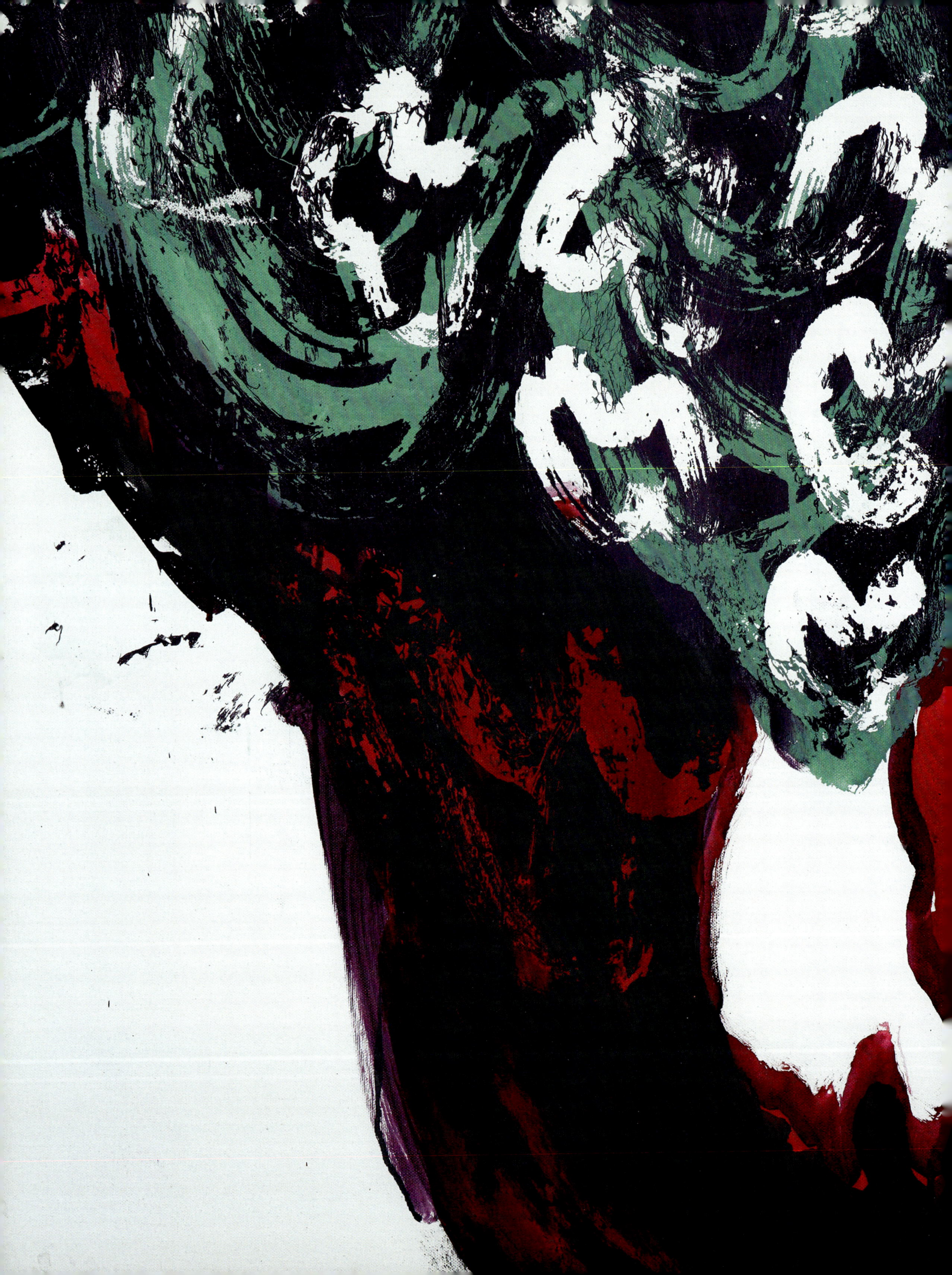

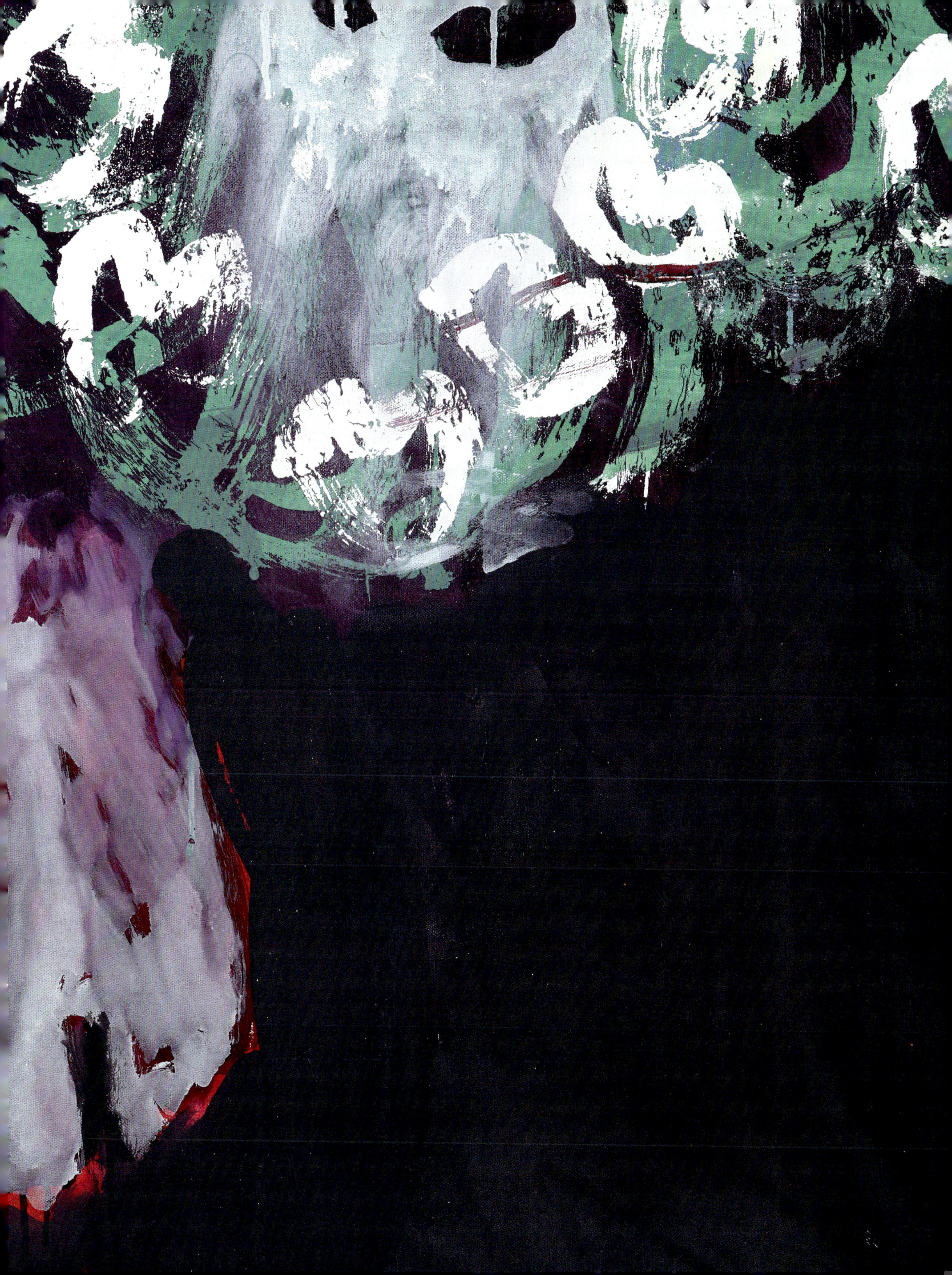

this challenge that Zvavahera first experimented with combining printing and painting, an exercise with which she still remains engaged, milking its capacity to deal with the poetic possibilities of pattern, repetition, rhythm and decorative distortion while allowing the tension between opacity and transparency, concealment and revelation, layering and lifting, to prevail.

Zvakazarurwa implies the potential for disclosure and exposure over time. Encoded, as we have seen, in the very idea of 'revelation' is that of 'unveiling', itself a translation of the Greek word 'apokalypsis', suggesting a future vision (apocalyptic or redemptive) that is neither foretold nor pre-known.[21] It presupposes a 'veil' or filter that masks the meaning it occludes. It even raises the possibility that stories and surfaces harbour secrets or riddles that are difficult (perhaps impossible) to decipher. If meaning is 'veiled', therefore, perhaps even through the process of translation, then it is tempting to think that it might reside as much in the fabric or process of representation as in that which is hidden beneath. The literalisation of veiling, as part of the language of printing/painting, makes its appearance in Zvavahera's practice early on. Associated exclusively with women, patterned veils shroud many of her female figures, who appear like amorous brides, wrapped and enfolded in cloth. *Handidi Kuzviona* (2016, p.51), for example, shows a proliferation of lace-like marks and gestural brush strokes that define the dress of the figure but exceed its contours as if to describe the surface of the canvas itself. The veil becomes a cypher for the dynamic of inscription and concealment that defines the work of art, suspended as it is between the depiction and deferral of meaning, which is both cryptic and difficult to unravel. While Zvavahera's early works were more descriptive and literal in content, taking on women's worlds and gynocentric concerns, from childbirth to falling in love, maternal desire to erotic fantasies and feelings, even these resisted an illustrative or naturalistic approach. Instead, the recourse to pattern and linear distortion, exaggeration and hyperbole, enveloped the scenes and scenarios in a paroxysm of decorative excess. See for example the monumental *Embraced and Protected in You* (2016, pp.58–59) with its accretion of female figures, whose arched bodies and haptically distorted arms and limbs, swathed in volumes of cloth or covered in print and pattern, seem to writhe in orgasmic bliss or agonising pain (who can tell the difference?) like goddesses or graces plucked or displaced from the past. What we are left with is an awareness of the heightened intensity of female power and vitality, which feels both erotically and maternally charged, and is encapsulated in the animated figures as much as in the visceral traces that come from the artist's hand.

The mother is a powerful figure in Zvavahera's panoply. She appears as a vital, if vulnerable, force and the fulcrum of passion and energy that fires both life and art. In Zvavahera's own self narrative, the role of her mother and grandmother is key. Carriers of cultural memory and guardians of language and love, they provide the affective bond that roots her to place and past.

In *Pane rima rakakomba (1)*, as we have seen, the supine body of the pregnant woman (surrogate for the artist/dreamer herself) provides the focal point for the surrounding figures whose presence promises some protection from the threats and dangers of the night. In the studio, and the light of day, the dream is filtered and processed, dismantled and disrupted so that it reappears in multiple forms and shapes, recurring and reworked over time. Its meaning is neither pregiven nor clear. Its articulation is dialogical and self-reflexive, worked through in multiple versions that help to constitute it after the event so that its 'energy' as much as its 'content' finds form.[22] Sometimes it is only through prayer and meditation that the imagery of the dream takes shape. Mostly it is the act of making that teaches the dreamer what it is that she saw. In recent variations and iterations, the maternal cypher, like a proverbial Madonna della Misericordia, stretches out her mantle and arms to envelop her siblings or offspring in the protective cloak of art. In some versions, she is seen in prayer, kneeling or bowed or bent, a ghost-like creature who fuses both figure and ground in the patterned expanse of *Fighting Energies 2* (2024, pp.65–67) and *Ndirikukutsvagai ndirimugomo* (2024, pp.77–79). On occasion, she appears to fly in, like a descending angel, poised to gather the demonic rats in her outstretched arms so as to dissipate or destroy their power (*Ndirikumabvisa*, 2024, pp.61–63). In each instance the concentrated energy of the work exceeds its narrative spur.

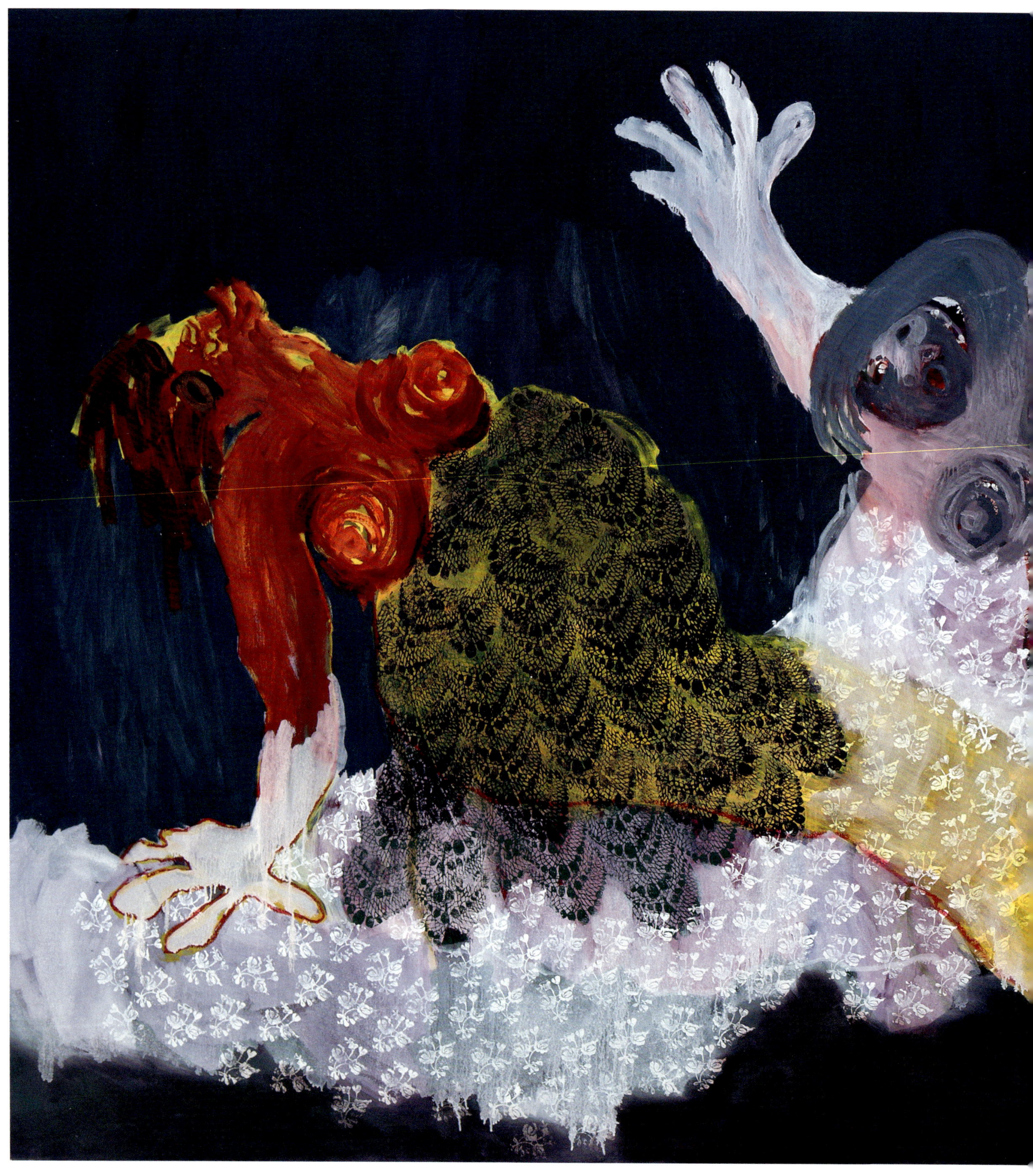

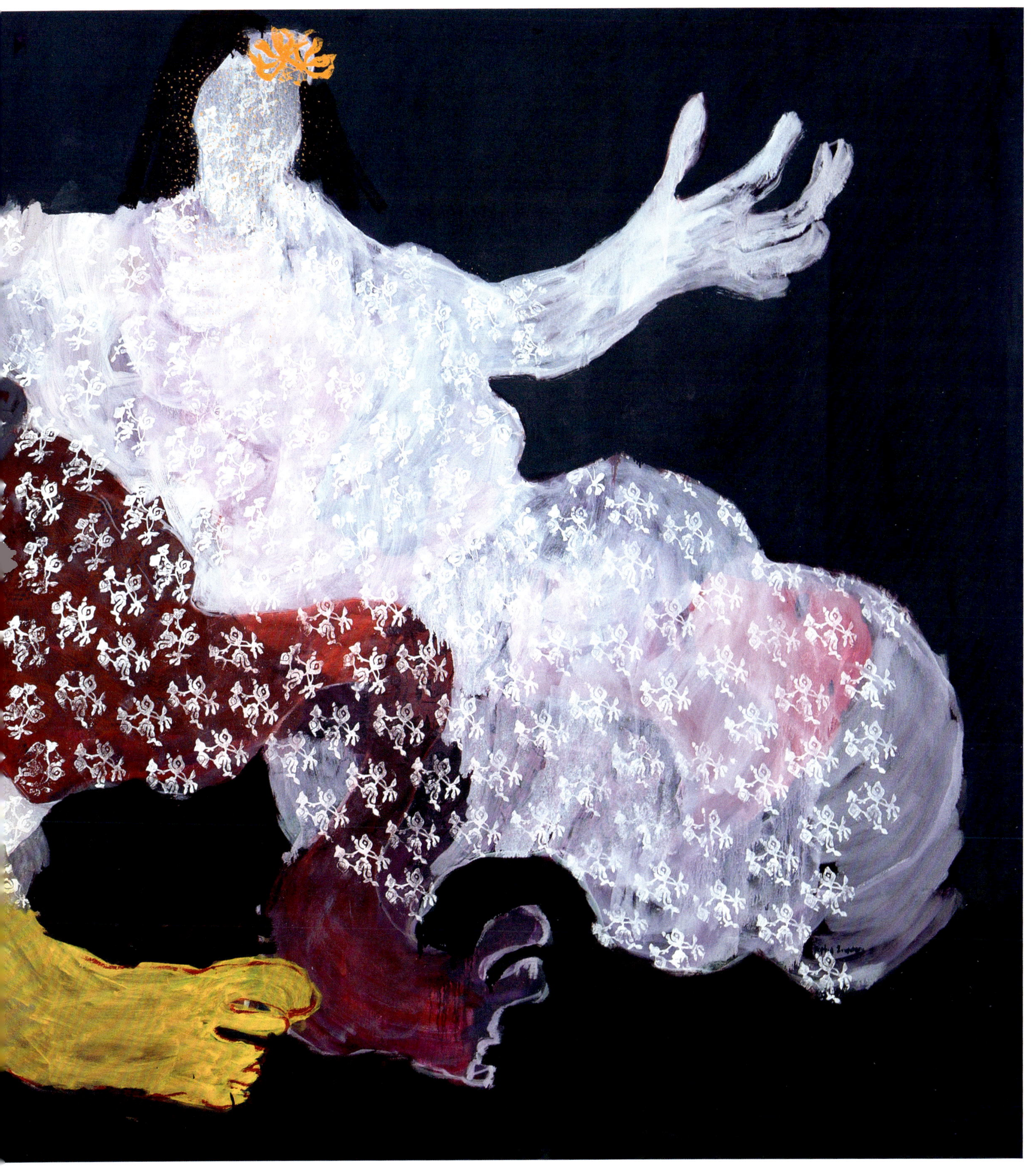

Embraced and Protected in You
2016
Oil-based printing ink and oil bar on canvas
210 × 400 cm

Ndirikumabvisa
2024
Oil-based printing ink
and oil bar on linen
253 × 210 cm

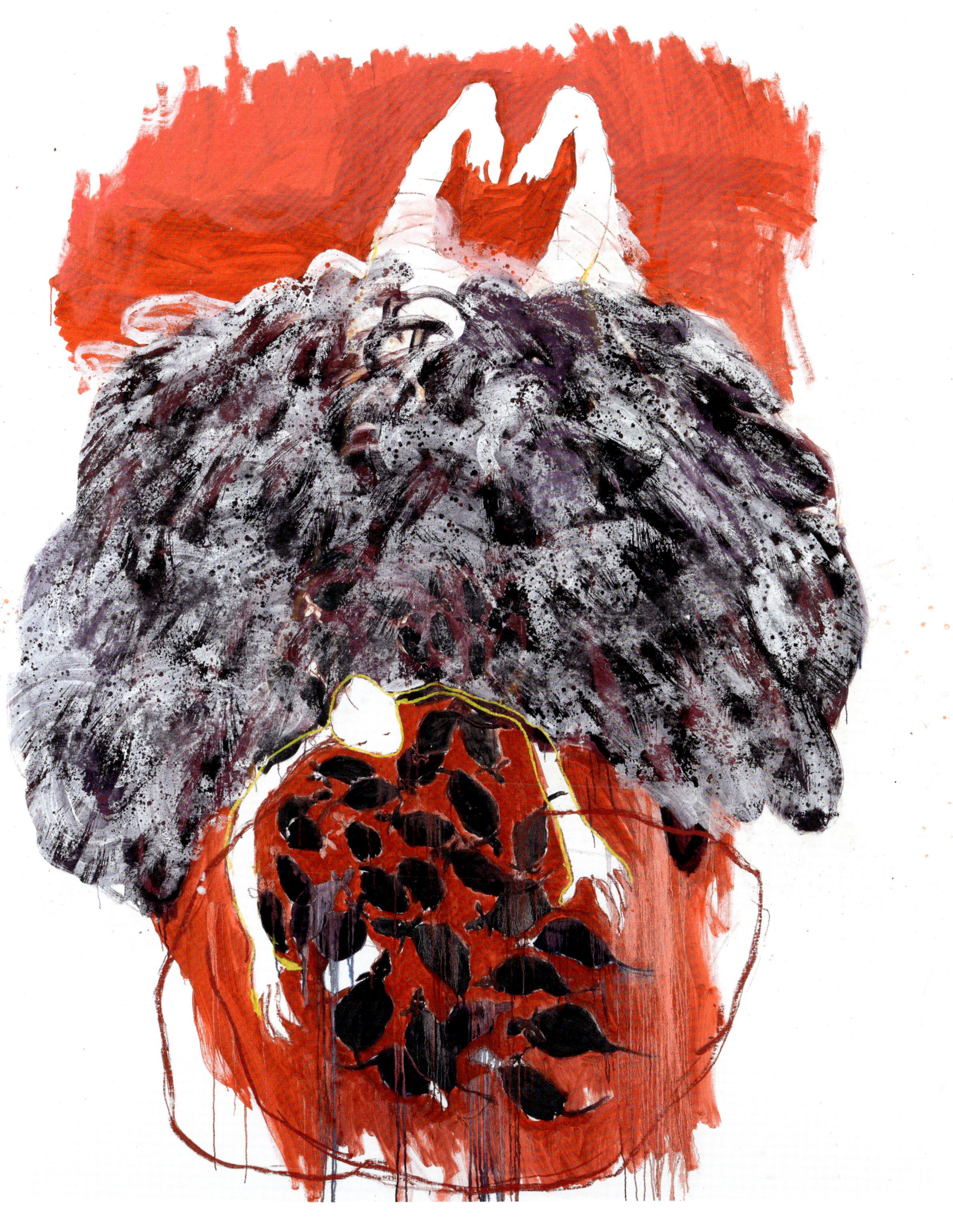

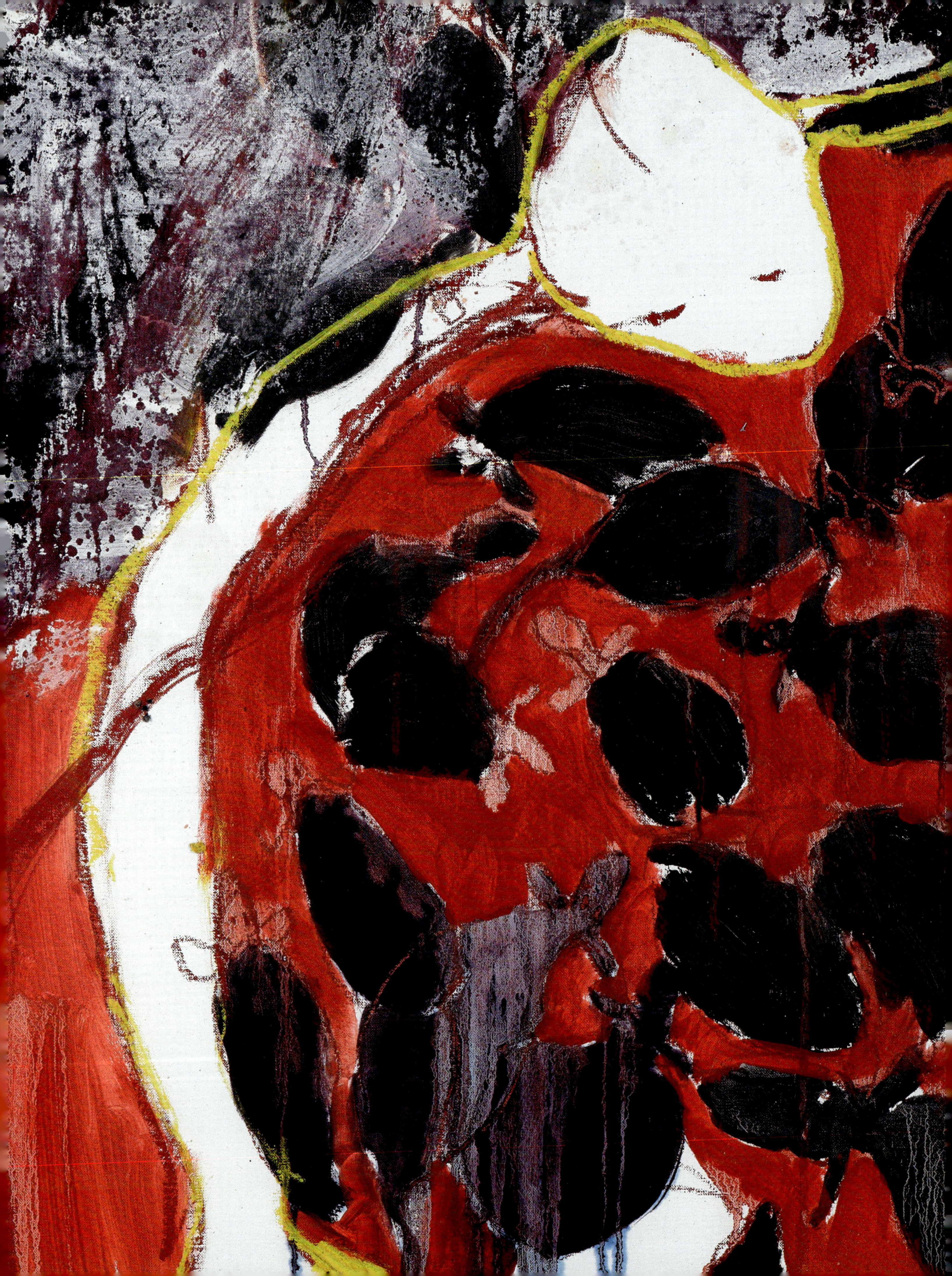

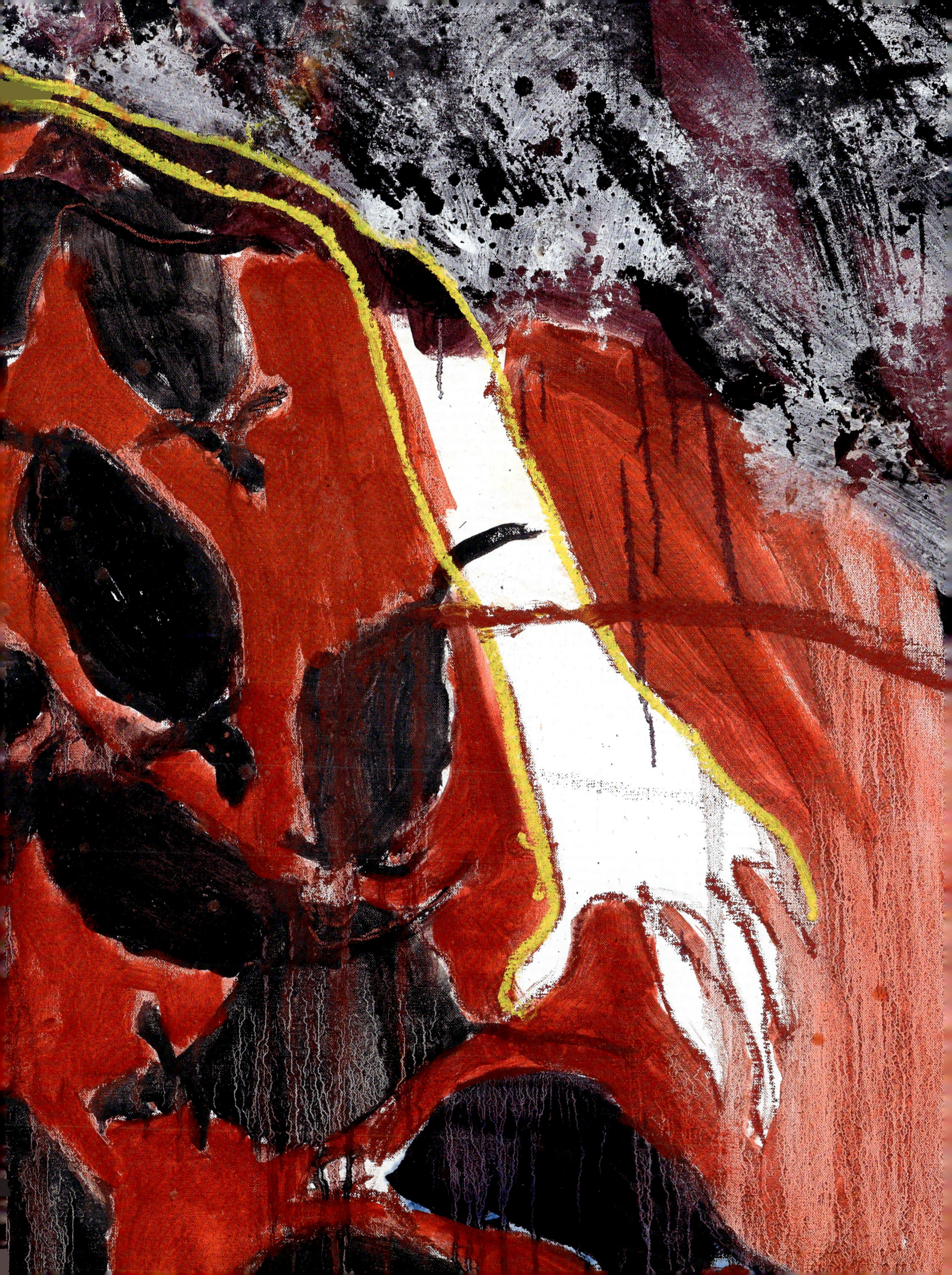

Fighting Energies 2
2024
Oil-based printing
ink and oil bar on linen
228.4 × 212 cm

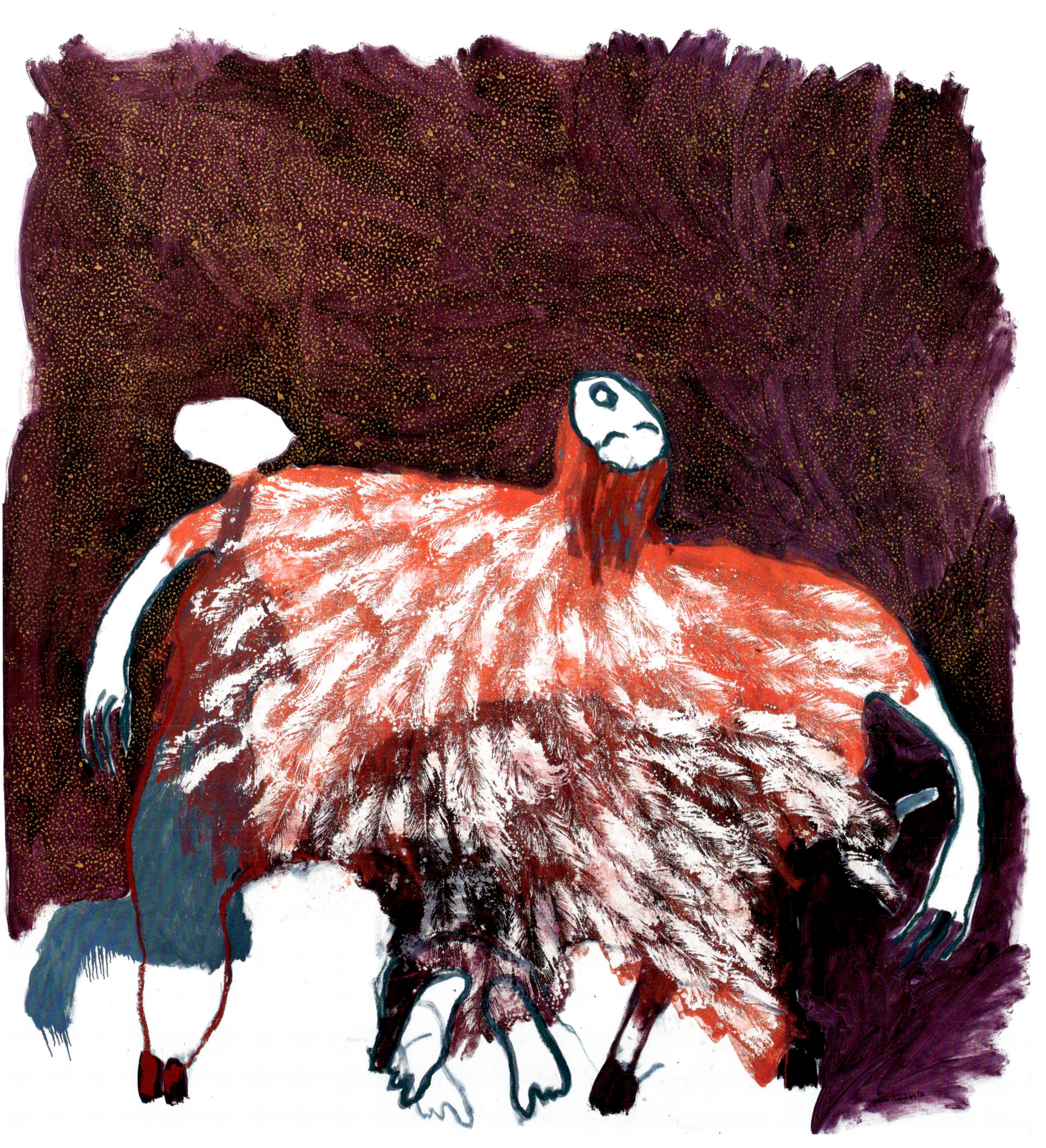

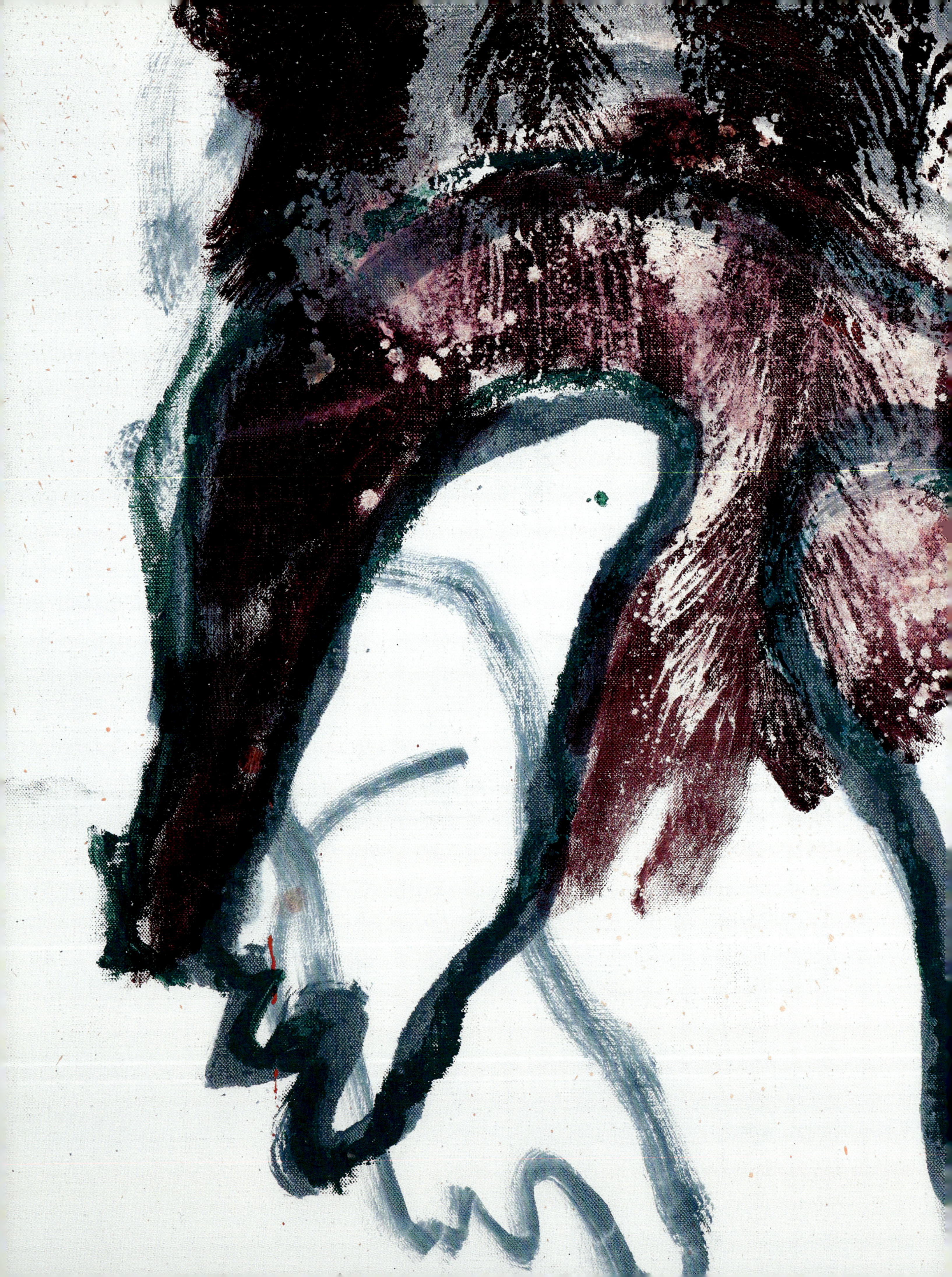

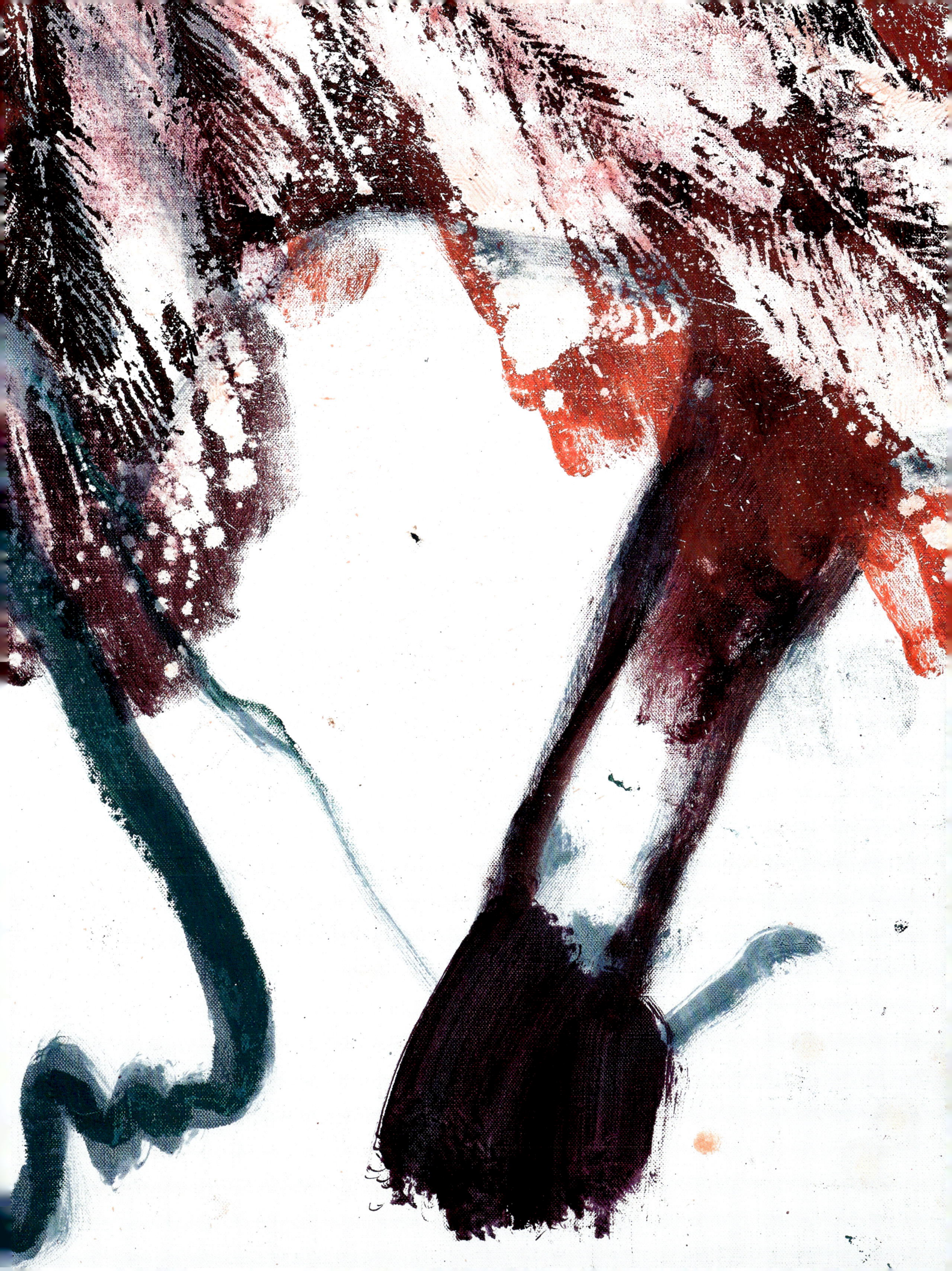

Imprinted with lace and leaves, lino and cut-out card, or layered through wax resist and ink-based wash, the surfaces of Zvavahera's works reveal the indexical traces of their locatedness in place and time. In their very materiality and texture is their embeddedness in a Shona-speaking world, that is itself constituted by and permeated with the languages and literatures of others. Whether referencing the printed cloths worn by local women or the surrounding vegetation, the works encode an environmental and aesthetic sensibility that has recognisable roots and associations. We see this, for example, in the curvilinear patterns of *Hide There* (2024, pp.70, 72–73), made by pressing actual ink-soaked, lacy fabric onto the surface of recent canvases, thereby suggesting domesticity and intimacy.

Worn universally by Christian brides in their veils and wedding gowns, white lace serves as the vehicle for a physical stamp that references its customary use but also transposes it into a syncretic and multi-faceted world. Accompanying the delicacy of the 'lacework' is the rough imprint of a palm frond that has been slapped onto the surface after being coated in ink. Taken from Zvavahera's own Harare-based garden, onto which her studio spills out, the foliage literally encrypts the local vegetation into the landscape of the work while also being abstracted as a series of striations and shapes. It both describes the outdoor growth and animates the imaginary scene. The overall pictorial effect is of a multitude of marks and stains, rubbings and smears, which connect the world of visions and dreams right back down to earth.

For it is on the ground and in the studio that the concatenation of material and visionary elements are given shape. The enigma of the dream is made manifest through the staging of the dreamer as a supplicating creature, deep in prayer, who bears the weight of the vision she carries. But the separation between imagined and actual worlds remains porous. For, while the imprint of lace and leaves brings the substance of the quotidian into the work of art, the vision it encodes feels anything but real or observed. *Kune chauraya zizi harifi nemhepo* (something has caused the death of the owl; it does not die of the wind) goes the Shona saying, capturing the mystery of causation: like the wind it is felt but invisible, effective but intangible, material but ineffable.

The relationship between the physical and metaphysical is posed as a problematic, a matter of fable and faith. So too is the language of painting: linked to life but not descriptive of it, art provides the space for the questioning of this relationship to be staged, without prospect of closure or resolution, but for the sake and the interest of the quest. *Zvakazarurwa* is a way of intimating just how much is at stake.

ENDNOTES

1. See interview between Chiya and Zvavahera, in *9 More Weeks*, published in Stevenson, 2018, p.134.
2. The idea of the pluriversal suggests a decolonial alternative to 'universalism' and posits an equivalence between multiple worlds and worldviews that does not exclude Western knowledge systems but also does not accord them supremacy. See Achille Mbembe, 'Decolonizing Knowledge and the Question of the Archive', Wits Institute for Social and Economic Research (WISER), University of the Witwatersrand, Johannesburg. https://wiser.wits.ac.za/system/files/Achille%20Mbembe%20-%20Decolonizing%20Knowledge%20and%20the%20Question%20of%20the%20Archive.pdf. Accessed 05.07.24.
3. For a discussion of time and religion in southern Africa and the refusal of Western binaries of the secular and the religious, see Jean Comaroff, 'Missionaries and Mechanical Clocks', in *The Journal of Religion*, vol. 71, no. 1, 1991, pp.1–17. See also Joel Cabrita and David Maxwell, 'Introduction', in *Relocating World Christianity*, Brill, Boston, 2017, pp.1–44; David Maxwell, 'Writing the History of African Christianity: Reflections of an Editor', in *Journal of Religion in Africa*, vol. 36, pp.3–4, 2006 and 'The Missionary Movement in Africa and World History: Mission Sources and Religious Encounter, in *Historical Journal*, vol. 58, no. 4, Dec 2015, pp.901–30. For a feminist account of the encounter between Christianity and Shona culture, see Francisca Chimhanda, 'The liberation potential of the Shona culture and the Gospel: a post-feminist perspective', in *Studia Historiae Ecclesiasticae*, vol. 40, supplement, pp.305–28.
4. I am indebted to Tsitsi Dangarembga who alerted me to the complex historical formation of Shona identity in a lecture she gave at the Stellenbosch Institute for Advanced Study in 2020. See also Herbert Chimhundu, 'Early Missionaries and the Ethnolinguistic Factor during the "Invention of Tribalism" in Zimbabwe', in *Journal of African History*, vol. 33, issue 1, 1992, pp.87–109 and Ephraim Taurin Gwaravanda, *A Critical analysis of the contribution of selected Shona proverbs to Applied Psychology*, University of South Africa, Pretoria, 2016, http://hdl.handle.net/10500/20980. Accessed 05.07.24.
5. I am grateful to Valerie Kabov for alerting me to the relationship between Shona proverbs and aesthetics and for sharing her text with me: 'Shona philosophy the secret at the heart of the rise of contemporary Zimbabwean art: Greshem Taplwa Nyaude a case study', 2018.

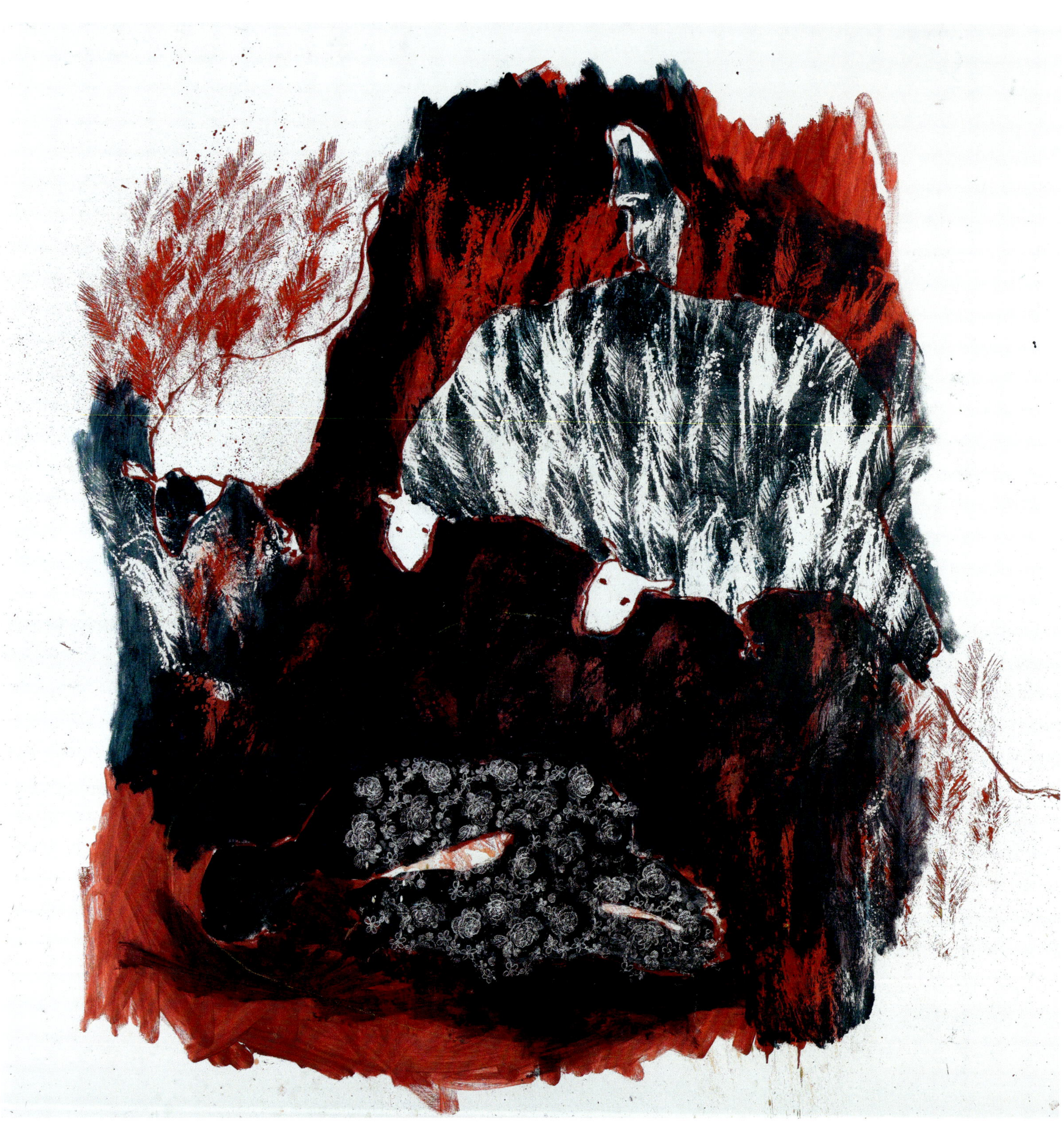

Hide There
2024
Oil-based printing
ink and oil bar on linen
207 × 205 cm

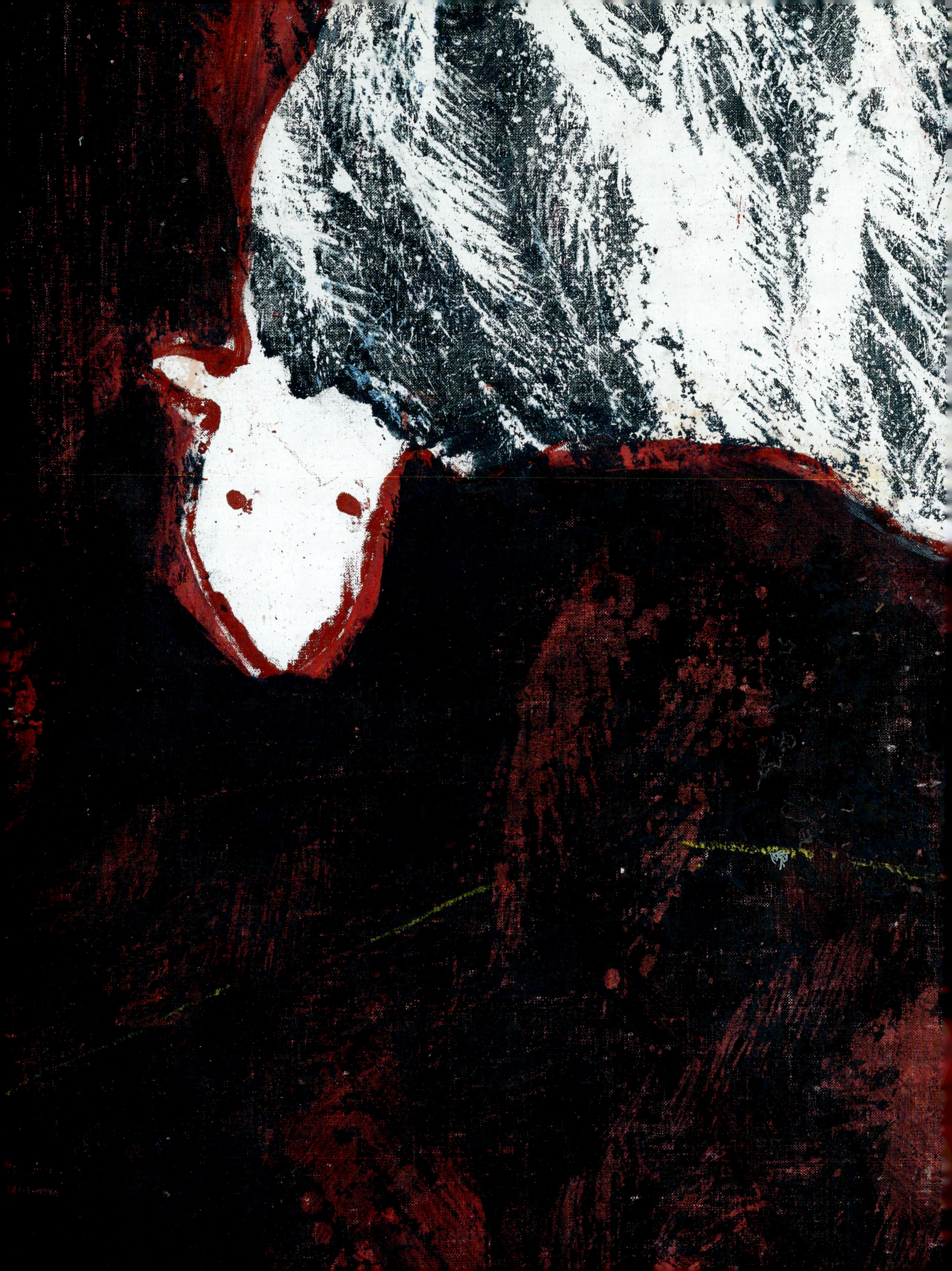

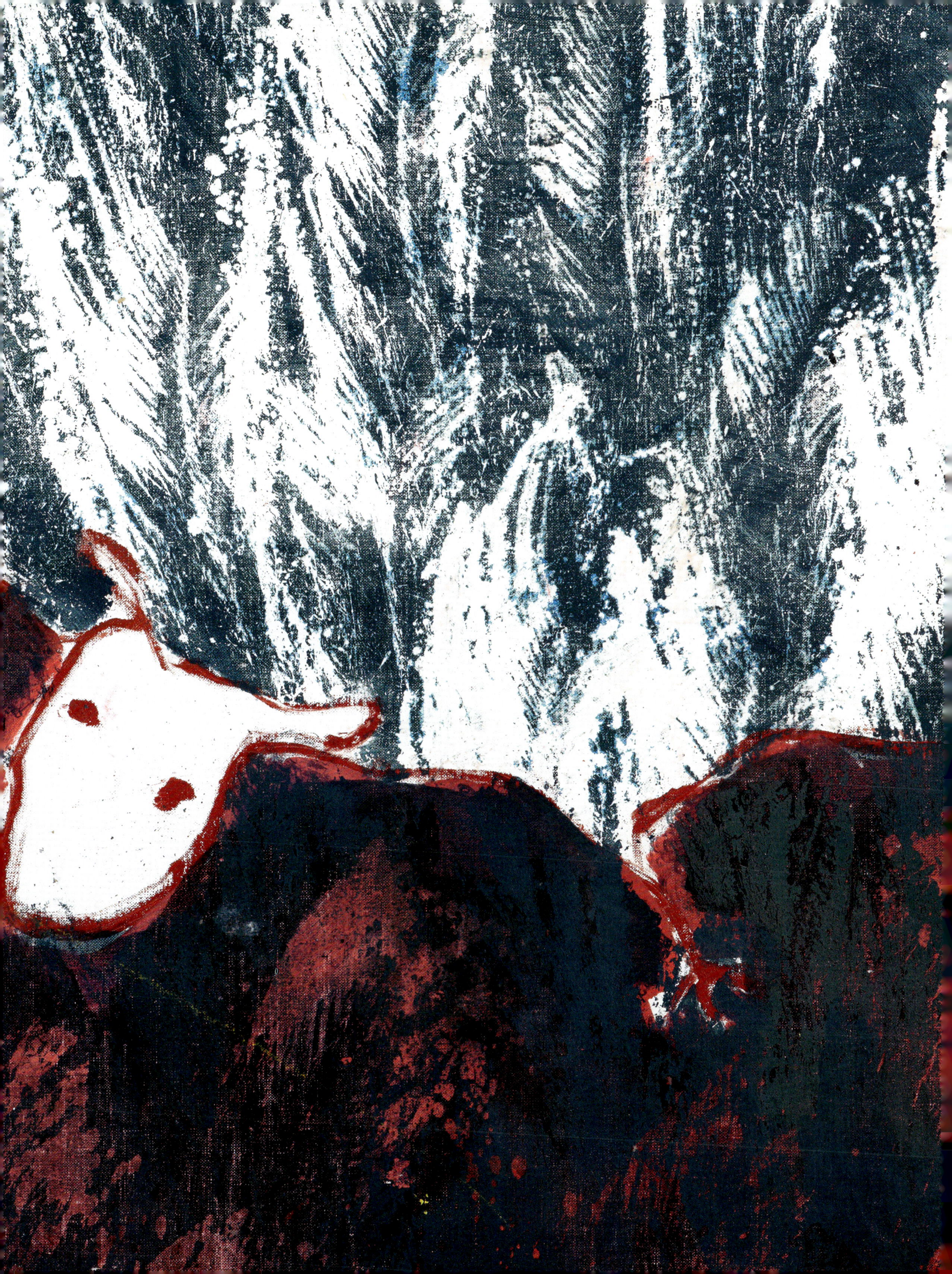

See also Gwarvanda (2016); G. Fortune, 'Form and Imagery in Shona Proverbs', in *Zambezia*, vol. 4, issue 2, 1975–76.

6. For a discussion of the particularities of dreaming in African contexts, see Augustine Nwoye, 'Dreaming in Africa', in *African Psychology*, Oxford University Press, 2022, pp.176–200.
7. A *chitenge* is a characteristic African garment, made in colourful wax printed fabric, that is wrapped around the body like a sarong or worn draped over the body or head like a scarf or shawl.
8. For Zvavahera's use of fashion magazines as sources, see Nomaduma Rosa Masilela, 'Ekphrasis for a Veiled Dream', in *Portia Zvavahera: I'm With You*, Stevenson, 2017, p.22.
9. For a discussion of the prevalence of 'expressionist figuration' in contemporary Zimbabwean painting, see Sean O'Toole, 'Carnivorous Politics, Defiant Bodies: Harare Painting in Turbulent Times', *Frieze*, 26 May, 2018. Accessed 25.06.24. In this article he places Zvavahera alongside Virginia Chihota, Misheck Masamvu, Gareth Nyandoro and Gresham Tapiwa Nyaude and traces their visual language to an earlier generation of painter/printmakers active in Harare from the 1950s onwards. See also Gemma Rodrigues, 'Traditions of Abstraction: Feeling Our Way Forward', in *Five Bhobh: Painting at the End of an Era*, Zeitz Museum of Contemporary Art Africa (MOCAA), Cape Town, 2018–2019.
10. For useful accounts of contemporary painting in Zimbabwe see Tandazani Dhlakama, in *Five Bhobh: Painting at the End of an Era*, op. cit., Valerie Kabov, 'Committed to the Medium', in *Art South Africa*, vol. 13, no. 4, Jun 2015, pp.22–24.
11. On the challenges faced by gender in this masculine-dominated environment, see Meredith Brown, 'Into the Greater Light', in *Portia Zvavahera*, David Zwirner Books, New York, p.12.
12. See Elizabeth Morton, 'Frank McEwen and Joram Maringa: Patron and Artist in the Rhodesian Workshop School Setting, Zimbabwe', and Christine Scherer, 'Working on the Small Difference: Notes on the Making of Sculpture in Tengenenge, Zimbabwe', in Sidney L. Kasfir and Till Forster (eds) *African Art and Agency in the Workshop*, Indiana University Press, Bloomington, 2013, pp.274–97 and pp.180–206.
13. See McEwen (1968) p.436. See Frank McEwen, 'Shona Art Today', *African Arts*, summer, 1972, vol. 5, no. 4, pp.8–11.
14. See Jonathan Zilberg on McEwen's invention of a tradition, which he ascribed with a history and context, in 'Shona Sculpture's Struggle for Authenticity and Value', p.21. See also the entry on Shona Sculpture in the British Museum catalogue: https://www.britishmuseum.org/collection/object/E_Af1996-18-27. Accessed 25.06.24.
15. For an appreciation of McEwen's role as the 'father figure' of Zimbabwean art history, see Raphael Chikukwa, 'Before and Beyond, A Tribute to those who Came Before Us', in *Five Bhobh: Painting at the End of an Era*, op. cit.
16. Modernism's debt to African conceptualism and abstraction is widely acknowledged, even though it went under the now discredited mantle of 'primitivism' with its projections and prejudices intact.

17. Of course Harare was then called Salisbury. Its name was only changed in 1982 when the newly elected Zimbabwean government sought to change the old Rhodesian and colonial nomenclature.
18. See Rodrigues, 'Traditions of Abstraction: Feeling Our Way Forward', op. cit., pp.70–75. She describes the ostracisation of McEwen by the white Rhodesian establishment for his support of and belief in African artists' creativity and selfhood.
19. Four of his paintings were included in Okwui Enwezor's groundbreaking show *The Short Century: Independence and Liberation Movements in Africa, 1945–1994*, held at MoMA PS1, New York in 2002. They were subsequently acquired by MoMA. See https://www.moma.org/artists/4144. Accessed 27.06.24. Mukarobgwa was far from untutored but he was astute enough to conceal his formation from his patron. McEwen was unaware that he had been trained by a local missionary, Canon Ned Paterson, who taught art to many young male artists of his generation and whom McEwen despised as he regarded him as imposing a Western/Christian worldview on his pupils. See Morton (2013) p.276. An exhibition entitled *The Stars Are Bright* (2022) of Paterson's pupils during the 1930s/1940s, held at the Zimbabwean National Gallery, revealed some of the characteristics that prevail in subsequent generations of artists: a recourse to biblical subjects and visionary themes, local landscapes and settings, and the use of pattern, repetition, stylisation as well as a commitment to personal self-expression as the mark of artistic integrity.
19. Artists like Gustav Klimt, Egon Schiele, Francis Bacon and Edvard Munch were all on Zvavahera's radar and even though she denies any overt 'influence', the exposure to European painting, through magazines and books which she would page through, must have helped to inform her sensibility, however subliminally or subtly. See Nomaduma Rose Masilela, 'Ekphrasis for a Veiled Dream', op.cit., p.23.
20. For a discussion of the relationship between contemporary art and revelation, see E. Coomasaru and T. Deichert, *Imagining the Apocalypse: Art and the End Times*, Courtauld Books Online, https://courtauld-website.s3.amazonaws.com/pub/e-books/cbo/Imagining%20the%20Apocalypse-%20Art%20and%20the%20End%20Times.pdf. Accessed 03.07.24.
21. I am grateful to Portia Zvavahera for many hours of conversation in which she described her process to me. These took place over two extended studio visits to Harare in August 2022 and April 2024. Her grace, hospitality and generosity were unbounded. Thanks too to Gideon Gomo for his wisdom and willingness to share.

Ndirikukutsvagai ndirimugomo
2024
Oil-based printing ink and oil bar on linen
213 × 209 cm

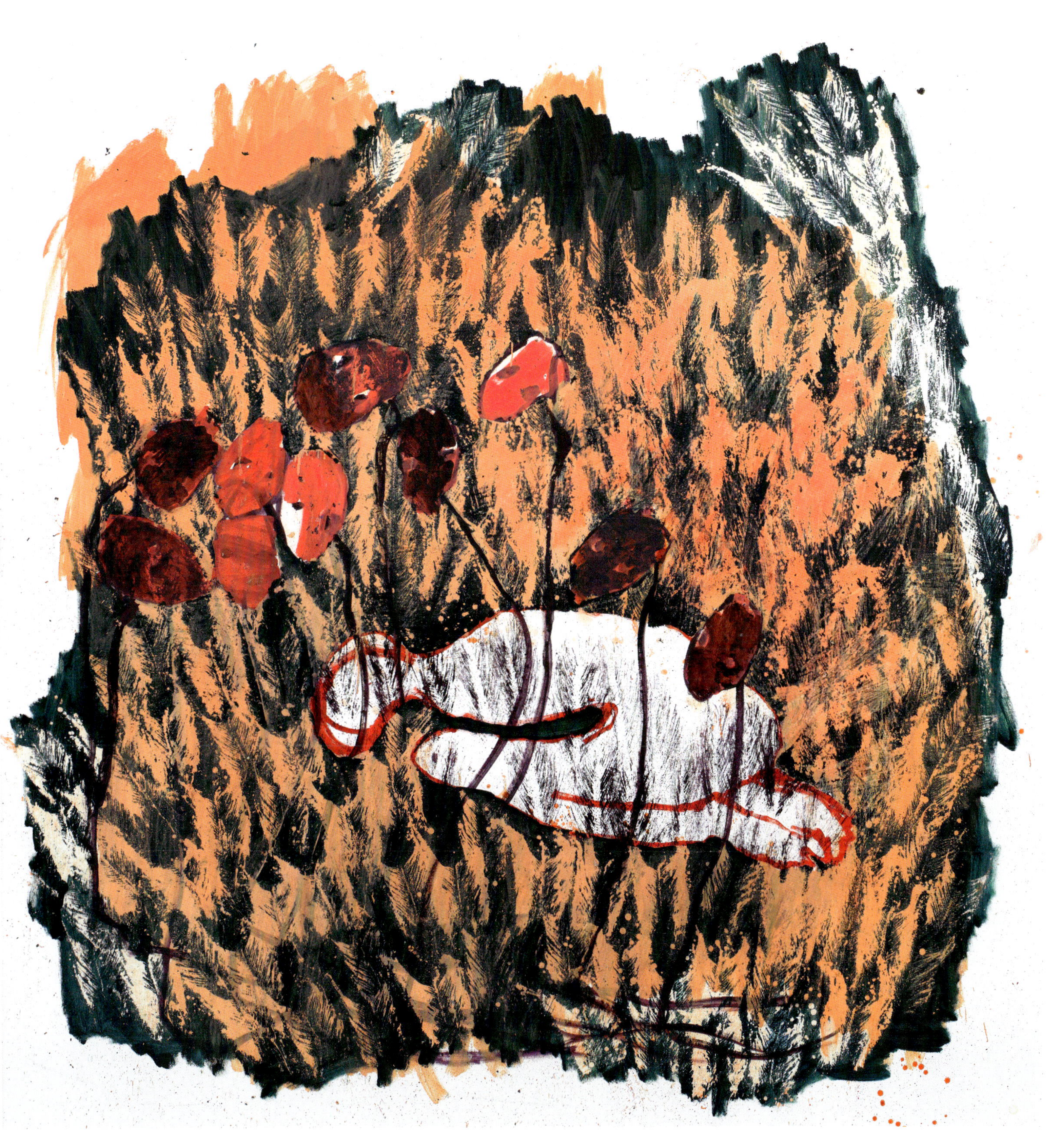

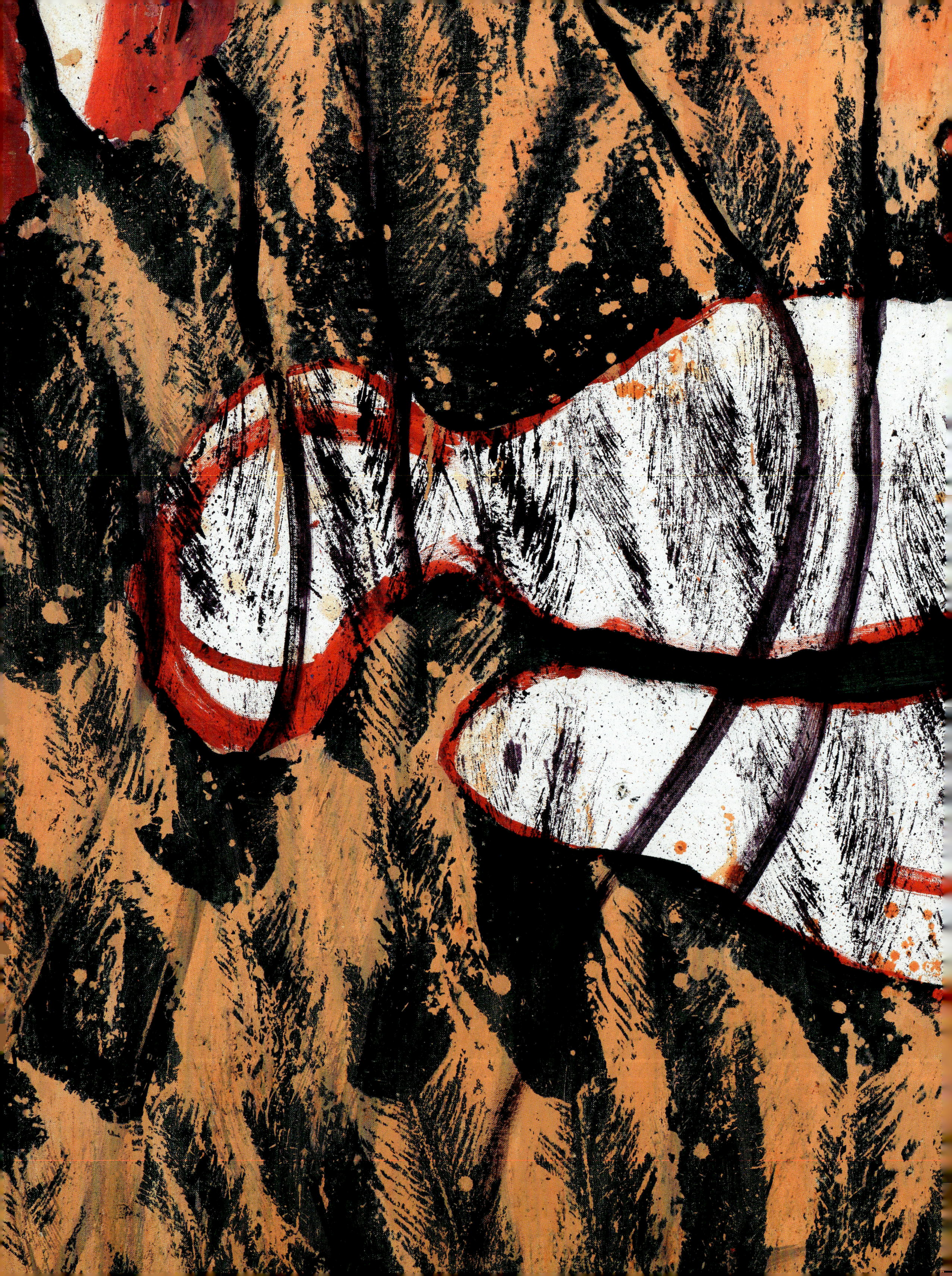

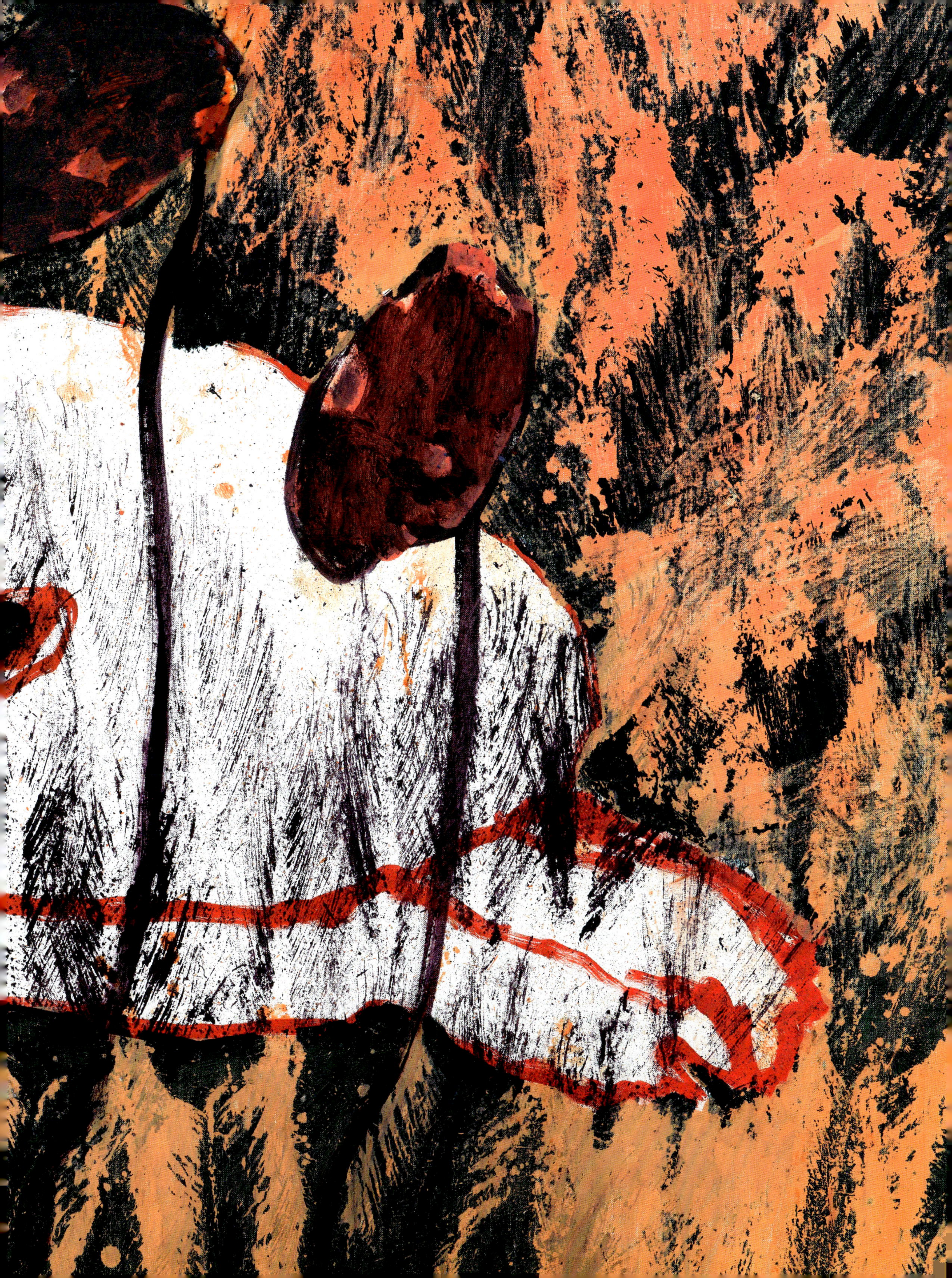

The Energy Present
2024
Oil-based printing
ink and oil bar on linen
195.4 × 197.5 cm

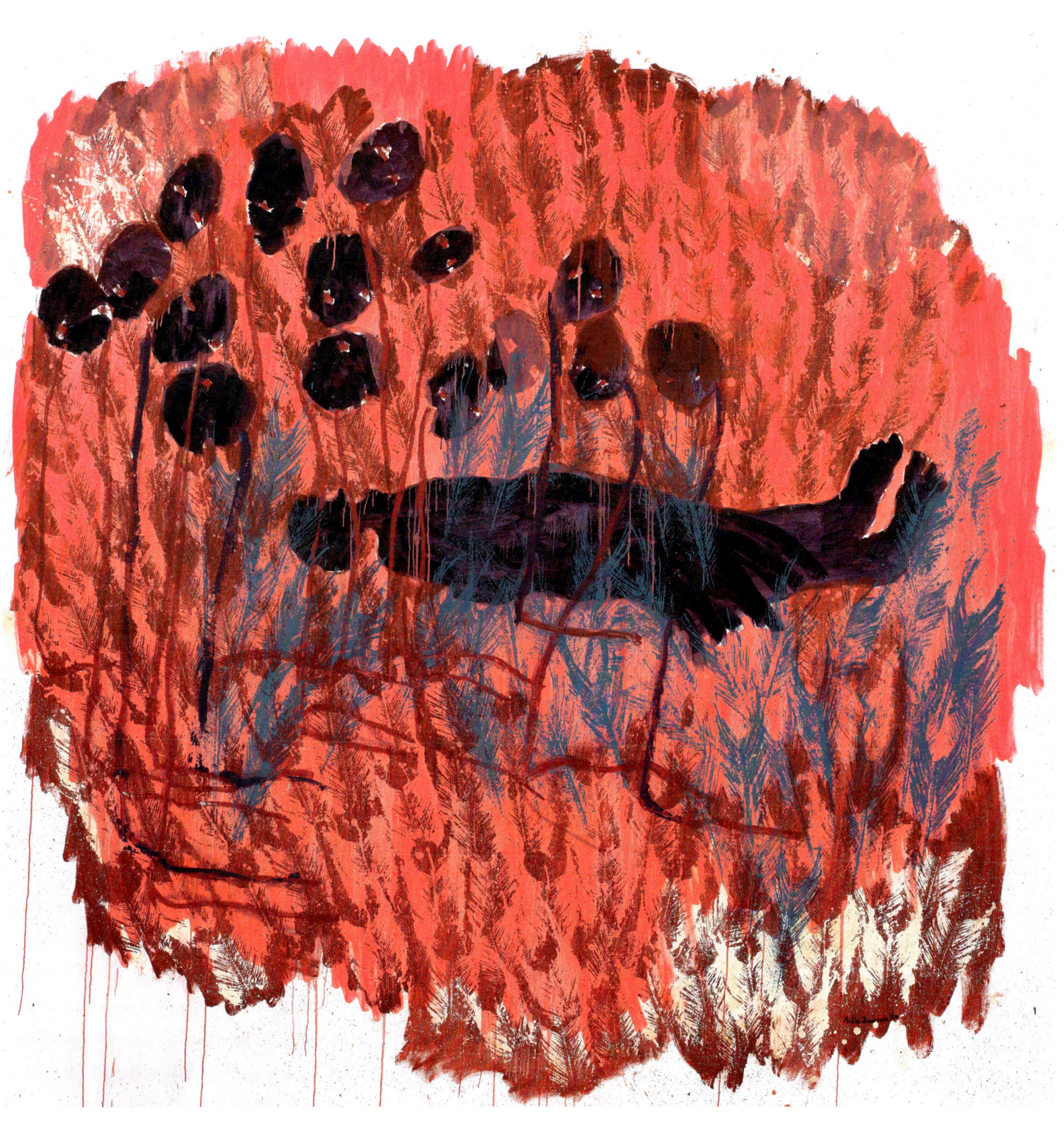

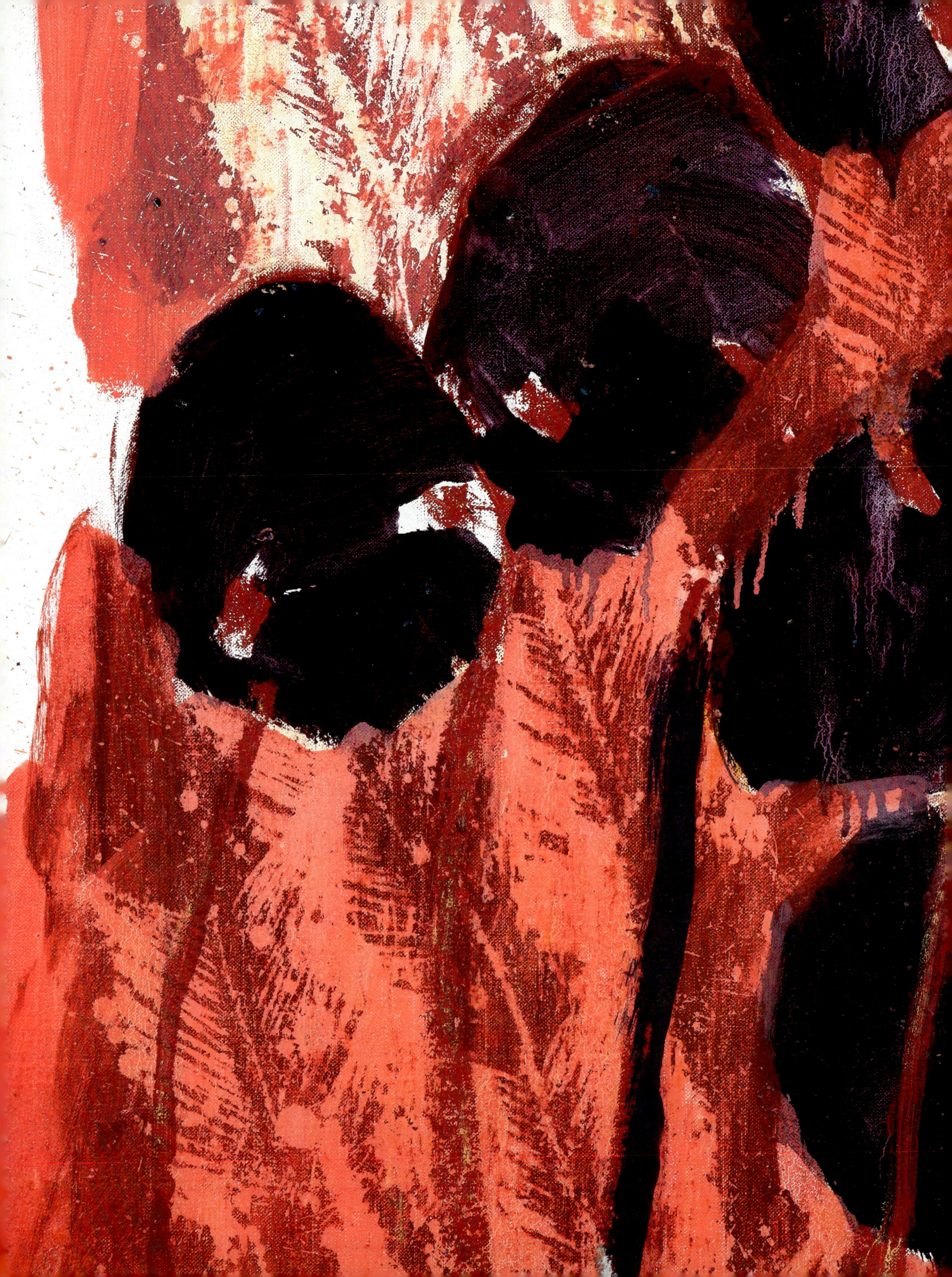

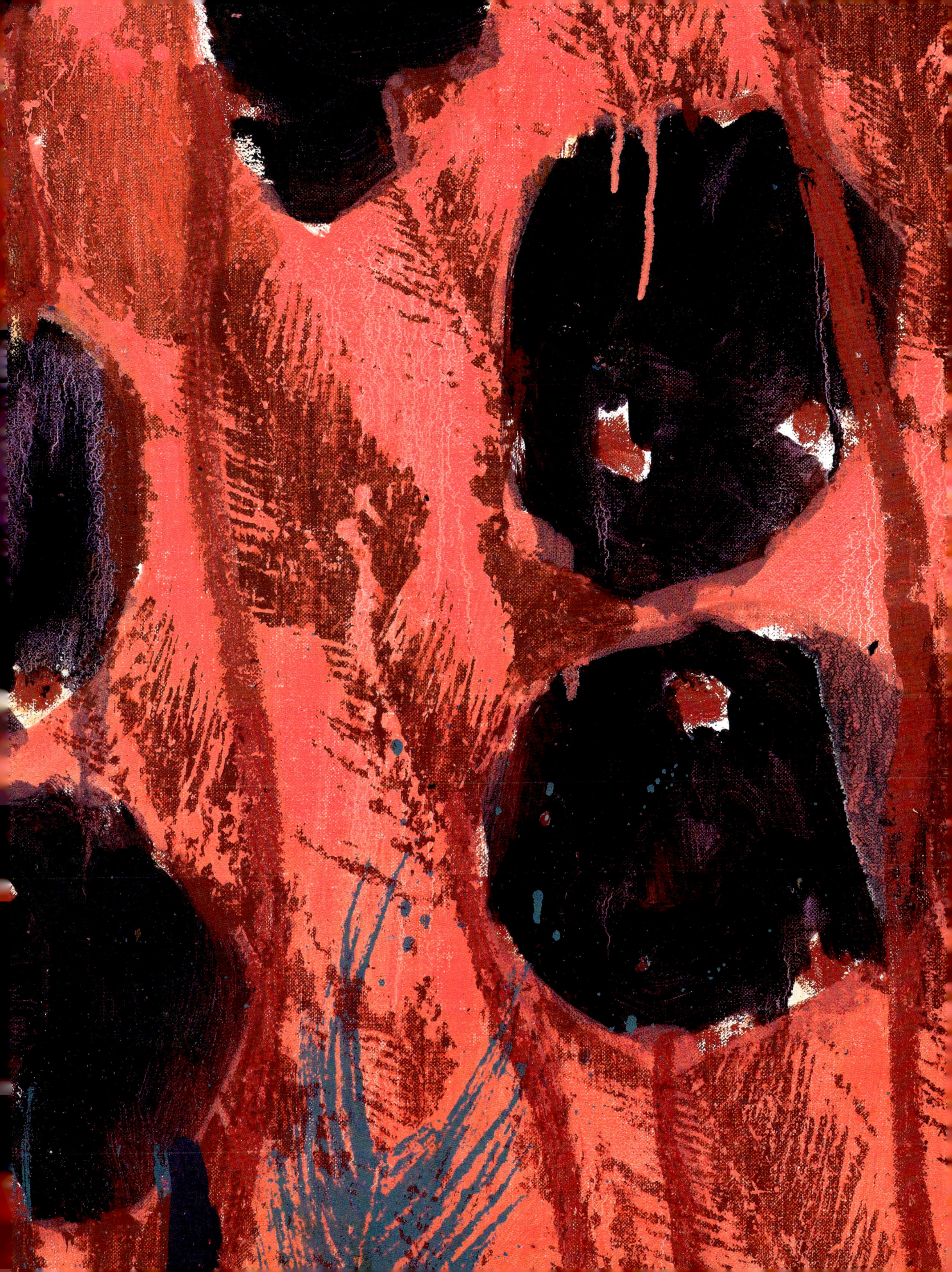

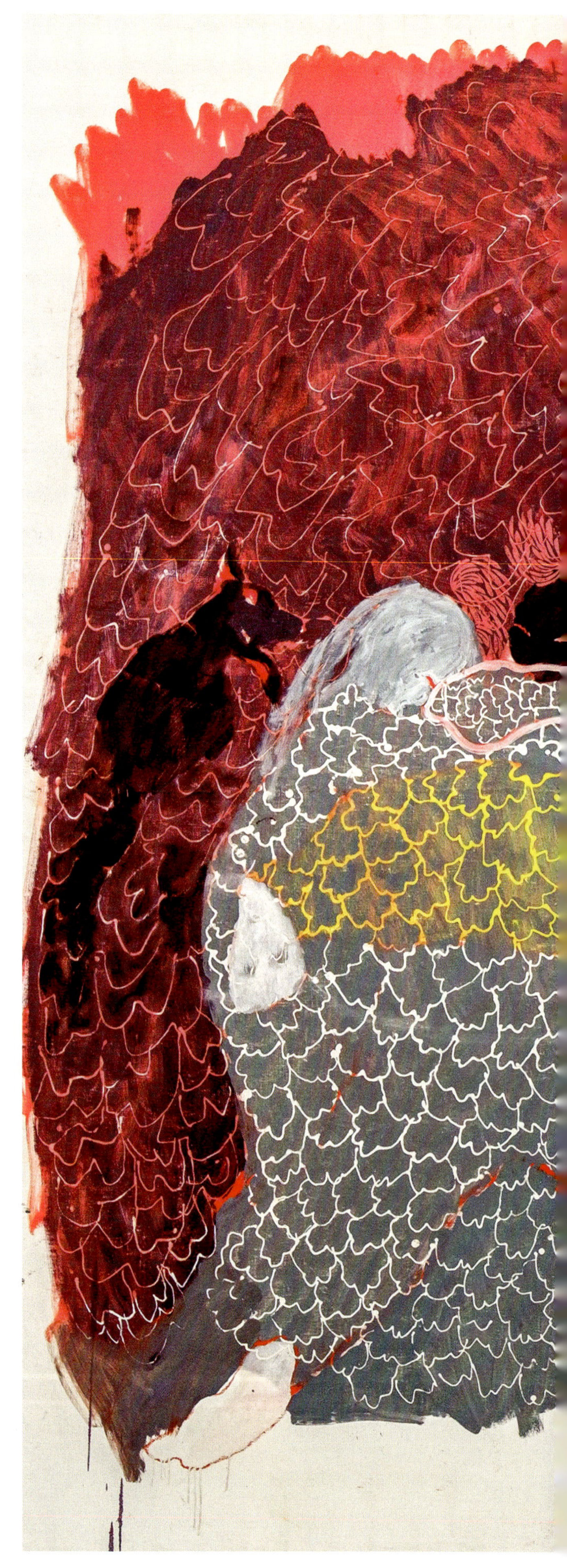

Ranganai henyu
(Devise your strategy)
2022
Oil-based printing ink
and oil bar on linen
215 × 265 cm

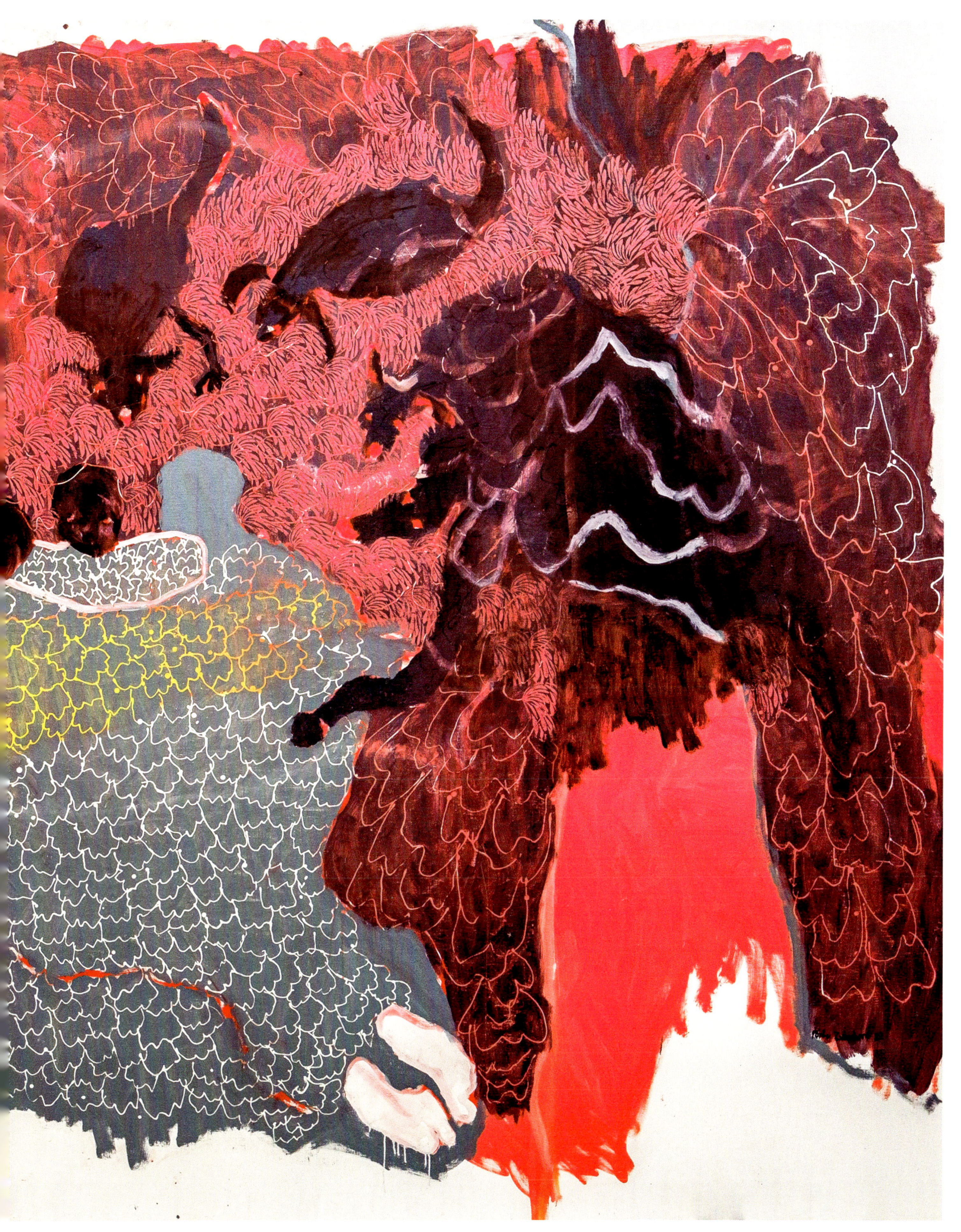

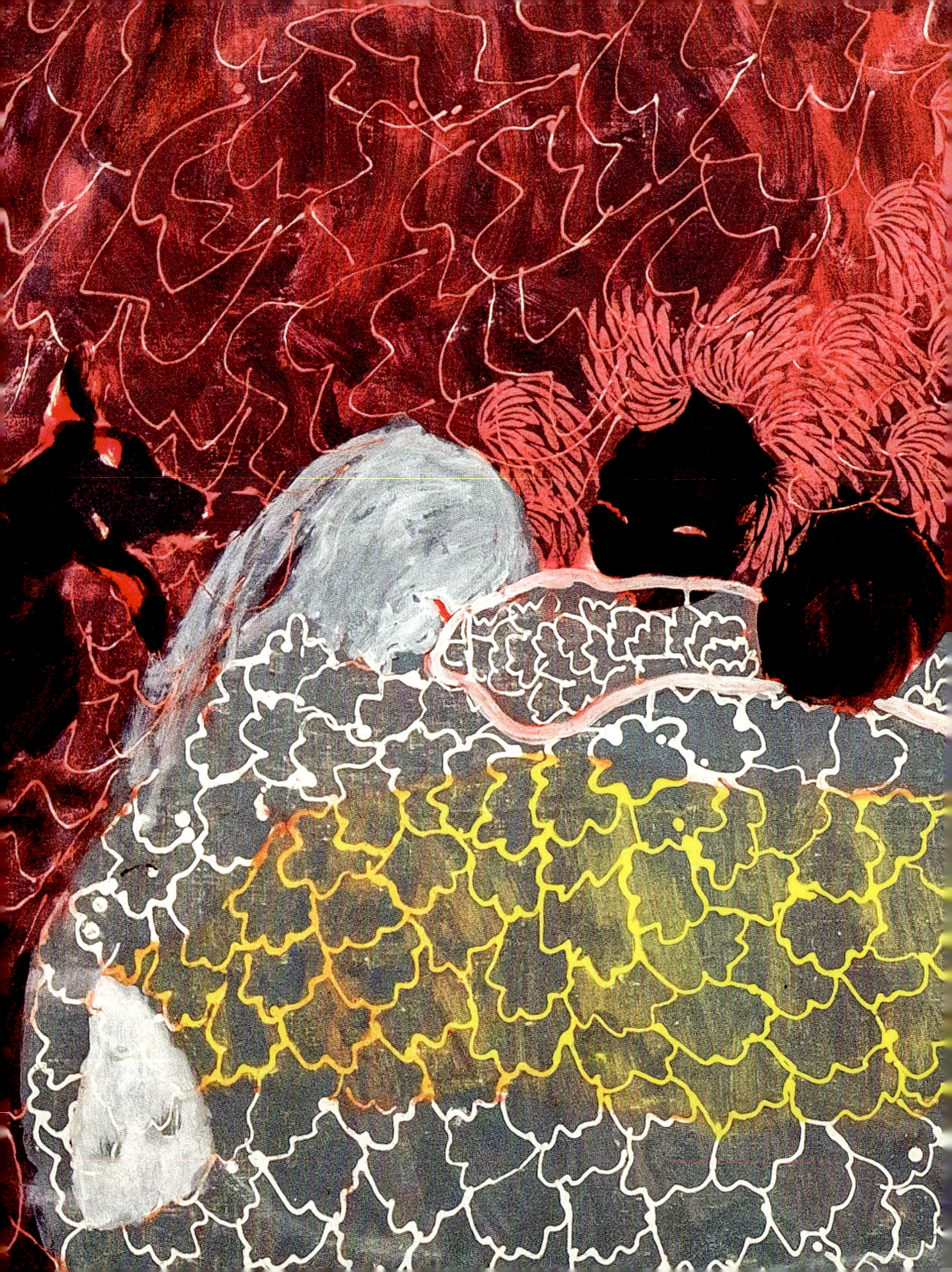

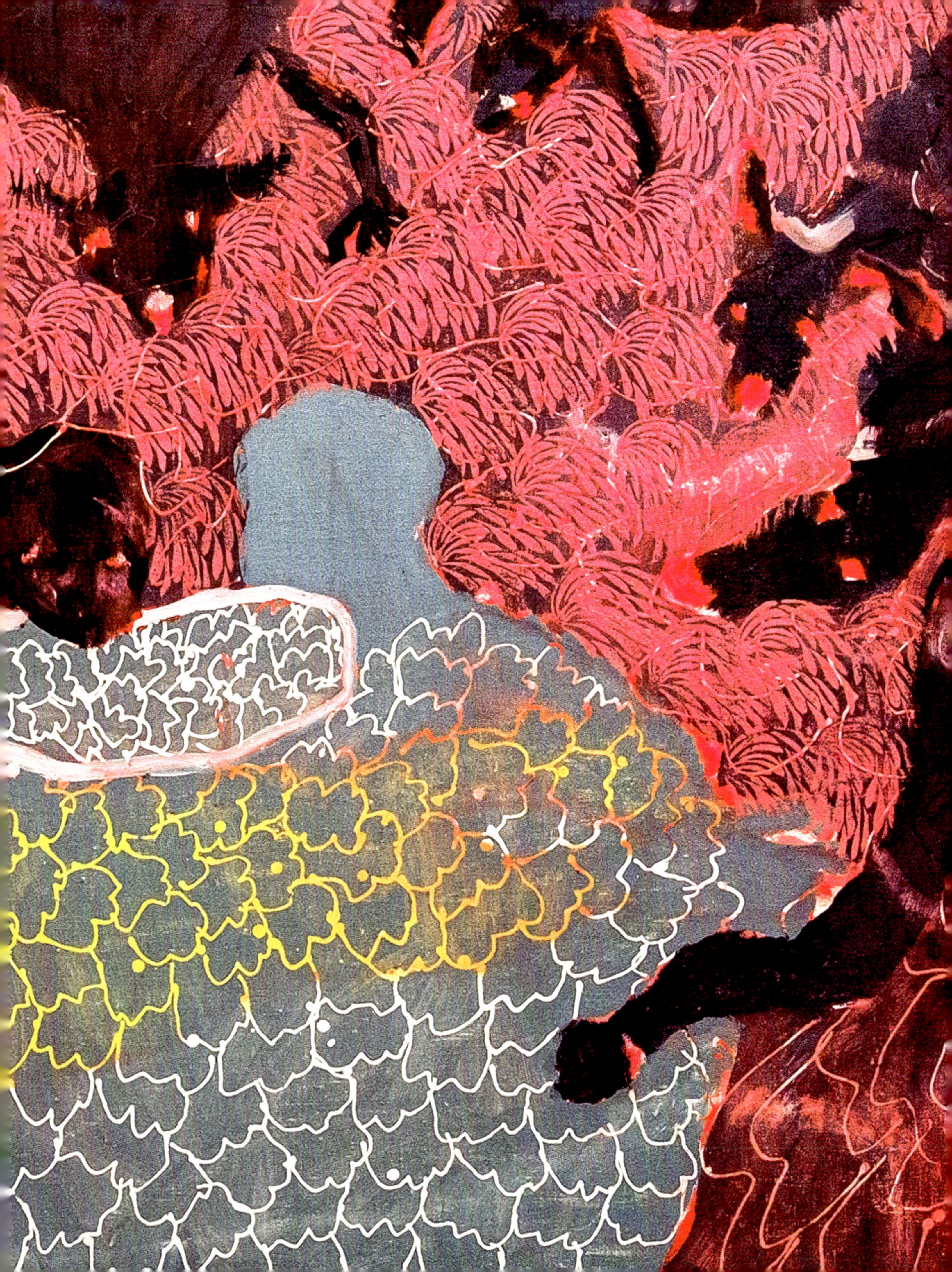

DREAMING IN SHONA

TAMAR GARB IN CONVERSATION WITH
SINAZO CHIYA
TANDAZANI DHLAKAMA
PUMLA GOBODO-MADIKIZELA

following pages:
Pane rima rakakomba (1)
(There's too much darkness)
2023
Oil-based printing ink
and oil bar on canvas
222 × 332 cm

In July 2023, I invited three women to sit with me in the Stevenson gallery in Cape Town, on the occasion of Portia Zvavahera's show, *Pane rima rakakomba (1)* (There's too much darkness). We talked surrounded by her works and in front of the eponymous canvas that has become a pivotal piece for our exhibitions at Kettle's Yard, Cambridge and Fruitmarket, Edinburgh. What follows is an edited version of the conversation we shared. Four women, of and from Southern Africa, confronted Zvavahera's practice, its locatedness and cultural specificity while exploring its connection to a planetary consciousness and the learned and shared languages of art.

TAMAR GARB (TG): About 10 years ago, before Portia Zvavahera became the international phenomenon she now is, I was introduced to her work by her gallerist, Michael Stevenson, and I've been talking with him about the work ever since. From the start, I was fascinated by what I think of as a kind of unique language that she has invented – this interface between painting and printmaking that serves as a medium for a personal cosmology and vision. I have only written on her work once before, and that was in the context of a book on the experimental and peripatetic African art school/workshop, *ÀSÌKÒ*, set up by my dear friend, the late Bisi Silva, who ran it from CCA Lagos, which she founded and directed between 2010 and 2019.[1] Portia was one of the first graduates of this programme and Bisi was one of her earliest mentors and guides. She encouraged me to work on Portia and we talked about her work a lot. So, these shows in the UK feel like a tribute to the prescience and brilliance of one of the first African women curators to change the contemporary landscape of art and to bring Black women from the continent into global visibility and prominence.

It would be good to start with an introductory remark from each of you about your own work and your knowledge of and engagement with Portia's practice.

TANDAZANI DHLAKAMA (TD): I'm a Zimbabwean curator, currently working at Zeitz Museum of Contemporary Art Africa (MOCAA) in Cape Town. My first memory of encountering Portia's work was in 2011 when I started working at the National Gallery of Zimbabwe. I saw Portia's work at Gallery Delta which closed down last year, but which was one of the oldest contemporary art spaces in Harare. Portia always used to have shows with one of her best friends, Virginia Chihota, who also works with printing but in her case in combination with other mediums – drawing, collage etc.

I feel like Portia and Virginia speak a similar language. Virginia uses a lot of printing with

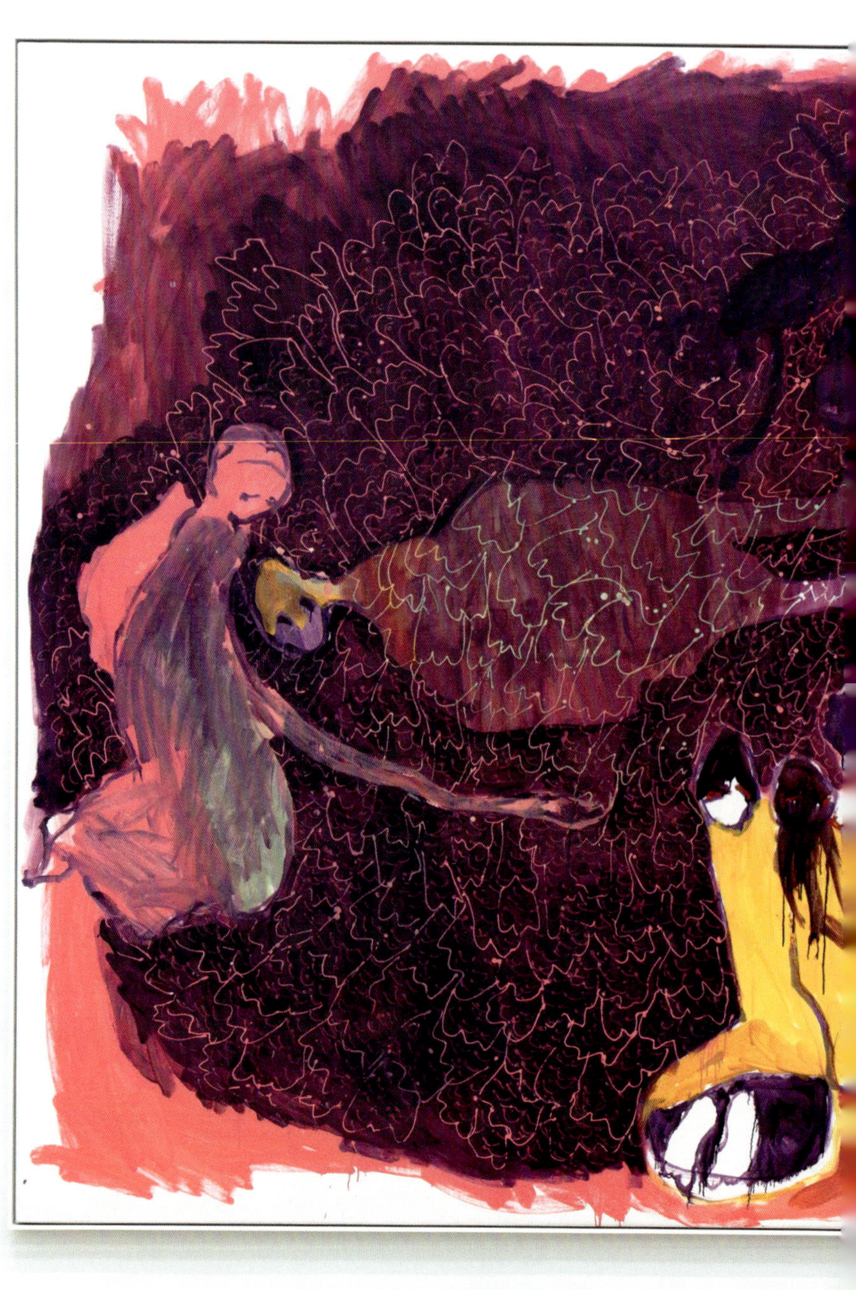

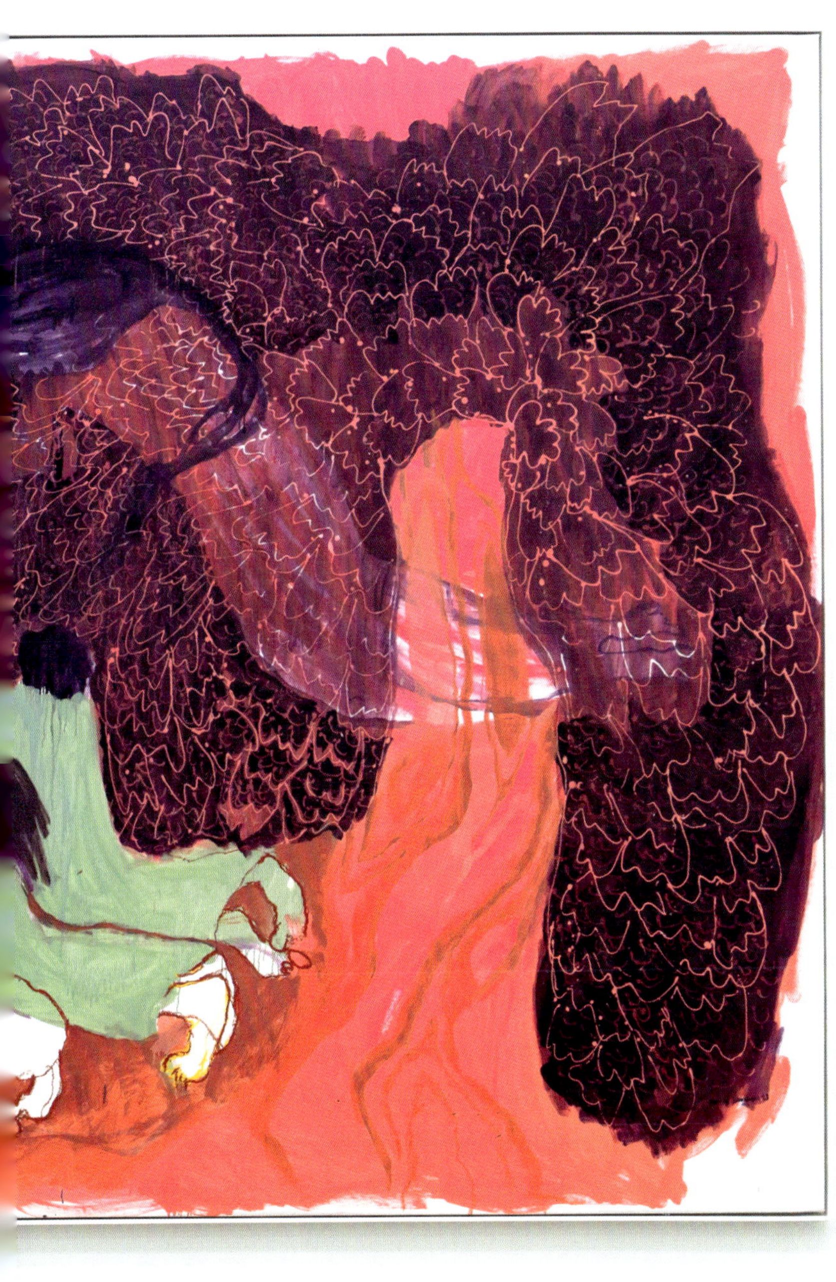

repetition and patterns as well as themes around motherhood and the body and so I've always seen Portia and Virginia's work together. At that time, Portia's work was much smaller in scale and it was darker – visually darker but also the themes were darker. Now, when we talk about Portia's work, dreams inevitably come to mind, but then these were invariably nightmares. I remember people having different reactions from their own perspectives. And then for me personally, a defining moment with Portia was when she represented Zimbabwe at the Venice Biennale in the Zimbabwean Pavilion in 2013. That iteration was curated by Raphael Chikukwa, who's now the Director of the National Gallery of Zimbabwe. At that point, the work became much larger, and I think we started seeing the specific colours that we see today. Before then, there had been more blacks and browns and oranges. She started using a different palette and I think she started getting much more international attention. When I moved to Cape Town in 2017 to work at Zeitz MOCAA, one of the first shows I started working on was titled *Five Bhobh – Painting at the End of an Era*, which was a survey of painting from Zimbabwe. 2017 marked the end of a political era – the end of Robert Mugabe's rule. So, I was investigating how artists were interpreting such a dramatic change – the longest-standing president had just been forced to resign. And I felt that it was artists who would give us a perspective on this significant moment. For me selecting Portia was a no-brainer – she had to be in the show. So, we included two works by Portia in the section on 'spirituality', which was fitting because in general her work often engages with the metaphysical.

PUMLA GOBODO-MADIKIZELA (PG-M): When I first saw Portia's work a few years ago, I was struck by the scale and ambition of the paintings. But then I started reading about it, and particularly enjoyed a few interviews that she did which are available online, and I became particularly intrigued by how she paints from her dreams. I find this so evocative, the fact that she finds a visual language through which to record or recall dream imagery as well as a private, esoteric world of symbols and shapes and signs. My work is increasingly engaged with the languages of art and the role of the aesthetic in relation to histories of systemic violence and trauma. I'm at Stellenbosch University, where I hold the position of Founding Director of the Centre for the Study of the Afterlife of Violence and the Reparative Quest. Thinking about concepts of healing, as well as mechanisms of coping and the way we manage trauma, has led me to turn to the arts and artists to explore how they use diverse artistic languages to work through trauma and transform it or give it meaning. My training is in psychology, and specifically psychodynamic psychology. What people must confront to work through trauma is something that is at the heart of our work at the Centre. So, when Tamar invited me to join the conversation around Portia's work, there was no question that I wanted to be part of it.

SINAZO CHIYA (SC): I'm one of the partners at Stevenson gallery so I have worked closely with Portia over the last few years. I've been fortunate enough to get a front-row seat into how she thinks and how to piece things together, how we're going to frame certain aspects of our shows, what to emphasise, what not to emphasise, what's necessary and what's not. I encountered Portia's work before I started working here. I remember being struck by it, and even now working with it, it still somehow resists language. And that's an amazing experience to have with art. Portia's like a seer. And the work engages with the unconscious, conveyed obliquely sometimes through the intricacy, the colour and the pattern of it. It's so difficult to articulate everything that she's doing here. How to put it into words …

Pane rima rakakomba (1)
(There's too much darkness)
2023 (detail)

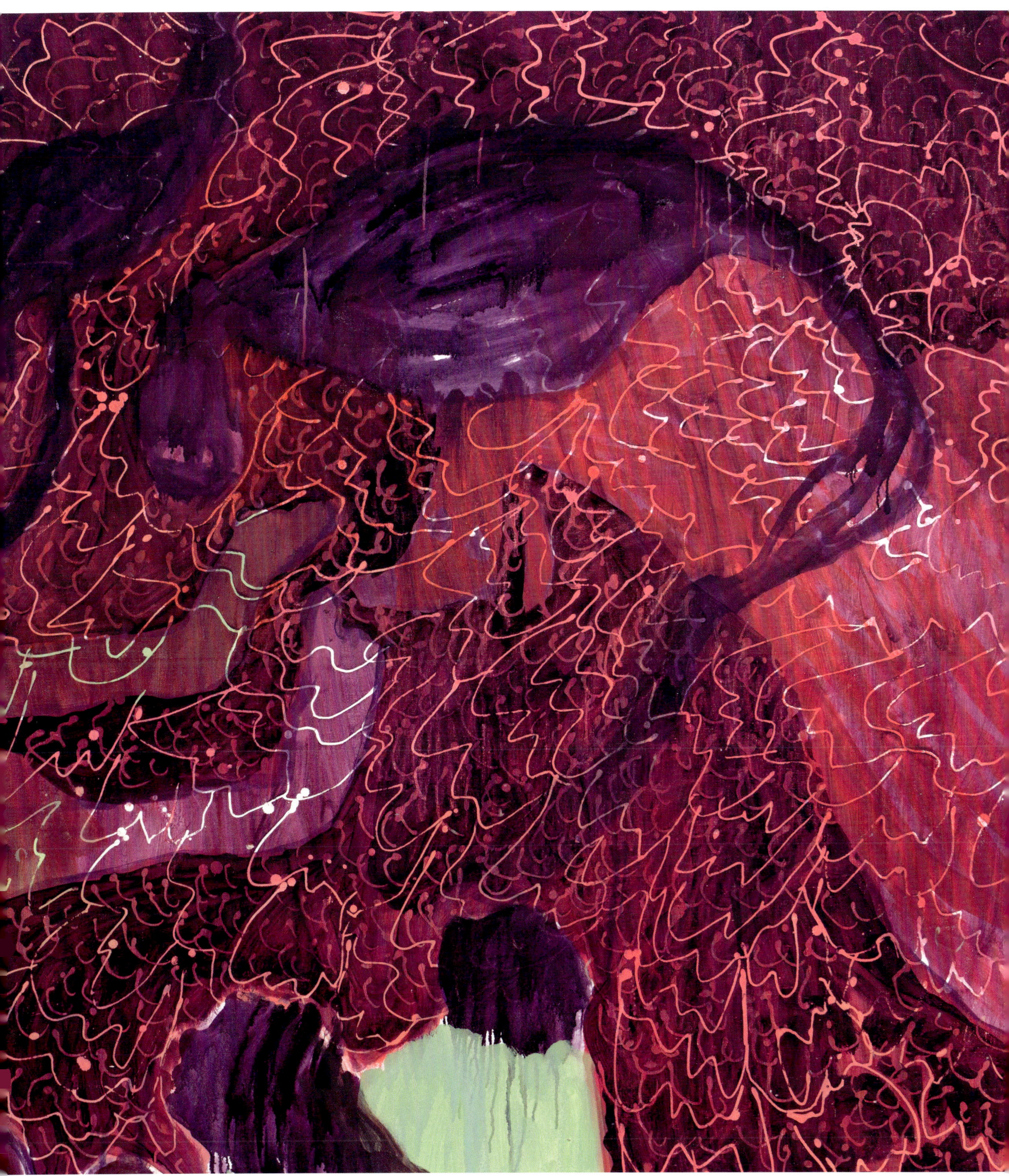

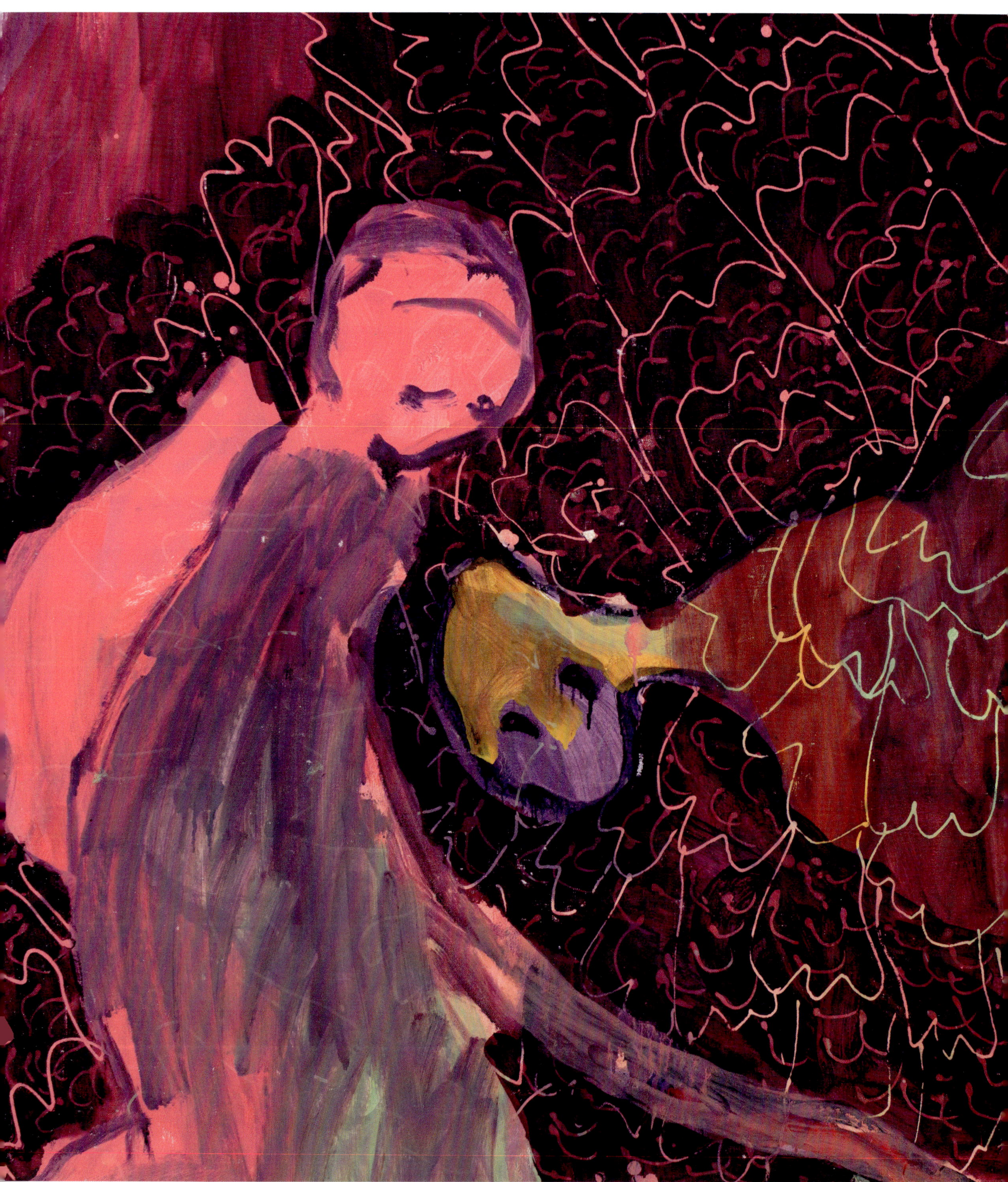

Pane rima rakakomba (1)
(There's too much darkness)
2023 (detail)

TG: Thank you all so much for those introductory remarks. Perhaps a good place to start would be with the notions of dreaming and dream work. Portia described herself to me as 'dreaming in Shona', and dreams constitute the font from which she works. What do you think Portia understands by connecting painting and dreaming so intricately? I am thinking of dreaming as a practice, and the experience of dreaming as a resource, or perhaps a repository or a storehouse – of mood, of atmosphere, of imagery, of anecdote. How do you think Portia sees that?

SC: From what I've seen it seems like Portia almost understands the dream as concrete information. The dream is not necessarily something that's speculative. Yes, it's something to be interpreted, to be teased out, but it's a real phenomenon that's happening. It's not just a subconscious residue of something that's a consequence of everyday life. Rather, it's a level of experience that has a direct import to how she lives her life, how she steers her life, and when it's not something that's necessarily guiding her, it seems like it's a way for her to process the fact of being in reality. So, it's like the dream constitutes a separate context, but also one vitally connected to who she is as a person, and also as an artist.

I remember a conversation we had when she was in London during her Gasworks residency in 2017. She felt blocked because she couldn't dream. And there was so much of her world that was thrown off kilter by the fact of not being able to dream that I think I gained a newfound respect for what it means to have this relationship with the unconscious self, the 'sleeping' self. It's not about getting your set many hours of rest, it's another life that she has. And that's where she gathers strength. That's the place from where she understands her world, how she understands her relationships, how she understands her fears. So, the dream is a place that's vital to her, like a secondary context, or like a co-primary context. How it works with the painting is that it seems like it's the organic source for her creations. Perhaps she's figuring out what love looks like. So, whether it's in the earlier shows like *I Can Feel It in My Eyes* in 2015, when she was in the gardens, or whether in shows like this one, *Pane rima rakakomba (1)* (There's too much darkness), many years later, when it's about motherhood, it seems like dreams provide the root of so much of her production. It's not as if she's creating from a somnambulist state. Rather it's like being acutely awake, but also so completely tied into this other state.

TG: I like this idea of being both profoundly asleep and intensely awake at the same time. The sense of the equivalence of the sleeping life and the waking life, the nocturnal and the diurnal, the entanglement of conscious and unconscious experience, if they are separable at all …

PG-M: I was struck, Sinazo, by what you said about the dream as real information. This evokes for me the question of the tension between sleeping and waking life in culturally specific African contexts. You know, dreams are sometimes considered to be messages that convey urgent information, and this seems relevant considering the role of dreams in Portia's artistic process, and the way in which her art reflects a dreamy aesthetic. When I started looking into her work, for me, there was this palpable link to her dreams, but also to an archetypal set of references for her dreams that speaks to a much broader cultural context, experiences that extend beyond herself, and which have affected women in her community. As private as dreams are, there's also something collective about them. I can't help thinking of a sense of mourning together, of connecting with other women's pain. Yes, the imagery might come from a specific dream, but it's a dream that connects her to a much wider circle of others. Maybe that's why she couldn't dream in London, being away from her cultural-communal context. For, dreaming can be like a call and response. You are called in a dream to act upon something. It's not just your story. You are called upon to speak to and on behalf of your community. You are 'chosen', in other words, to speak on behalf of others. That's what I find really so inspiring and fascinating about Portia's work – it brings us back to the meaning of dreams in a collective and culturally specific sense.

TG: I think you are right. Portia's paintings function as an expression of her experience but also as a conduit to a broader world and cosmology. While listening to you all speak, I was reminded of the dream as part of a matrilineal heritage. Portia talks about the fact that when she was a child, her grandmother, to whom she was very close, had vivid dreams and used to recount them in the mornings, in Shona. So, dreams and language/lineage are tied together, and it was through the powerful figure of her grandmother that she as a child took dreams very seriously. This makes me think of the matrilineal imaginary, a kind of feminine consciousness that is both visceral and oneiric – perhaps an umbilical and symbolic connectedness that is made manifest through the dream.

TD: I would say I think Portia shares a prophetic inclination or a gift, and it can be said that that gift can be passed down through the family line. It's as if she is a seer or is able to receive messages that she then documents through painting. Painting then serves as a vehicle for interpreting or translating, activating or deactivating whatever messages she's receiving. So often 'spirituality' is invoked in relation to her work, but it's hard to define. It's not something that is necessarily separate from material or earthly life in a binary way. These categories are permeable – like waking and sleeping.
I would want to think of this in a culturally specific way. A lot of African cultures engage with spirituality as part of everyday life. There isn't always a separation of church and state. Religion or the spiritual life is part of your everyday; it's part of who you are, and I think Portia's work resists those binaries. And so, when I use the term prophetic or even spirituality, I'm not necessarily thinking about it in a Western sense that creates this dichotomy. Nevertheless, there are biblical references in her work as well and religious art that fills her imaginative universe, whether awake or asleep.

For example, if you look at her use of figures, they are often winged like angels or eagles. They can be part human, part animal, of this world and the next. I think that the dreams are not just dreams, but they serve as a coded kind of messaging of aspects of life that she's meant to wrestle with. And so, painting too is a form of interrogating whatever it is that is coming through the dreams. At the same time, I think for Portia painting enables reflection. It's self-reflexive, for example, when thinking through relationships (motherhood, marriage, sisterhood), but also feelings of fear and anxiety and unease.

TG: Would it be accurate to say that the dream is like an interface? It is drawn from what we might want to call the spiritual or metaphysical or another zone of being. But it's also informed by the fears and the anxieties and the nightmares of life and living. So, it's as if the language of the dream, without wanting to use a Freudian model here, transforms everyday experience: the anxieties of life, whether in relation to motherhood or love or intimacy or whatever, those relationships and encounters and stories get transformed and reappear in the language of dreams. Sometimes these are forbidding and dark and dangerous. And sometimes they seem to be infused with a kind of warmth and energy and love. Sometimes they're mixed. But the dream feels like a storehouse between waking and sleeping, between

***Hauvatore* (You cannot take them)**
2023
Oil-based printing ink and oil bar on canvas
209 × 182 cm

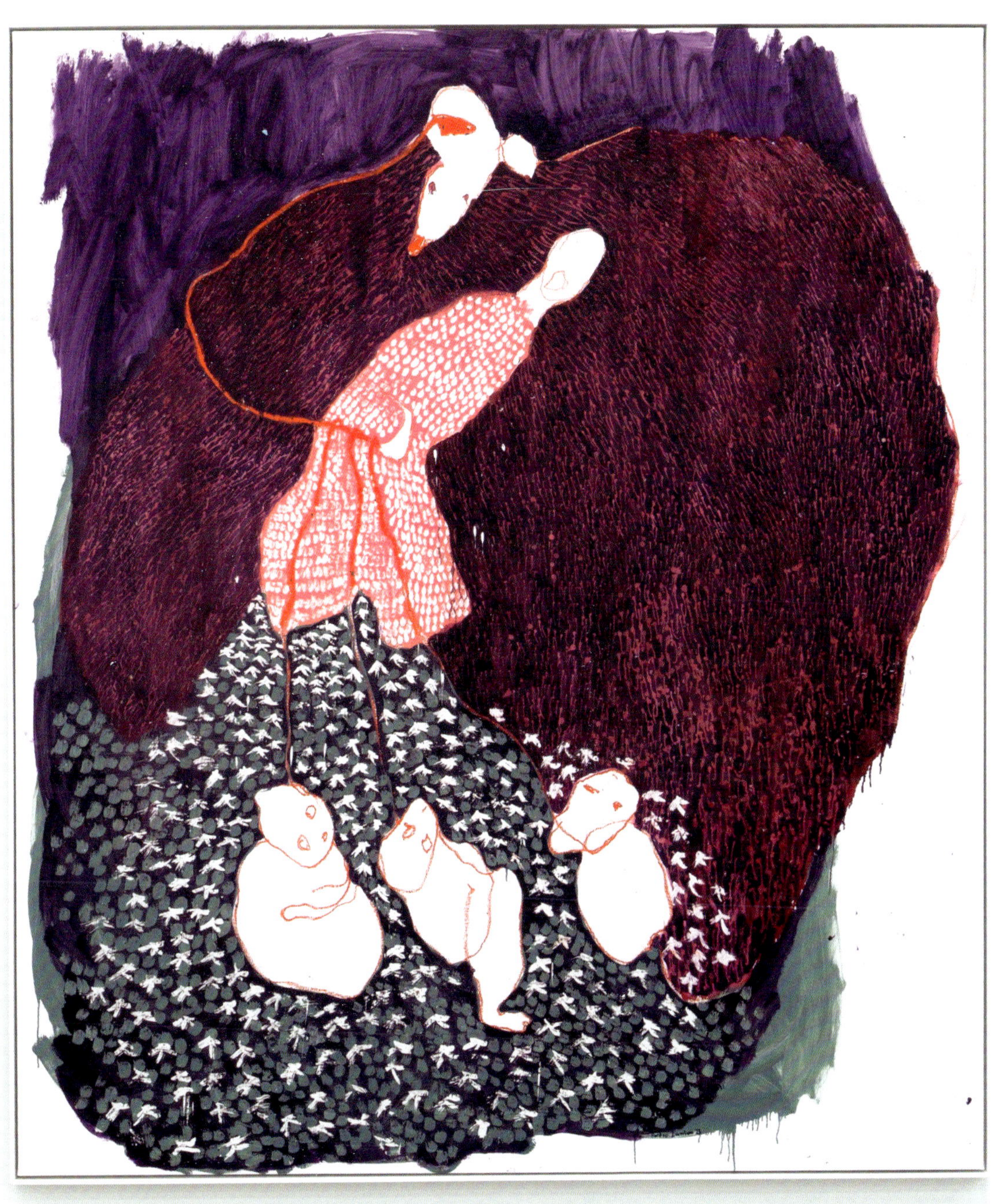

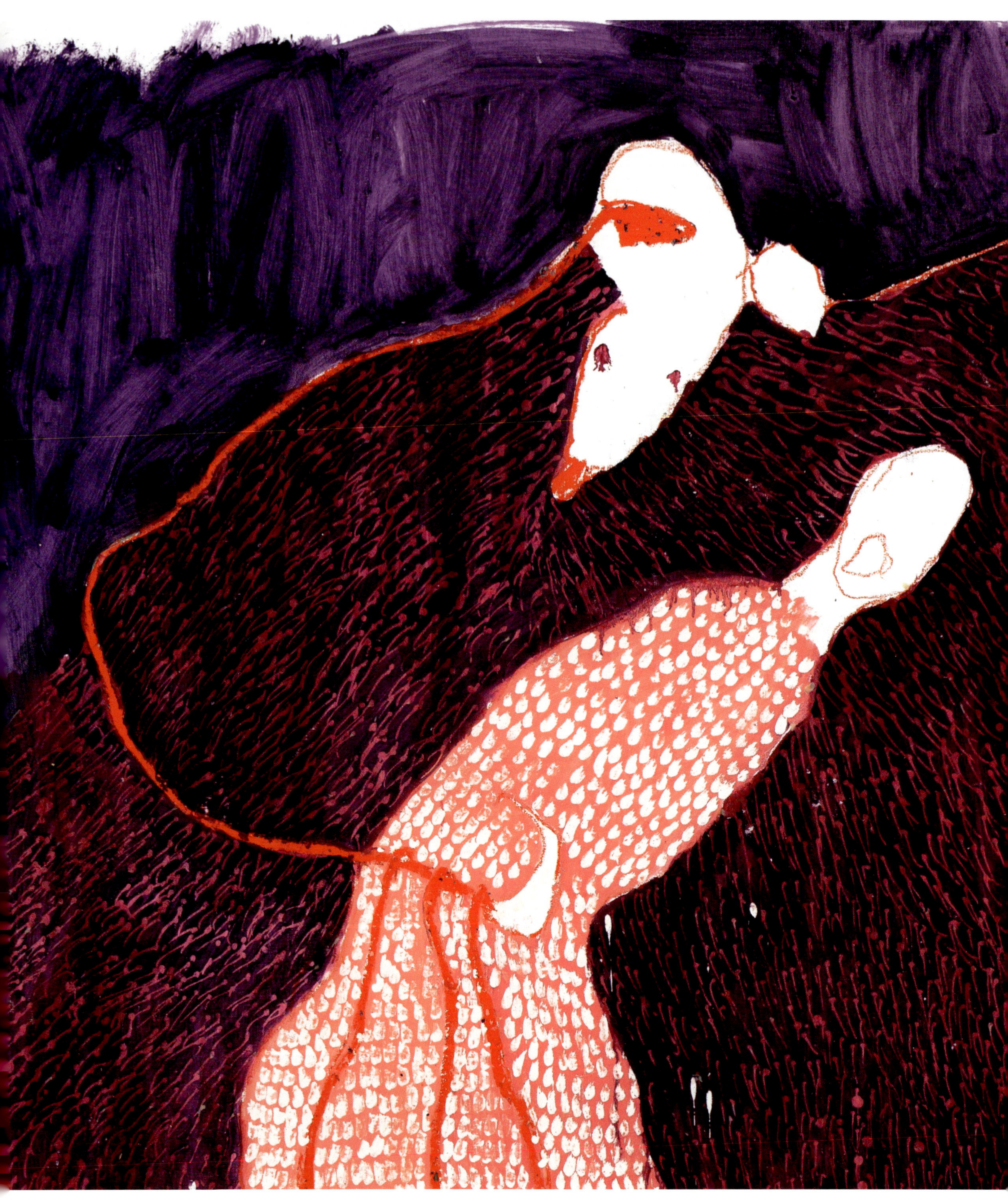

Hauvatore **(You cannot take them)**
2023 (detail)

consciousness and unconsciousness. I'm not sure if there's a Shona-specific way of articulating this, or a particularly Zimbabwean and African way of understanding it. Of course, I'm not looking for some kind of 'authentic' or 'pure' African experience. There's no such thing. Portia lives between multiple cultures and languages, from her Christian faith to her connection to the ancestors. Dreaming, like waking life, moves between these porous and intermingled identities.

PG-M: Yes, no one wants to use the overused term intersectionality, but I do think we need to integrate various models for understanding dreams, and the Freudian is an unavoidable one. There is an unconscious life, which requires that we consider thinking psychoanalytically. But there's also the fact of people's everyday lives, their cultural embeddedness, and the stories and suffering this generates. We need this cultural context, you know? Call it African if you will, and I wouldn't avoid calling it 'African', because this is the cultural heritage from which Portia draws inspiration for her work. And we need to consider the way dreams are a gateway to something that transcends consciousness, perhaps to something in the realm of the spiritual. Here we also need an expansive notion of the spiritual. It's not necessarily religious, but it's the spiritual in a much broader sense, something which we often struggle to articulate. How do we think about the spiritual in her paintings? Do the paintings offer a bridge between consciousness and the spiritual, and convey her gift of understanding or seeing beyond? Sometimes people speak about the gift of speaking through the spiritual or articulating the spiritual for the rest of us. In the African context, there is the acceptance that some people are gifted with a power or capacity to transform what is unspoken and exists in the deep unconscious into meaningful messages that can be presented and taken in multiple directions. There is always something central in the messages. Whether it is: 'behold, this is what is happening to the rest of us womenfolk', or 'behold, this is (a calamity) that awaits us as a community'. Some kind of foretelling or prescience. So, we can understand the unconscious – the wellspring of dreams – in these terms, as a source that can be tapped for new knowledge and inspiration for art. Through the unconscious all of the provocations of life and its anxieties and the unsettling stuff that's happening, that is beyond rational articulation or narration, find a voice. And here's where I find artists so interesting. With them there is this connection of the unsayable and ineffable to the hand and the work of the hand. It's an action, an embodied deeply unconscious action that speaks through the body and the movement of the pen/brush of the artist. So, it's an integration of the unconscious, the embodied, you know, stuff that is really embedded within the body. All those memories that may be unconscious, but are situated in the body, and how these memories explode into shape and colour and form. So, the dream becomes a mediator between the unconscious and the body. It is integrated and intersected and ultimately explodes or finds form on the canvas or on the page.

TD: In Pentecostal Christianity, a message could either be coming from an evil place or from a holy place. And if it's coming from an evil place, you need to cancel it – speak against it or do something to stop it. If it is coming from a holy place it's unveiling truth, which is still linked to the everyday, because we're talking in this context about not separating spirituality from the natural, what we would call the natural realm. And there's also this idea that if you don't write it down, if you don't document it, you'll forget the dream. So, I think in Portia's case, there is this embodied act of painting, but it's her way of cancelling or inscribing or documenting. It's tantamount to capturing a message, which of course doesn't resemble the dream exactly. For Portia, one dream can become ten paintings or ten paintings can be ten dreams. And the dreams can be freely interpreted or drawn out, stretched and altered. So, I think even though you don't see the urgency in the brush strokes, there is this tension which comes from the need to capture whatever the message is, on the one hand, and to make sense of the associated anxiety or subconscious affect on the other. Pumla, you spoke of how the body carries memories, anxieties and hopes. Portia puts these on the canvas. And the body is present in every single painting that I've ever seen of hers. I've personally never seen a Portia painting without a figure.

TG: That brings us to the question of figuration and the way that the body, usually a female figure, perhaps a surrogate for the artist herself, is so central to all her work.

TD: Yes, it's very striking. But it also escapes the binary of abstraction and figuration. Without being didactic, it is always evocative ... What the body does in Portia's work is create this tension, this agony, this ambiguousness.

SC: Yes, for me I see a profound integration or unity that happens in her practice. From the prophetic to the reflective; from being the 'streaming of experience' to being profoundly embodied; from a kind of secular knowledge to metaphysical inquiry; from Judeo-Christian dogma to ancestral beliefs and traditional practices. It seems like across all these oppositions there's a profound unity that she holds while still maintaining an interesting narrative and aesthetic tension. But it seems like for her the boundaries don't exist. They don't need to exist. Her practice has a very subjective kind of wholeness that she's making and figuring out through each painting, through each dream. In a way it's a gift that is then there for other people to see from, and it veers from the deeply personal to the collective. It seems like all these spheres find some kind of answer through her practice.

TG: I love your idea that the painting becomes a space for the meeting of these apparent dichotomies. But what is also crucial, and this goes back a little bit to the translation of daily life and dream life into the physical material conditions of painting, is that the process is made possible through an incredibly knowing, technical skill that comes out of an immersion in traditions of making and training and learning. Whether drawn from the wax-resist techniques of batik that characterises fabric printing in local communities and cultures or from European painting and printing practices, I think it's very important to understand that this is a learned process, built on the acquisition of skills honed over time and through repetition and experimentation. Look at the way in which these surfaces are orchestrated, look at the way in which the edges of the canvas/paper are left bare; look at the integration of pattern and flatness and shape and contour. These are so highly calibrated and carefully composed. I think that I'd like us to talk a little bit about what it is to be so engaged with technologies of making and printing. Of course, the materials Portia uses are quite unique. To paint in printer's ink and to paint under and over print and pattern and with the resistant and subtractive process of wax – these are techniques of her own making. Here once again we have an irreverent confection of methods that knows no obeisance to hierarchies of art and craft, medium and material, the earthly and the divine.

TD: As you say that, I'm immediately reminded of the National Gallery School of Visual Arts and Design (NGSVAD), which twenty four years ago was known as the BAT Visual Art Studios, and the Harare Polytechnic Art Department, where Portia studied. At those two institutions she was taught by extraordinary people who really

Nhai shiri waitasei nyanga?
2023
Oil-based printing ink
and oil bar on canvas
249 × 138 cm

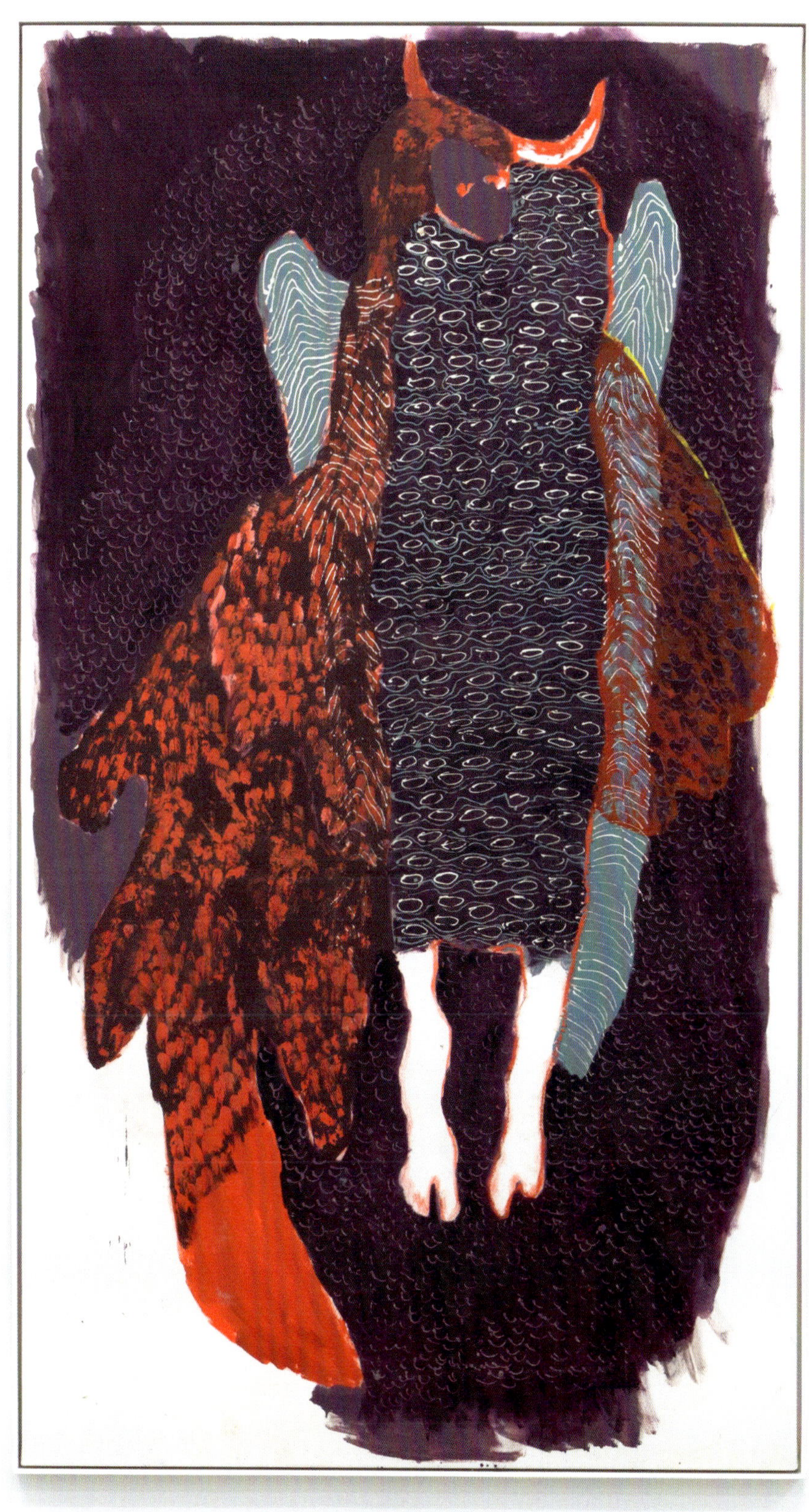

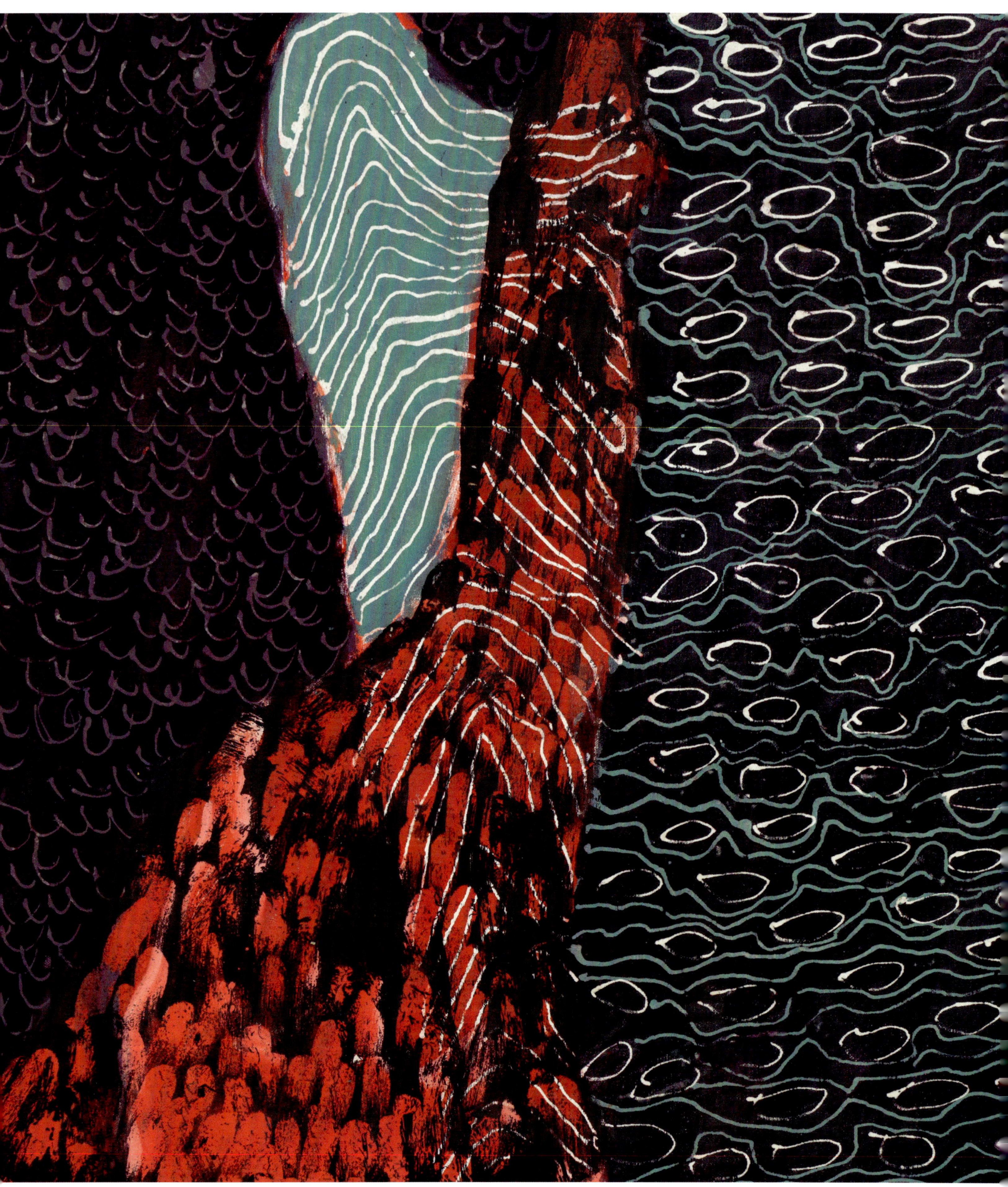

Nhai shiri waitasei nyanga?
2023 (detail)

challenged the status quo and shifted art pedagogy in Zimbabwe. These schools were, and still are, very modest spaces. The NGSVAD, for example, was started in the 1960s or 1970s, during colonisation, by the then director of the National Gallery, Frank McEwen. At that time, Black people really were not encouraged to study the arts. They were not seen as serious artists and their work was referred to as primitive. So, the National Gallery, of what was then Rhodesia, started what was called the Workshop School. Here McEwen wanted to give Black artists an opportunity to express themselves on their own terms. This might sound slightly patronising today, but it was seen as radical at the time. The art lessons for this school took place in the basement of the National Gallery, and he gave the students art materials and basic guidance and important art lineages emerged from that time. The school then became formalised over time after independence. And today it's based in a high density, historically significant part of Harare called Mbare, which started off as a place for dormitories that were created to house Black men who had come to the city for work.

And so, the foundation of the NGSVAD where Portia studied is that of resistance. The school has historically been a radical space. And then if you think of the Harare Polytechnic, there was an incredible artist, mentor and lecturer named Chiko Chazunguza, warmly known locally as Mukoma (brother) Chiko. He was head of the department of arts in the 2000s, which is when Portia attended the Harare Polytechnic. By 2007, Zimbabwe was going through an economic crisis with world record hyperinflation, to the extent that basic commodities were very hard to come by. Yet though it was a difficult economic time, Chiko had high expectations for the students. If they said that they couldn't finish the assignment because there was no paint, he would say to the students, 'listen, if you can't find yellow paint, go and find something yellow on the street and put it on your painting and make an artwork'. They had to be inventive. He also directed them to self-reflect and look at references from around them, in their own world. He was encouraging them to think about our histories and our contexts in a material and visceral way. Other art spaces were still emphasising looking at old European Masters. As a result of Chiko's direction some of the most ingenious Zimbabwean artists emerged under that tutelage. Portia is a product of those two important institutions, their training, their rigour, their curriculum. I've never heard anyone call her work 'primitive.' I can see why someone seeing it for the first time might just assume that this African artist is somehow intuitively working in this way, but it's important to assert that it's coming from a place of incredible resourcefulness, and radical pedagogies.

PG-M: Listening to you, Tandazani, I am so struck by the site specificity of this trajectory. You trace the pre-history of Black art training in Zimbabwe to the 1960s. Thinking about the way it started reminds us how even during the colonial era, the colonisers might have assumed that they were situating African people in a particular context or mindset of 'backwardness' or 'primitiveness', assuming that they were incapable of being creative, of producing original work. They locked African people in, so to speak. But, people find a way of rising above and being inventive and that to me is what is so extraordinary about Black experience – its transcendence beyond the confines of colonial or apartheid victimhood. I am so moved to hear you speak about the site of training, of where art was born, and how the work of Portia and others emerges from it. It's almost like it's a metaphor itself for how people rise up and defy the limitations placed upon them. You are told where you belong, what your limits are. You belong in Soweto, you belong in Langa, or any of the other townships created to lock you in. You are an object of someone else's fantasy, in their minds, an embodiment of a total absence of imagination, and yet you use imagination to redefine who you are and to reclaim your sense of identity, what you know yourself to be. I am interested in the way we form a sense of identity in relation to place, even to a place whose very purpose is to keep you down. You can't really write people off as objects. That project is bound to fail every time. It's so important to remember that people do not exist simply as objects of someone else's gaze and can reclaim their sense of agency. In a way, art then becomes a metaphor for subverting all that, a vehicle for the expression of that reclamation.

TG: I guess this is interesting too in relation to our discussion of dreams and dreaming. These processes are so powerfully connected to the imaginative life, the inner life, which no one can rob anybody of. And then there is the question of how the inner life can be mediated, translated into something that others can apprehend or access. How is it made manifest materially and in language? I am so struck by the image you have all created of the expansive growth of a world of dreaming and thinking and making, notwithstanding the delimitations of colonial expectation or physical constraints. Within that space, skills were developed and honed and something special could grow. Out of that, creative life can flourish and technologies and skills are developed to reflect upon the situatedness of subjectivity at the same time as it navigates an imaginative capacity that is without boundaries and borders. The dream I guess, translated into painting, stands for this. It comes from somewhere specific but it reaches out into the world, and into other worlds.

SC: I think Tandazani's story sheds an amazing light on Portia's practice. And what you, Tamar and Pumla are saying about how pedagogic practices and human resourcefulness can end up working for one, even as they themselves are beating the 'structural' odds, is an interesting idea. It is a unique tightrope to walk, where one assimilates to a learning practice or working style but must also be alert to keeping boundaries so that these influences don't end up determining who one is, and one is not having to fashion one's self in relation to them. This is important. It's a matter of people sharing creativity, focusing on their own stories and histories, being willing to share skills, resources, perspectives, so that artists are given the scope to privilege their own subjectivity. It's not prescriptive. It's not a matter of being told to make a response to this regime in a particular way in order for your art to be recognised. It's a creative community. A little cabal of artists making work that is for them. Or even an artist like Portia who is making work for herself.

You can call Portia's work political in its own way, but it also doesn't need that kind of label. She's so completely assured about what labels she uses and what she doesn't use in relation to her practice. And as regards the skill, the technique of it, I think she paints as if she's got nothing to prove. She paints with every kind of sensibility and tone that she wants to and produces this amazing balance between precision and gesture that is absolutely self-owned and confident. It's beholden to no one. With Portia, everything is in its right place according to an instinct that she's worked on, learned and honed for a very long time. It's built on years of practice and perseverance, and the 'mastery' of a set of skills and technologies that she has made her own.

TG: That's so important. There is nothing naïve or untutored about her practice. And through curatorial initiatives, museum collecting and displays, books, magazines as well as the experience of her teachers there was exposure, from early on, to European oil painting. Figures like Pablo Picasso, Gustav Klimt and Egon Schiele were engaged with and processed. Our debates on cultural borrowing and appropriation can be so

***Ndirikukuona* (I'm watching you)**
2023
Oil-based printing ink and oil bar on canvas
249.5 × 142 cm

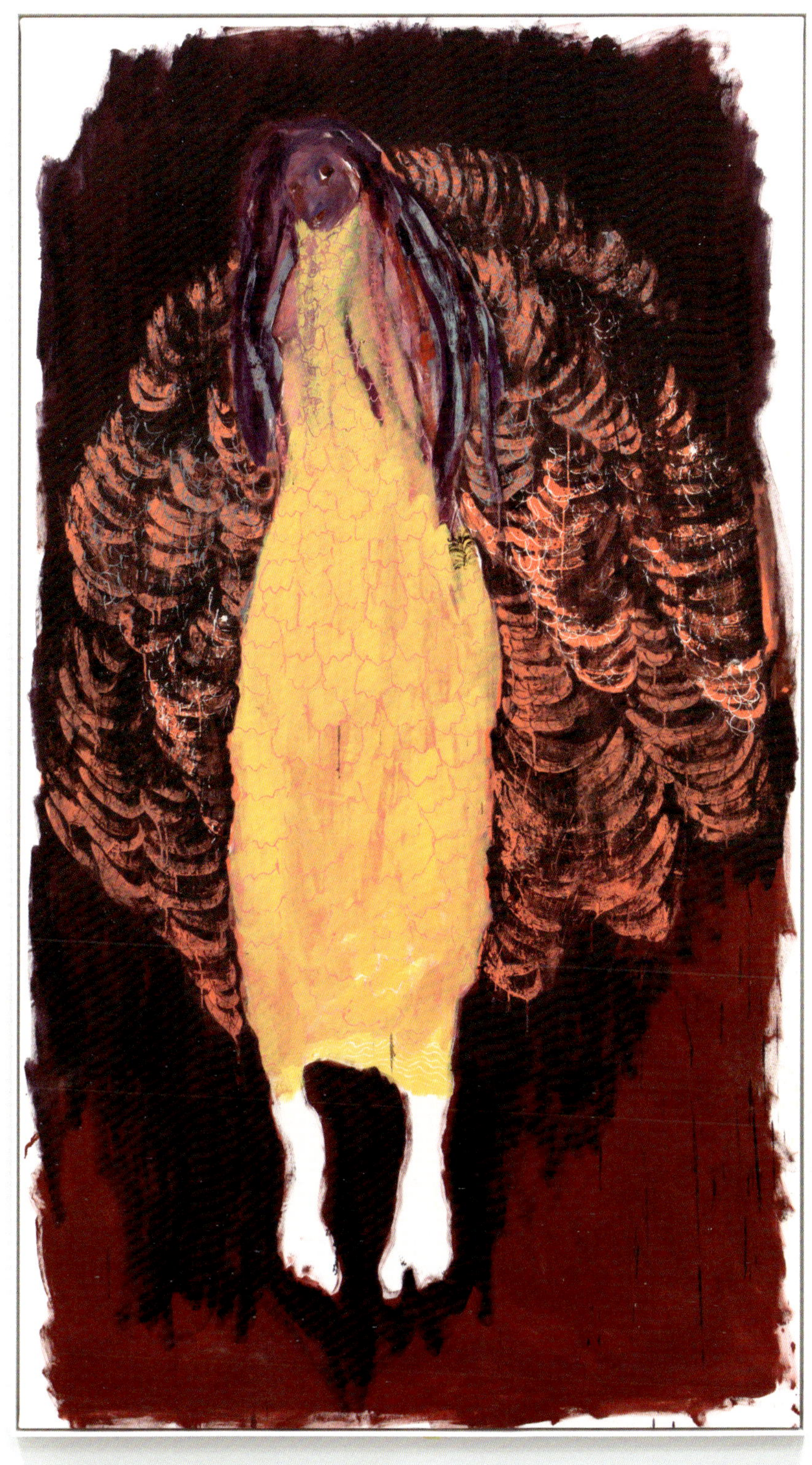

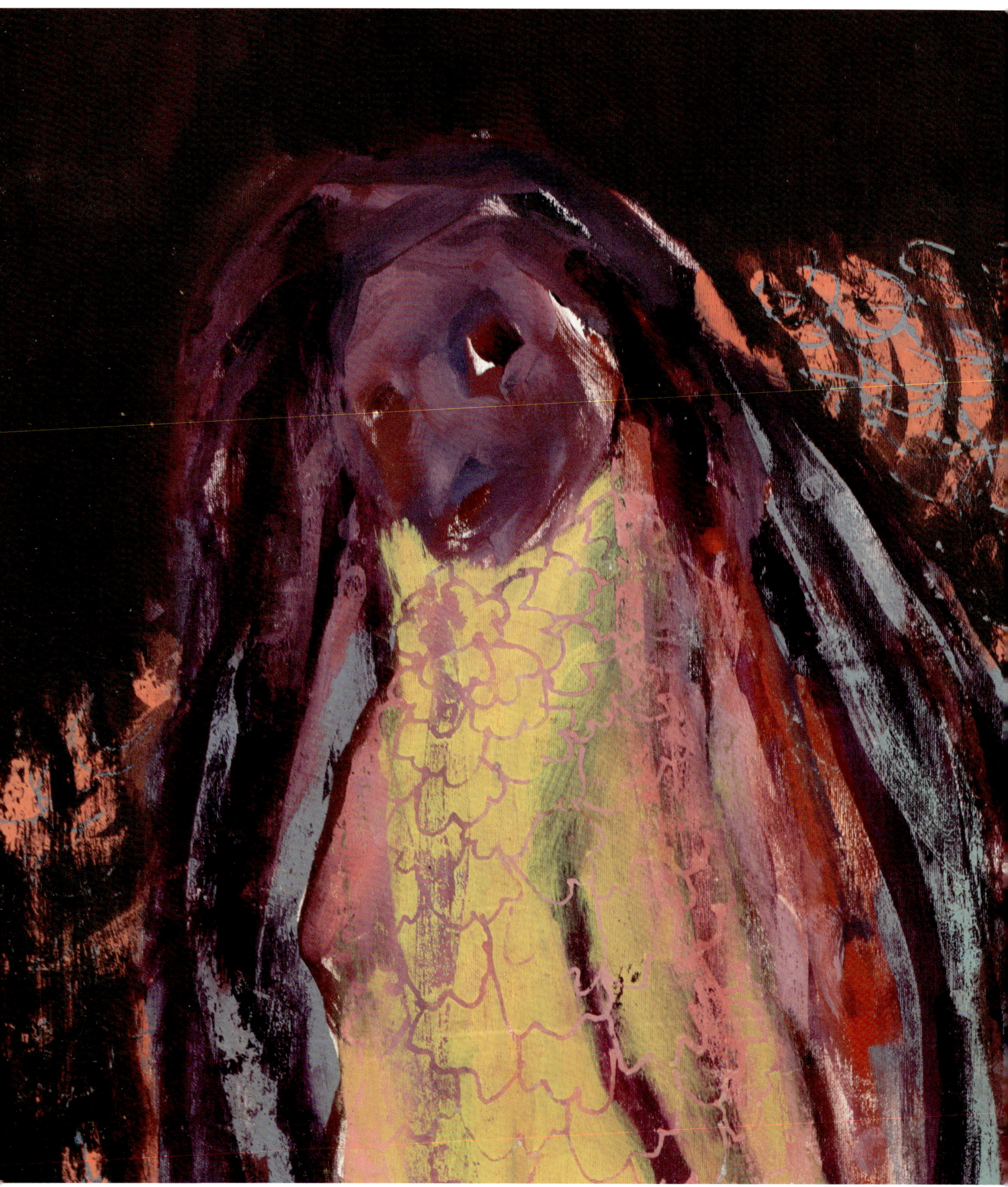

Ndirikukuona
(I'm watching you)
2023 (detail)

impoverishing if we lock everyone into their own autochthonous culture. So, while Portia and her colleagues might have been being encouraged to work from an essentialist vantage point, they were also exposed to a wider world of cultural and artistic references and they made use of these in order to forge a language that was theirs. There is no (and never was) pure 'Zimbabwean' space that is sequestered from the rest of the world. And while I wouldn't want to subsume Portia's practice back into the narrative of European oil painting, I also don't want to deny its multivalent references and resources. Even now, when you sit in Portia's Harare studio and look at her bookshelf, you see all sorts of books including volumes on medieval painting, from whose figural models and icons she draws. You see this in her winged figures and angels and demons. They may figure in her dreams and private fantasies, but they also come from European art, consciously or subconsciously. At the same time, she's involved in the Pentecostal environment, in an African-based Christianity and congregation centred in communities of women, and she prays, like she dreams, in Shona. While working with local traditions of batik and printmaking and a set of references that are very located and culturally specific, she also feels completely at ease and entitled to raid the cultures of the world for her own purposes. So, whether it's an angel from a medieval painting with a kind of haptically extended arm or whether it's a decorative surface reminiscent of a Klimt or whether it's the stuff of pattern making which comes from local fabrics, there is a sense of authority about using all those languages, and this is what creates a unique and porous pictorial world.

TD: I love that you brought that up because there definitely is that sense of authority and an assertion of the right to reference and cite anything from everywhere. Of course, the Western world has been doing that forever, but it feels like for Africans, we have to ask for permission or we have to over-justify ourselves if we don't want the world to diminish our choices or if we don't conform to a pre-conceived idea of 'authenticity'. We forget that cultures have been cross-pollinating since time immemorial and that there have been many contacts and connections for centuries. For example, there was Chinese porcelain found in Great Zimbabwe, which means the Chinese were in conversation with the Monomotapa Kingdom or the Portuguese, before colonisation. We know that artists like Klimt would have likely gone to some museum in Brussels or Vienna and seen West African masks. So, maybe Klimt was referencing masks like Picasso was, but now Portia's referencing Klimt, and taking on board his points of reference and influences in all their complexity. And that's okay. I think my point is that human beings are constantly referencing each other and let's relieve Africans from this burden of having to justify that.

TG: And relieve Africans from the burden of having to be locked into a subjectivity which cannot transcend its own situation. The negotiation of locatedness on the one hand and access/participation in a wider world on the other is delicate and sometimes difficult to manage. On a studio visit in Harare, I asked Portia what language she dreamed in. And she said 'I'm dreaming in Shona'. Those were her words. The specificity of that is precise and telling. It is relevant to who she is as an artist and where she situates herself, linguistically and culturally as well as physically. So, I'm not wanting to downgrade that specificity, but at the same time I want to say that to dream in Shona is also to dream in the languages of the world. It doesn't mean that you're locked into dreaming in Shona but rather that that is the space from which you dream. And it's also a space from which you are entitled to claim whatever you want. This is relevant to what we were saying earlier

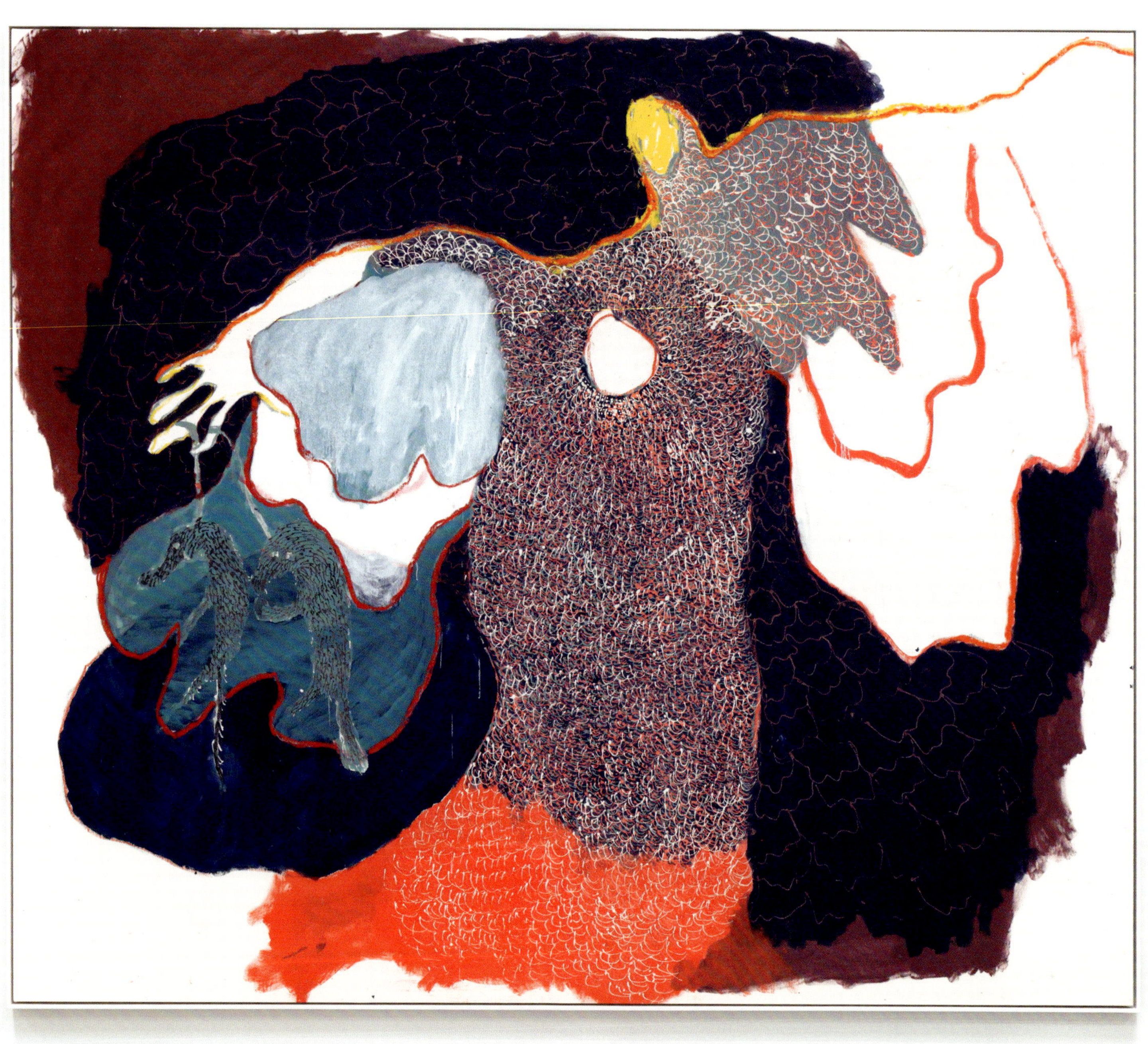

Abatwa
2023
Oil-based printing ink and oil bar on canvas
245 × 291 cm

about how we interpret or decode the dreams. What models of thinking do we use? Is it appropriate to shine a Freudian lens onto the question of dreaming in this context or do we need exclusively African-centred interpretive models? Can we use both and if so, how do we register the particularity of this practice, but without locking it into a parochial specificity? How do we see Africa as a centre from which you can navigate the world?

PG-M: But doesn't the dream announce itself in that way anyway because its origins are always located and specific, with peculiar details and reference points? But, at the same time, it evokes broader themes that interface with it. This reminds me of a dream of my own. When I started studying psychology, I was doing my honours degree with a supervisor who was a Jungian. And I had a very dramatic dream where I was going into the depths of the earth, and at the end of the dream I was standing on a podium and on this podium there was a Bible. And it was beaded. At the end of the dream, I felt like I was searching for something, as I was paging through the book and each page contained different colours of elaborate beadwork. For me, this object, this beaded book, references an infusion of cultures. Even though there is that sense of its location, its Africanness. It is also something else. Its very materiality speaks of multiplicity and of a co-mingling of cultures and cosmologies. It is not a case of either/or. It is both/and … I think of this in relation to Portia's exposure to books and images from the Western tradition. She is 'dreaming in Shona' but she is also looking with the eyes of an artist and a Christian and a mother, whether consciously or unconsciously. The encounter with the book happens in relation to her experience of daily life. Hers is a complex world. It is located in an African context. But it's a world that is also integrated with these other worlds that are part of her experience.

TG: I love that. It's the gift of double consciousness – or even of multiple consciousnesses. That is what it is to live in multiple spaces and languages simultaneously. So often, people complain of the tyranny of having to code-switch or to live in many spaces and registers simultaneously. I know that this can be a burden, especially when it is imposed, but it can also feel like a privilege. And that's what I feel in the face of Portia's work. It emerges as a gift of multiple consciousnesses, both in terms of the dream world and waking life with their numerous cultural references, their locatedness and their universalism. It's so big. As a world …

SC: I wonder if the clue is in what you're saying about these multiple consciousnesses, prompted by the phrase 'dreaming in Shona' and the tensions that can exist between the specific and the general. So, one doesn't want to be reductive but we also need to acknowledge (and celebrate) where the work comes from. I think what she gives us in a way is the gift of transcendence, and a way of remembering and accessing the fact that there's really so little that we know about what actually shapes our world. There's so much in our world that we don't understand. There's so much that we can't see. There are spectrums of light or sound or taste that are beyond our human senses. And I think there's something that Portia does even with this 'dreaming in Shona' and this combination of the unconscious on the one hand and the deeply historical matrilineal lineage which she comes from on the other; I think that she reminds us that it's okay to be inconclusive about certain things because there are so many mysteries and possibilities that are beyond our comprehension. What Portia does is to allow assured uncertainty to become a form of knowing – because she'll make drawings and paintings that take her, by her own admission, years to understand. She learns, only over time, whether a dream issued a warning, or whether it was inspiration for something else. Her approach makes it okay not to know what to do with where something sits. To let the work itself do some of that work. Maybe that's too optimistic a thing?

TG: No, I think that's very useful because Portia herself says that the painting teaches her. It's not like she's sorted out the dream in advance, that she understands it and then illustrates it. Portia's paintings are not illustrative. The process is that when she wakes up in the morning, she sketches and writes down the images and narrative of the dream of the night before. Sometimes she even does this in the middle of the night. These are kept as working drawings and notes, preserved in countless sketchbooks that are private. They are not meant for display or exhibition. They are repositories filled with personal notations and marks, like a secret storehouse or archive. Then, as you said, Tandazani, out of one dream many paintings can emerge and one dream can be a 'source' for many works over a long period in different iterations and forms. Only in the process of making does a personal meaning for the dream emerge. And then working is combined with other acts and ways of being in the studio, from worshipping to waiting to weaning or caring. The studio is not a rarified space that is sequestered from daily life. In it, mothering and daughtering and meditating and praying all happen in the presence of painting/printing. Portia's baby is often strapped to her back as she bends and crouches and climbs from flat surfaces laid out on the floor to unreachable canvases pinned to the wall. The movement between them is made in synergy with the breathing of a sleeping child, fused to the warmth of her mother's body. At a certain point the artist knows that the painting is done and something has been distilled in it. But it's not an illustration of the dream, even if some of the bits of iconography and imagery are suggested by the dream.

PG-M: I like it that you said something about waiting. You know, even in dreams there is that sense that you don't know what they mean, you know some dreams are epic. Dreams can have episodes that emerge in sequence, or chaotically and incoherently. They have their own temporality. The way that Portia processes the dream over time is a kind of waiting. Sometimes even in Freudian terms you may have to spend days or weeks to wait for a moment of revelation or clarity, particularly with dreams that suggest a kind of staging of something to happen. You know the dream feels like a staging, like an opening of something, a disclosure. So, the moment of the dream is the enactment of that moment. But you don't know what that moment is. So, there is the waiting, in Freudian terms, as you 'work through' the dream – to put it in the language of psychoanalysis. The painting then appears transcendent, of course. But it's also a kind of a working through that reveals itself gradually even to the dreamer herself, as well as to us as the viewers of her work. I assume that in the process, there is a transformation that registers a regional specificity but also that transcends it. But it's usually rooted in the need to work through a traumatic experience or anxiety.

TG: A nightmare?

PG-M: Yes, perhaps a vision that occurs through the dream and I suspect there's a kind of overlap between the unconscious or the subconscious in the moment of the actual enactment of the dream, but that some of it is lived in the moment of painting. You know, so that it collapses the border between the moment of dreaming and the moment of painting and processing. So that it's lived in the present.

TG: Would you say that we can think of prayer as a kind of analogous practice?

PG-M: I was gesturing towards that because there's something about you giving up yourself in prayer. You are almost handing yourself over to something else. And so, the

Abatwa
2023 (detail)

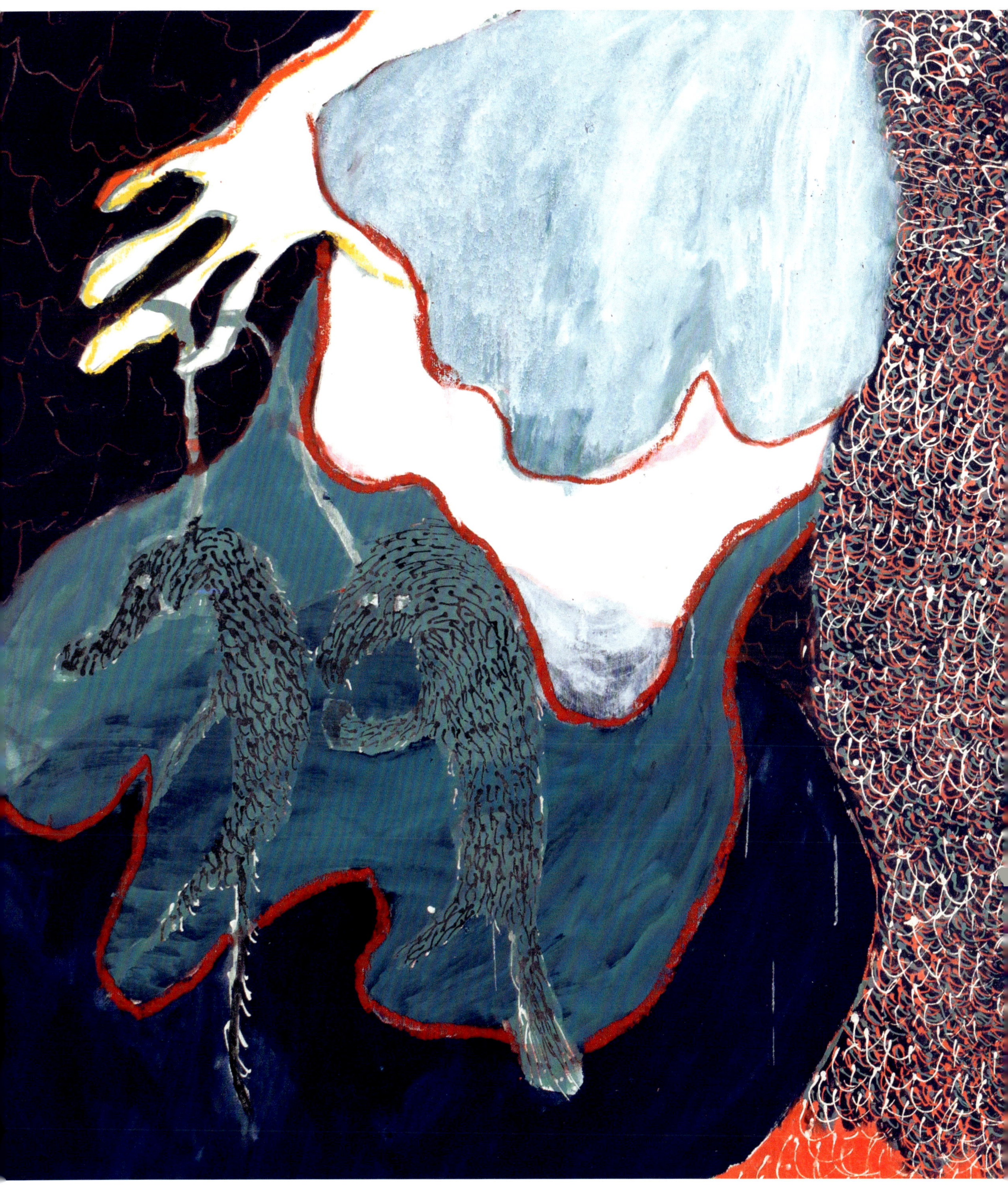

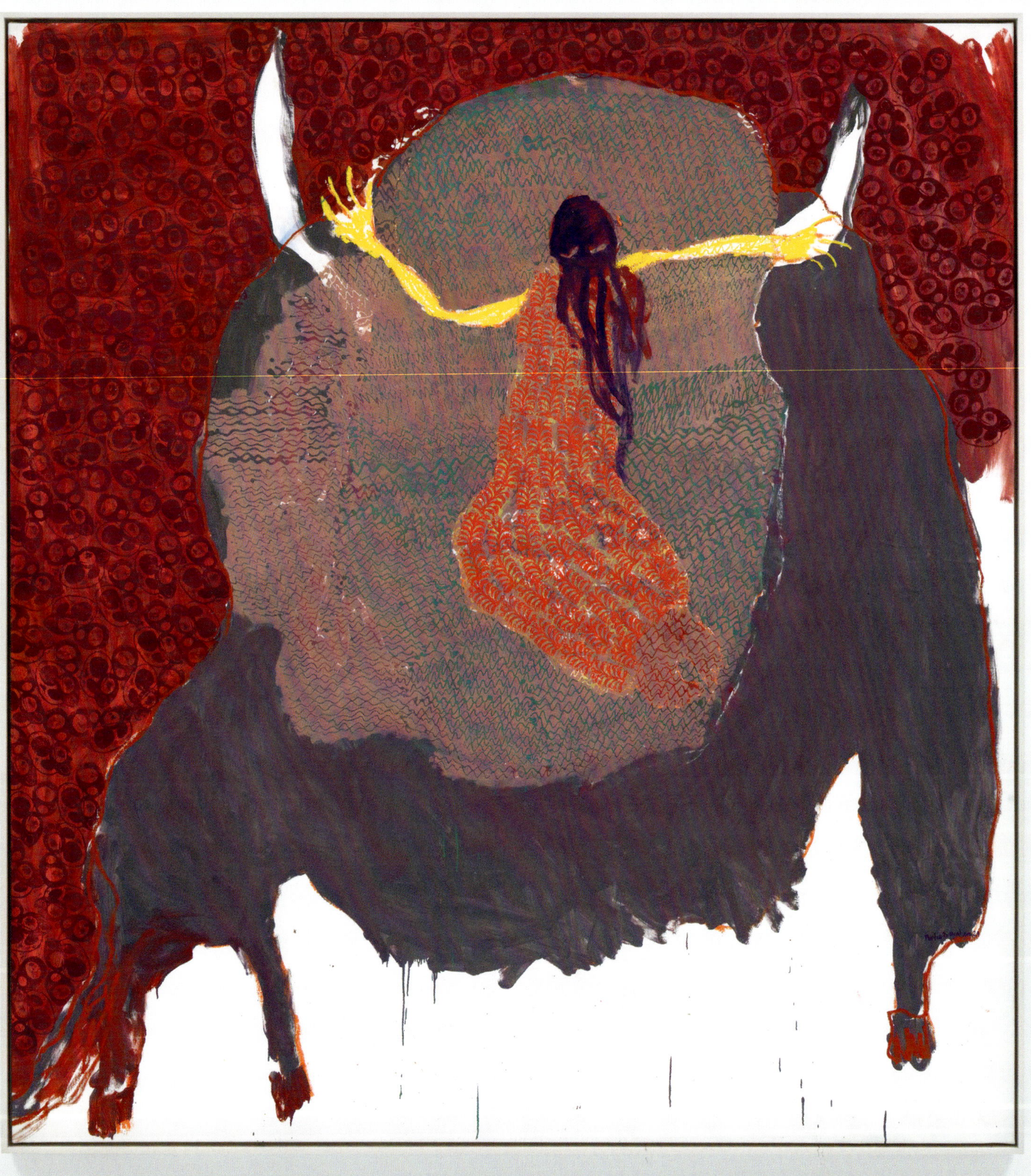

Prayer amid a battle
2021
Oil-based printing ink and oil bar on canvas
208.3 × 192.4 cm

practice of prayer, it's beyond meditating, you know, although it's aligned with meditation. But prayer takes you to another realm if you really give yourself up to the moment of prayer. So, Portia's being spiritual in prayerful pursuit is central here. That dynamic within the painting space, in the space where she's engaged in painting, she can do that with her mind. With her unconscious, with her body, she kind of gives herself up so that it's almost like it performs itself through her. It becomes something that you are living through the spirit, almost like the messages of the spiritual realm. Because in prayer you're speaking in words, but also through your body while imagining the existence of something beyond yourself. The painting becomes a kind of a dialogue. A prayerful dialogue.

SC: I'm interested in how you're positioning the connection between painting and praying. This makes sense of the way Portia can be both in the present with the canvas but also in another realm. So, the discrepancy between waking life and sleeping life narrows when she's working. It's almost as though she is praying on/through the canvas. It's an embodied action that allows her to connect to the negative messages and spirits animated in sleep by the dream: her demons, so to speak. It's as though she's excavating the 'within' in the act of painting, and then it all collapses, even if it's not illustrative. It's how she makes the collapse.

TD: I agree about the potential different states of being, but I wonder ... I'm grappling with the word sleeping because perhaps in the dream, you're more awake than when you are awake. And so, I think this is a different state of being because sleeping feels passive, but I think there's something active, whether she's physically asleep or awake. I think for me, her dreaming is more like a state of heightened awakeness.

And then relating this to the idea of multiple consciousnesses and the possibilities of 'dreaming in Shona' and being bilingual. I think being African is to have multiple consciousnesses, because that's just our heritage. So, in some cases it becomes laborious like compulsory code-switching, but in some cases it's just normal life. You know most Africans speak many languages and that affects our beings, into our thinking, and into our dreaming as well. I don't think many of us dream monolingually.

And then in relation to prayer, I'm reminded of the word wrestling. There is this tension, if you look at the artwork and the brushstrokes and the movement of the brush, it's not necessarily violent, but there is a tension, a wrestling. And if you think of biblical narratives as well and Portia's drawing from biblical sources amongst many things, the wrestling emerges in the imagery as well as the act of making. Jacob wrestled with God, and this stands for an inner struggle of faith and trust and surrender. So, there is this idea of wrestling through prayer or spiritual warfare, but it's not necessarily a violent thing – it can be meditative or contemplative. So, I really love what has come up around this idea of prayer. Of course, Portia did create a series of works where she was literally praying, or at least the figure in the work is shown to be praying or kneeling, and supplicating figures recur. Perhaps they stand against the darkness that engulfs her, in the night, in the unknowable half-light. With these praying figures. There are ominous creatures, like the rat, which serves as a metaphor for something antagonising or harmful. But she has to document it, or wrestle with it or face it in order for that prayer to unfold ...

PG-M: It has to be exorcised.

TG: I think also this goes back to what you were saying earlier, Tandazani, about having to understand that the mythology is not necessarily comforting and often works in terms of the menacing or gloomy. Take the rat, for example, it has a very particular kind of symbolism in Portia's work. It embodies something evil that has to be wrestled with and withstood. And the practice of painting feels like a way of managing fear, even of self-protection in the face of danger. But then there's also love and surrender. Perhaps this is figured in the supplicating Mary surrogates that come straight out of the Christian playbook. And the intimation of maternal figures, cradling bodies that are either dead or entombed and doubling perhaps as a birthing figure. Death and life feel so proximate in these works …

TD: But then you know, it can be much more prosaic than that. Take, for example, the use of flowers. These can just refer to floral dresses and cloths rather than some celestial universe. The references might be quite banal and to do with an alertness to daily life with its patterns and shapes.

TG: I think that's really important because of course one can overblow the portentous or the mythical. And it's not as if inspiration descends from above to an untrained hand. We have talked about the training Portia received and the facility with which she can wield her materials. This comes from daily practice and engagement producing a formal rigour. Everything, the visions, the narratives, the imaginary universe and the recurring images, is mediated through the technical skills that have been painstakingly acquired and learned laboriously over the years. Of course, as Portia has herself said, there was lots of talent to start with and she obviously was a very gifted child. She could draw from an early age. But that's not the same as inventing a whole new way of working through which to express the multiple consciousnesses we have talked of. And here I stress again that Portia is not an outsider artist. She's a trained practitioner within both African specific and Western traditions of making, and out of that she forges her own language that navigates multiple ideas of the decorative, the planar, the saturated surface...

SC: It's a very volitional practice, yes.

TD: And I think that's why I love Portia's work and why I think it's so important because it does resist being categorised and boxed into any deterministic notion of an 'African' identity. But yet it still feels political. Because there is something political about a Black woman artist deciding to resist whatever pressures from wherever and just making work about love, or about her three babies, or about pregnancy, or about anxiety. So, she refuses falling into stereotypical tropes. Why not make a whole body of work about the erotic or about intimacy or about whatever you want to?

TG: I think that's important and I think it also resists a certain kind of puritanical dogma. That's part of why I admire the erotic element of some of the earlier work. It offers an embrace of the capacity of the human for intimacy that is so powerful because there's nothing about it that is about prohibition and the law. It seems to me to be the opposite.

TD: And I love that. I love that she is very much a part of pretty much every painting. Somehow it emerges from a very personal space, whether it's connected to her husband Gideon, or to her children or her mother, you know it's always coming from a very subjective perspective, even if it becomes universal.

SC: And always so physical, even when it is connected to dreams, whether it's nightmares or dreams of love, there is such a profound respect for the somatic existence.

TG: Absolutely. And desire. I think the work is infused with desire and that is both something that is transcendent but also totally embodied. I mean, there are some very violent images of childbirth where you see the pain and the agony of parturition, the visceral physicality of giving birth.

Prayer amid a battle
2021 (detail)

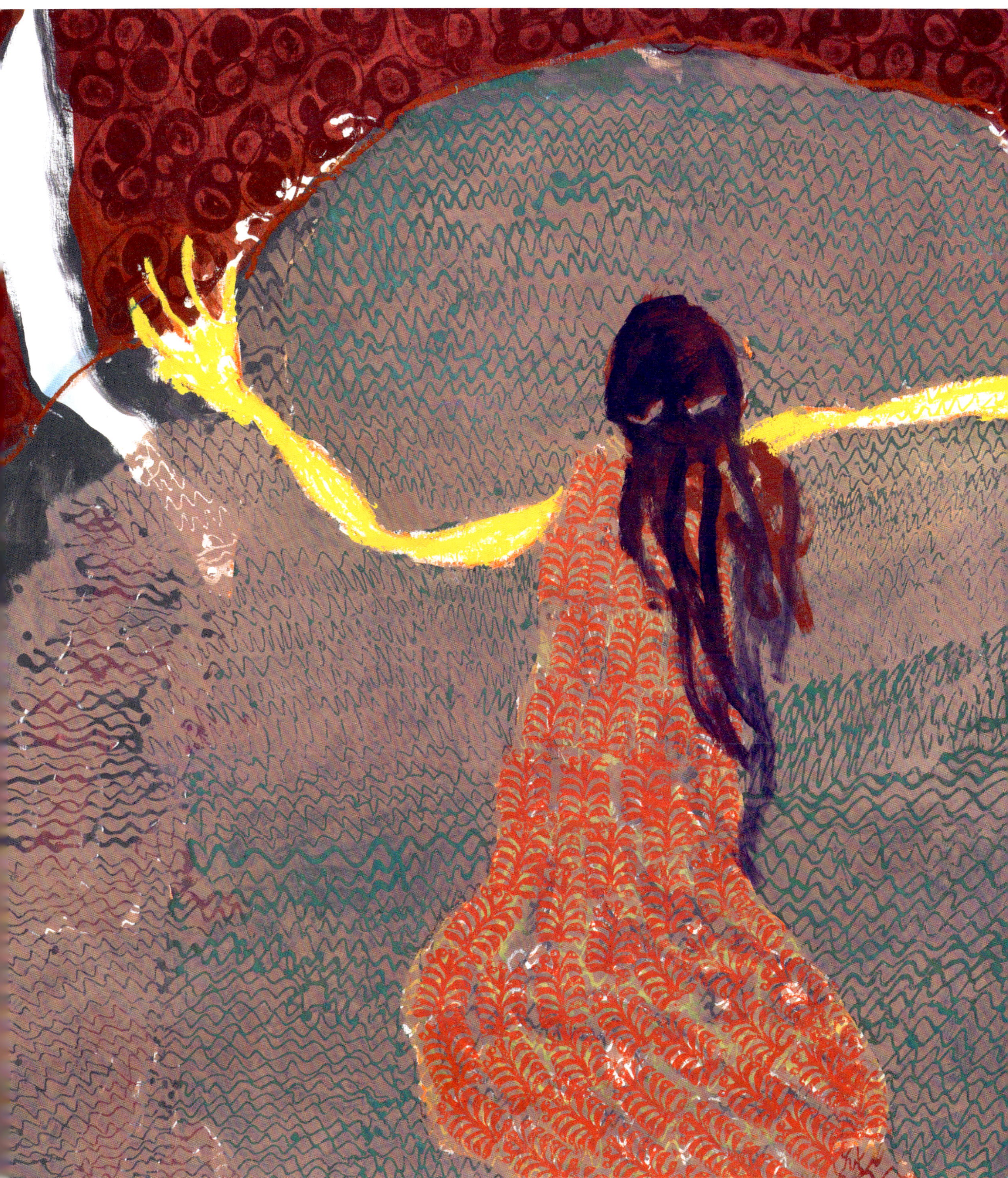

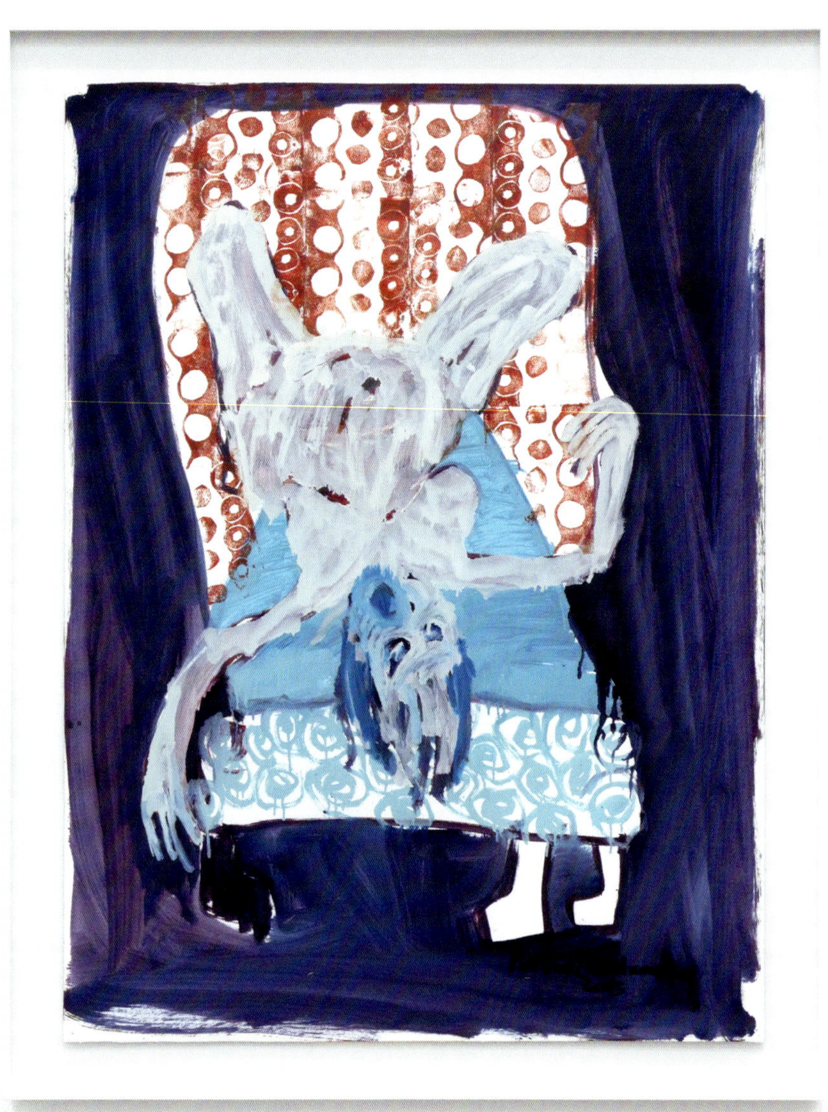

Labour Pains
2012
Oil-based printing ink on paper
100 × 75 cm

Then the physical intimacy with the child. Or the physical intimacy with the lover and what it is to be a desiring and doing figure in the world.

PG-M: Isn't that then the importance of the work? That it comes from the perspective of a woman who has lived in a world that, in the case of Zimbabwe, is so complicated for women. Women who write about violence come to mind, for instance Tsitsi Dangarembga: often those stories of violence are complicated and portray raw violence. Yet at the same time, they may convey a richer and more multifaceted exploration of a life infused with love in the midst of extreme depravity. And here the maternal is crucial, implicated as it is in a dynamic of love. We are women who experience that. I feel that the work has a special capacity to connect with women's experience transnationally. I think empathy is important here. I think of the possibility of empathy with the 'other', you know, with other women, with other suffering women, with women with similar experiences, with the possibility of love itself. There is the intimate familial love, romantic love, erotic love. But there's also the love of humanity; of life. You know we are surrounded by all this violence, but there is also something else, that as human beings, as women, we carry the possibility of loving.

TG: Listening to you, Pumla, it makes me realise that love is a practice. Perhaps it's an emotion, but to love is an act. It's a doing word. It's a practice like to paint or to pray and I think that in that sense, to me the act of making is also an act of loving, which doesn't mean it's uncomplicated or isn't without pain. Because to love is always to fear loss and to risk. There's no loving without risking. At the same time, it's the ultimate affirmation of life.

TD: That makes me think about the word 'vulnerable'. I think in pretty much every body of Portia's work there's a sense of vulnerability because we're granted an inside view into a private space. Whether it's an anxiety about these demonic rats, or it's anxiety about pregnancy or about childbirth or whatever. I think what makes her work powerful is that the vulnerability is just there, on the surface. And because there is that vulnerability, it's easy for us to engage because there isn't a block, there isn't a wall. She gives us a language for things that we can't always articulate, whether that's in the metaphysical dream world or in our daily lives.

The hands are interesting in this context. A little drawn/painted hand creates either tension or vulnerability, or an openness, or shows you toil, or passion or desire. It's in these little gestures, in the lines and abstract shapes and forms that the vulnerability is felt. There's a delicateness too in the feet. You know, it's literally just lines and brush strokes and dripping paint that create such fragile effects, and the sense of the vulnerability and contingency of life …

SC: It's almost as if she honours every single aspect of herself, even her vulnerability, which then turns it into a power. It's like there's no shame in her realm, whether that's like in intimate terms, or in her fears; she honours every part of it by sharing it with tenderness.

TG: I'm intrigued by the idea that there is no shame and that, I suppose, is a better way of saying what I was trying to say earlier about it being so unpuritanical. I mean, even when she draws on the erotic it evokes a love without censure, without moralising (or sanctimonious prohibition).

PG-M: Yes, you're so right – there's really no shame that's getting out there. And the body is very much physically holding, physically embracing, physically engaged … What happens when you see that physicality, you see that it's not just a touching, it's an actual enmeshment, you know. It's an enmeshment with the other. And the subject of love is felt in a really very tight way. It refuses to be denied.

SC: Yes, that word refusal is interesting. Portia refuses so much and thinking back to what we were saying earlier in relation to the line between psychoanalysis and the ancestral, she refuses to take part in that, or to make the distinction between the 'European' and the 'African', the 'Freudian' and the 'indigenous'. The line between the somatic and the metaphysical, she refuses to take part in that too, or the line between abstraction and figuration; she's just interested in wholeness.

TG: That's the work's integrity, its integrated, entangled wholeness. It is both emplaced and specific. She is 'dreaming in Shona', after all. But, it's also a language that reaches beyond the local and the specific to engage across binaries and borders. Its scope is planetary even though it can be traced in place and pattern and precedent.

1. See Tamar Garb, 'Archiving the In-Between', in *ÀSÌKÒ: On the Future of Artistic and Curatorial Pedagogies in Africa*, CCA Lagos, 2017, pp.115–28.

Labour Ward
2012
Oil-based printing ink on paper
147 × 121 cm

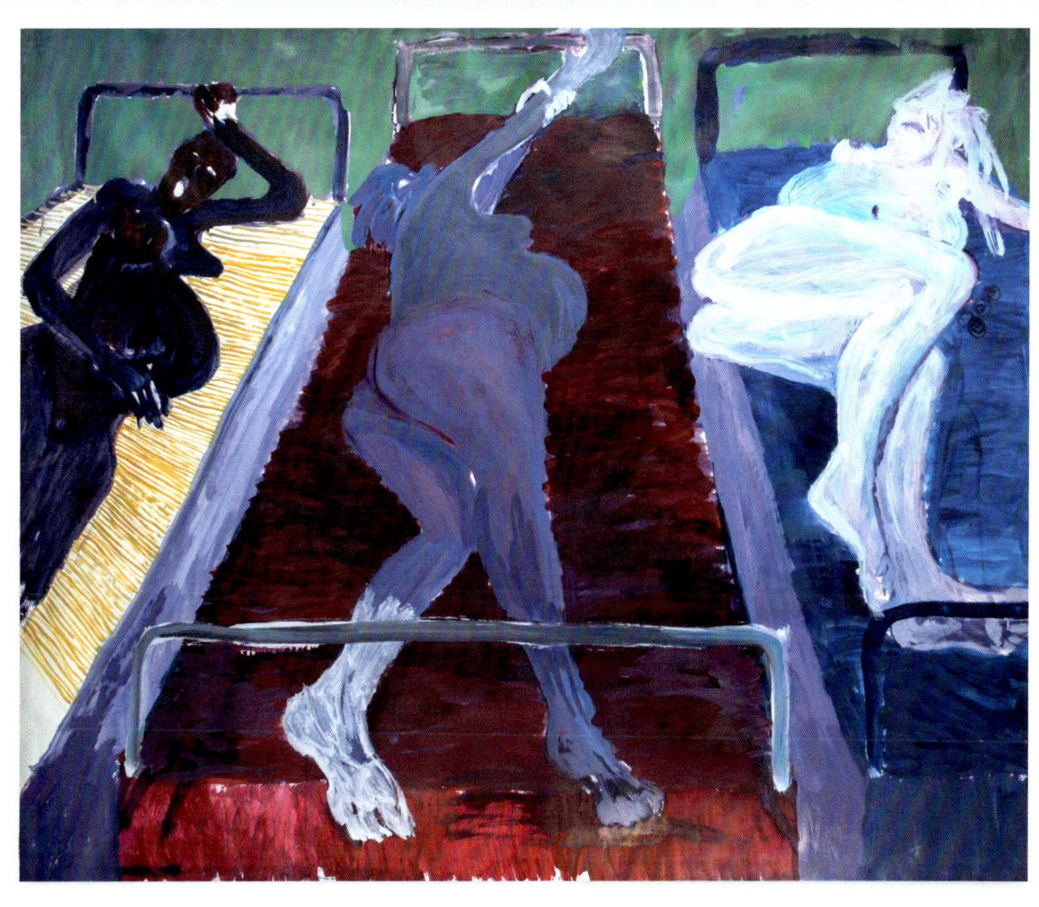

His Presence
2013
Oil-based printing
ink on paper
150 × 114 cm

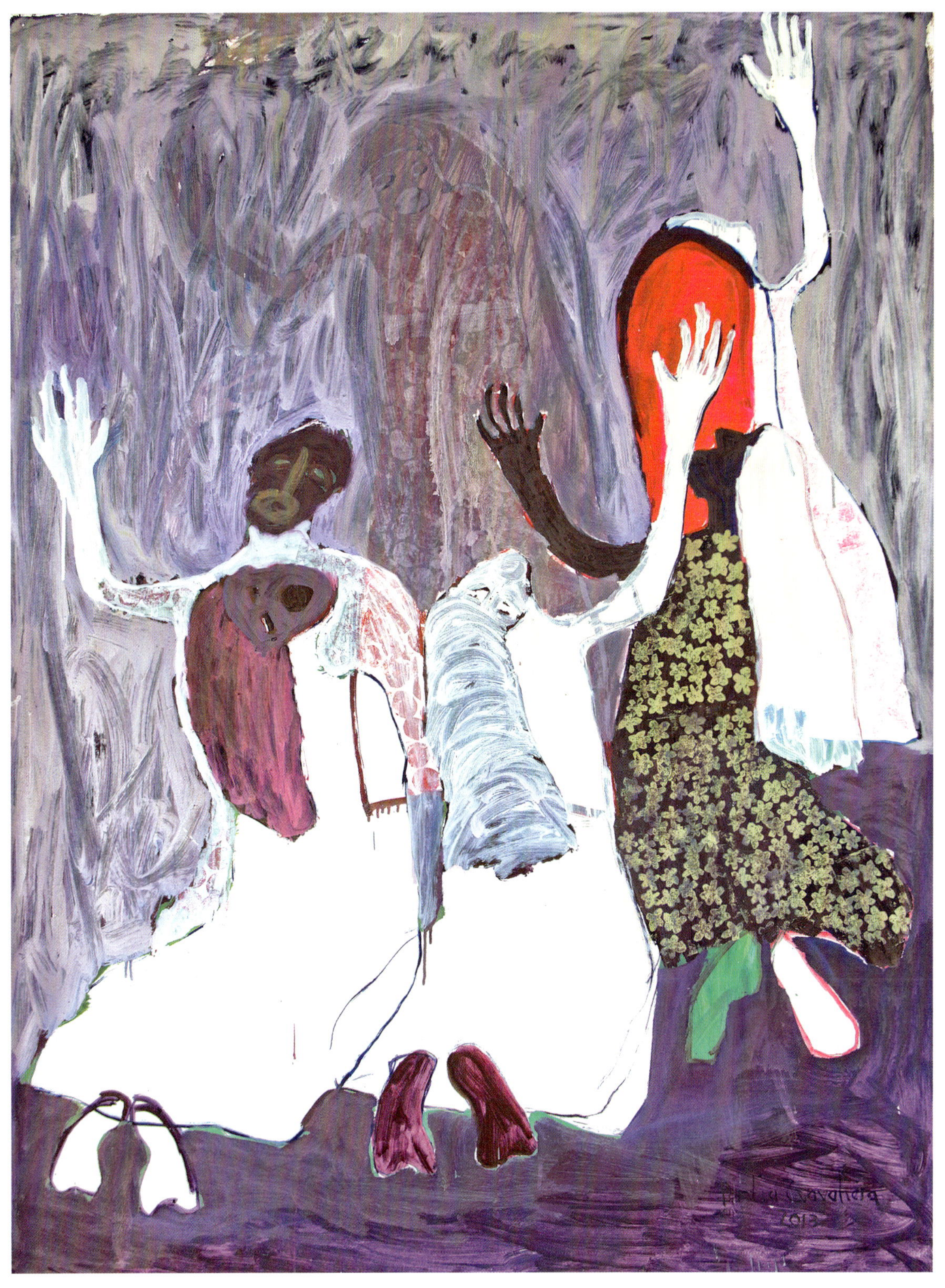

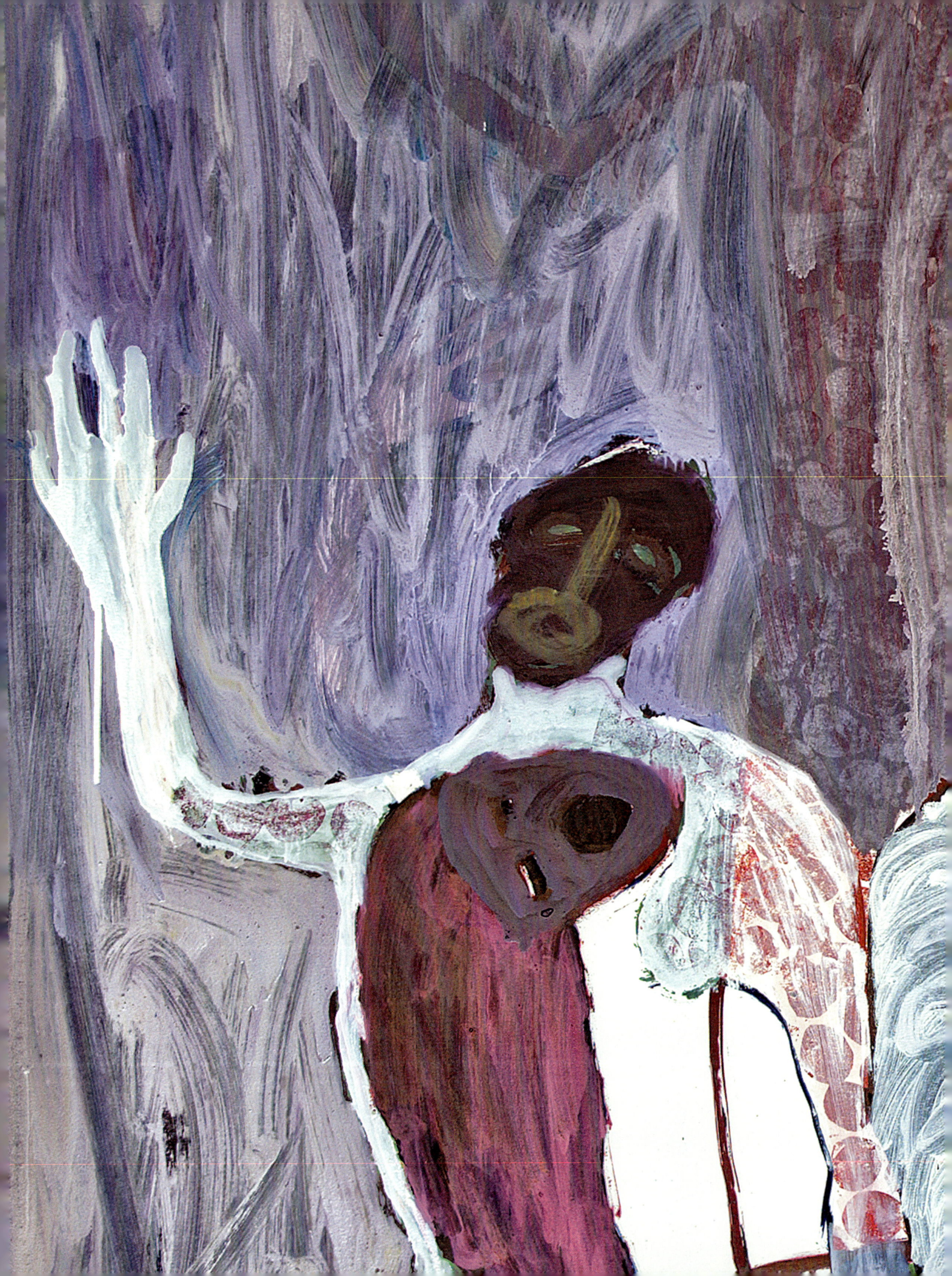

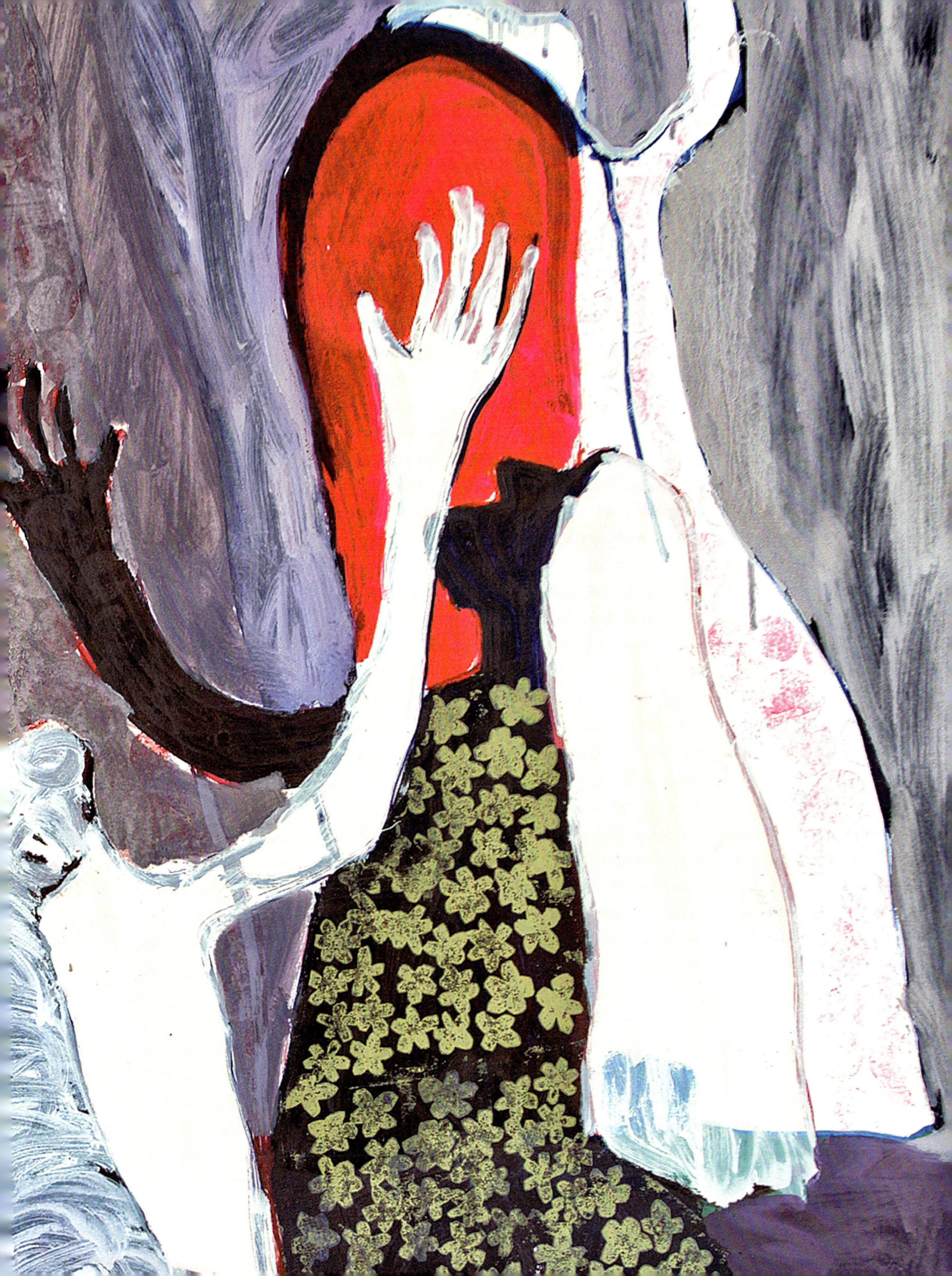

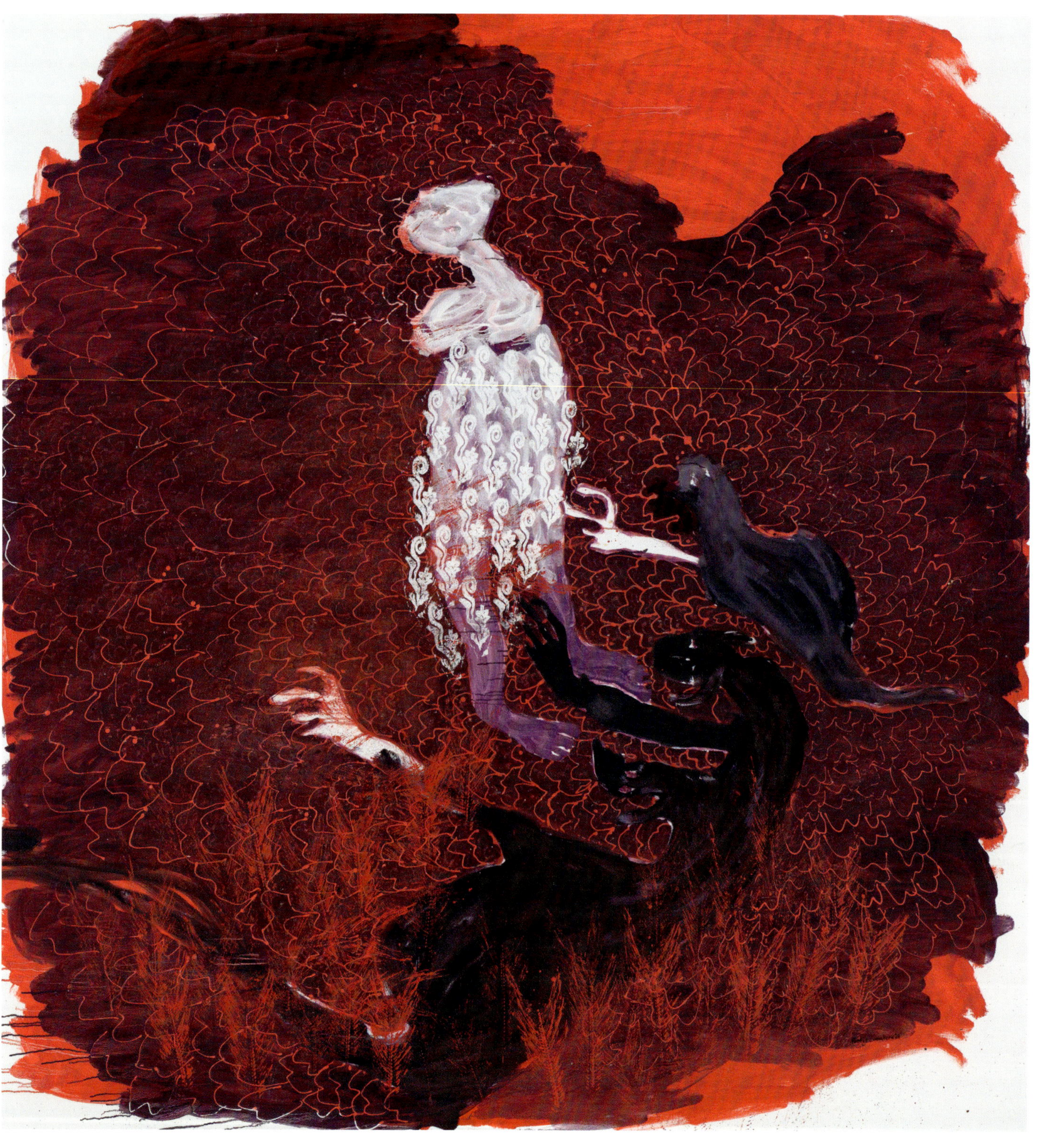

Fighting Energies
2024
Oil-based printing ink
and oil bar on linen
214.5 × 200.3 cm

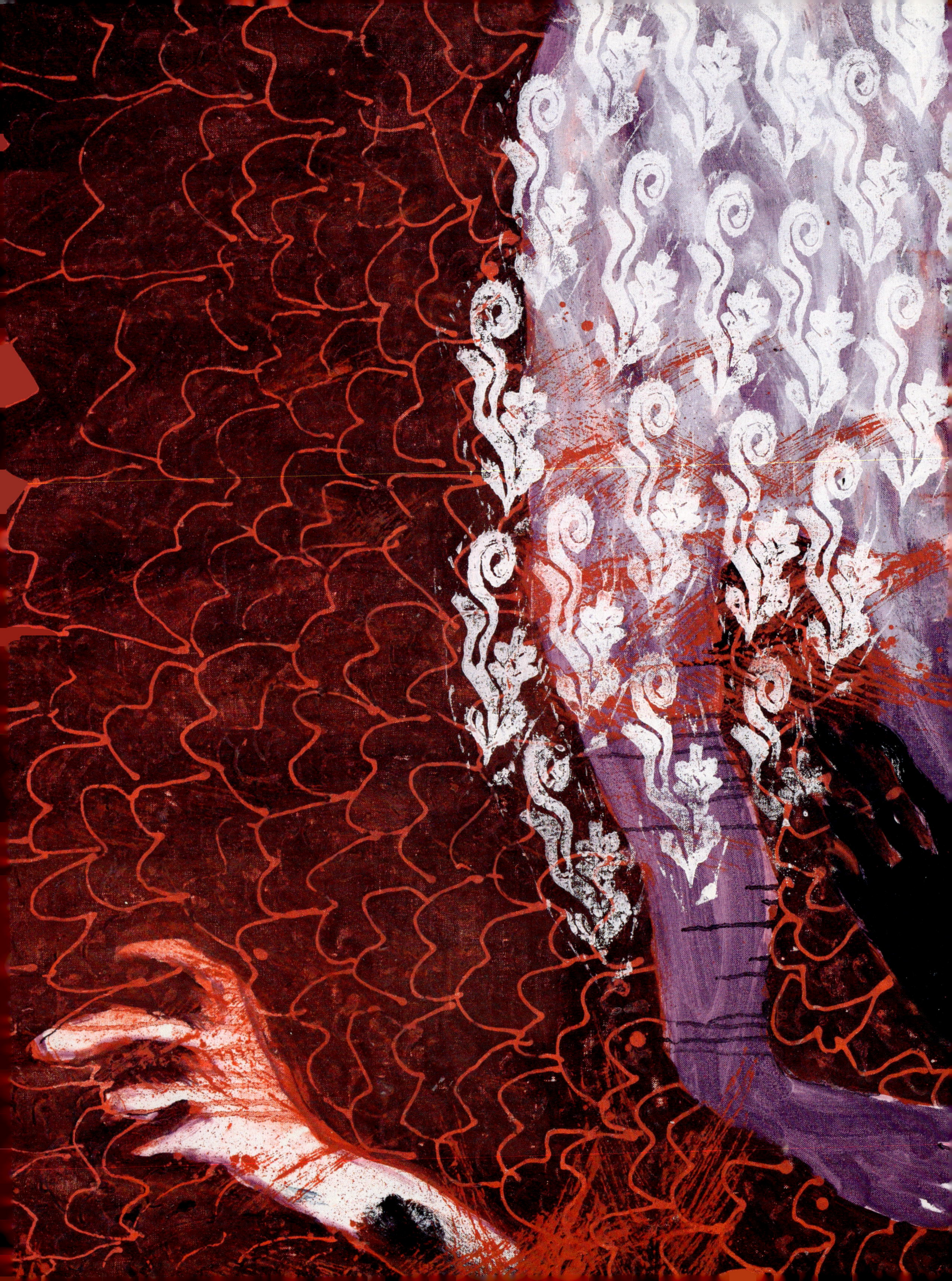

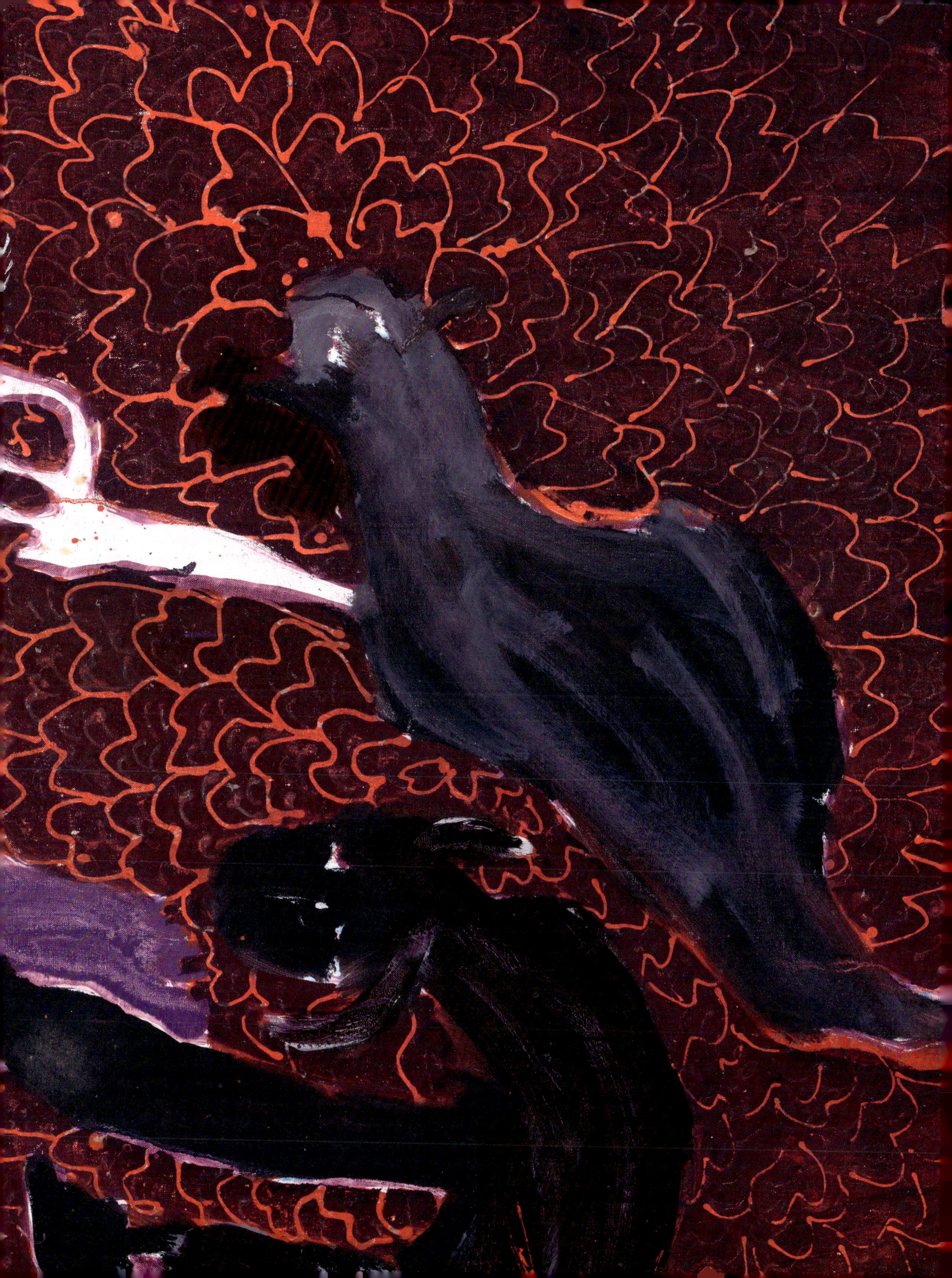

LIST OF WORKS

All works courtesy the artist, Stevenson and David Zwirner, unless otherwise stated

Works are listed in alphabetical order by title

All sizes height × width unframed

Embraced and Protected in You
2016
Oil-based printing ink and oil bar on canvas
210 × 390 cm
Private collection
pp.58–59

Fighting Energies
2024
Oil-based printing ink and oil bar on linen
214.5 × 200.3 cm
pp.124, 126–27

Fighting Energies 2
2024
Oil-based printing ink and oil bar on linen
228.4 × 212 cm
pp.65, 66–67

Handidi Kuzviona
2016
Oil-based printing ink on paper
238 × 140 cm
Private collection
p.51

His Presence
2013
Oil-based printing ink on paper
150 × 114 cm
Private collection, Mauritius
pp.120, 122–23

Hide There
2024
Oil-based printing ink and oil bar on linen
207 × 205 cm
pp.70, 72–73

I Want to Stay in Love
2017
Oil based printing ink and oil bar on paper
203 × 140 cm
Collection of Garth Holmes (South Africa)
p.46

***Kudonhedzwa kwevanhu* (Fallen people)**
2022
Oil-based printing ink and oil bar on linen
212.5 × 299.6 cm
Private collection
pp.16–17, 18–19

Labour Pains
2012
Oil-based printing ink on paper
100 × 75 cm
Private collection
p.116

Labour Ward
2012
Oil-based printing ink on paper
147 × 121 cm
Private collection, Mauritius
p.119

Lifted Away
2024
Oil-based printing ink and oil bar on linen
214 × 385 cm
pp.12–13, 14–15, 138–39

Ndahwarara
2014
Oil-based printing ink on paper
150.5 × 97 cm
Private collection
p.37

Ndirikukutsvagai ndirimugomo*
2024
Oil-based printing ink and oil bar on linen
213 × 209 cm
pp.77, 78–79

Ndirikumabvisa
2024
Oil-based printing ink and oil bar on linen
253 × 210 cm
pp.61, 62–63

Ndokumbirawo Ishe
2014
Oil-based printing ink on paper
98 × 150 cm
Private collection
p.38

***Pane rima rakakomba (1)* (There's too much darkness)**
2023
Oil-based printing ink and oil bar on canvas
222 × 332 cm
Norval Foundation
pp.26–27, 90–91, 93, 94

***Ranganai henyu* (Devise your strategy)**
2022
Oil-based printing ink and oil bar on linen
215 × 265 cm
The Nixon Collection
pp.84–85, 86–87

Tavingwa Nezvehusiku
2018
Oil-based printing ink and oil bar on canvas
198 × 198 cm
Private collection
pp.28, 30–31

The Energy Present
2024
Oil-based printing ink and oil bar on linen
195.4 × 197.5 cm
pp.81, 82–83

This is Where I Travelled (2)
2020
Oil-based printing ink and oil-bar on canvas
206.4 × 177.3 cm
Private collection
pp.53, 54–55

This is Where I Travelled (4)
2020
Oil-based printing ink and oil bar on canvas
242.5 × 201 cm
Tate: Purchased with funds provided by Simon Nixon and family 2022
p.33

***Vachengeti vangu* (My guardian)**
2020
Oil-based printing ink and oil bar on canvas
260 × 193 cm
Private collection
pp.40, 42–43

* not included at Kettle's Yard

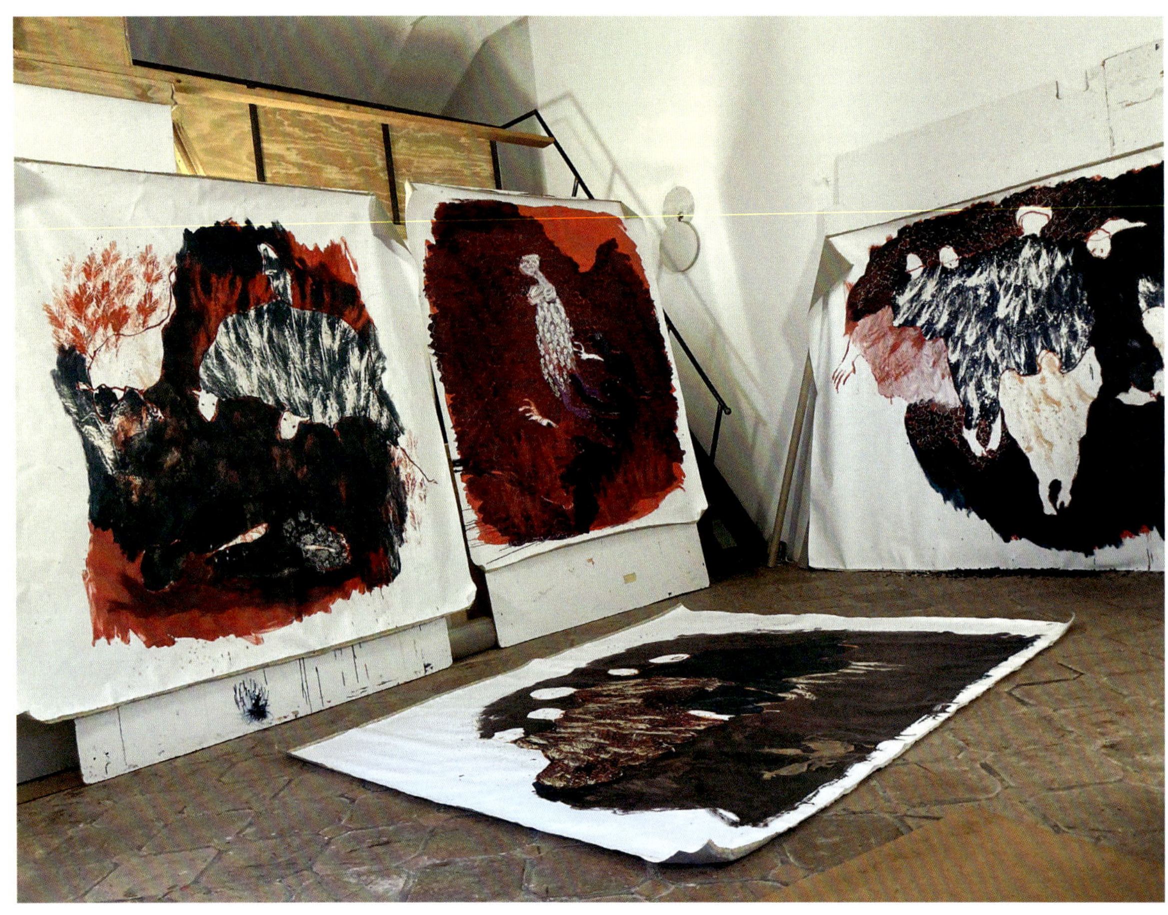

Studio view,
Harare, 2024

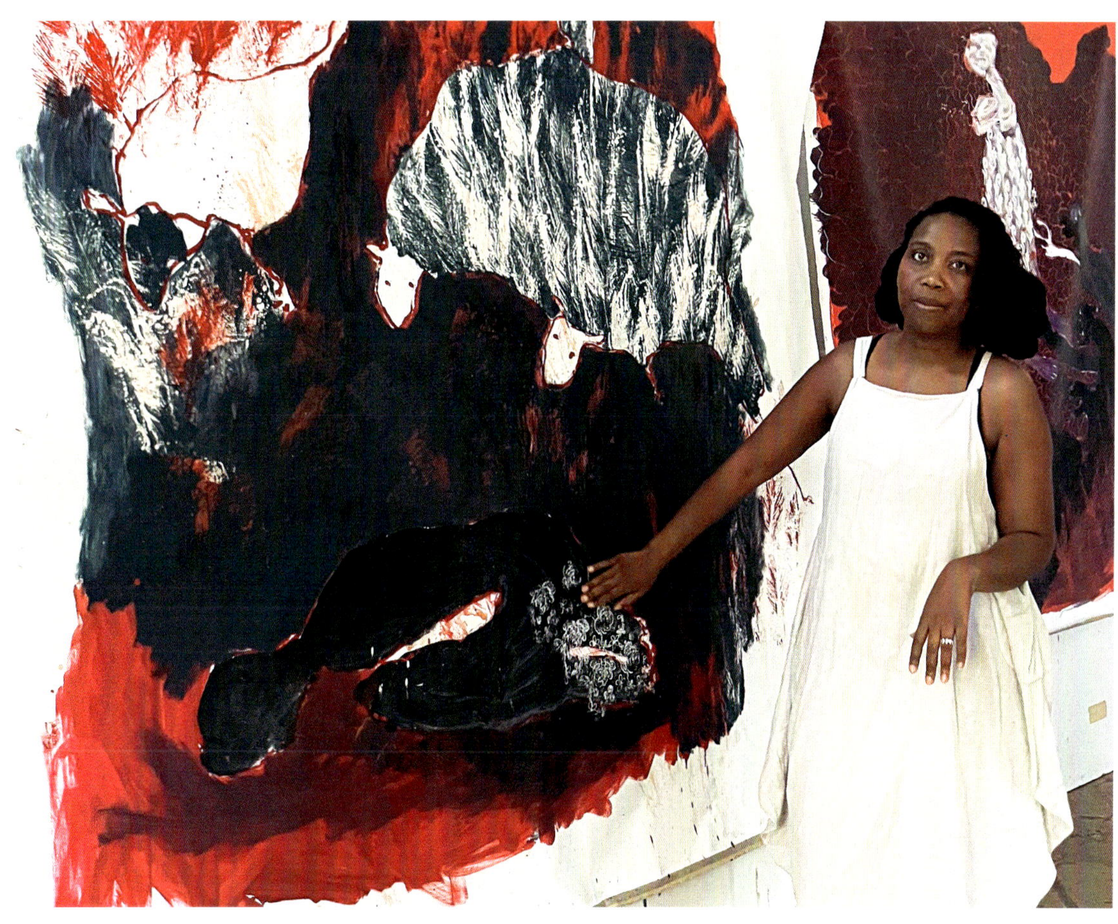

PORTIA ZVAVAHERA

Born 1985 in Harare, Zimbabwe
Lives in Harare

EDUCATION

2006
Diploma in Fine Art, Harare Polytechnic College, Zimbabwe

2004
Certificate in Art, BAT Visual Art Studios, National Gallery of Zimbabwe (now National Gallery School of Visual Art and Design), Harare

SOLO EXHIBITIONS

2024
Portia Zvavahera: Zvakazarurwa, Kettle's Yard, University of Cambridge; Fruitmarket, Edinburgh
Portia Zvavahera, Fondation Louis Vuitton, Paris

2023
Pane rima rakakomba, Stevenson, Cape Town

2021
Ndakaoneswa murima, David Zwirner, New York

2020
Walk of Life, Institute of Contemporary Art Indian Ocean, Port Louis
Ndichasvika rinhi ndionekwe, Stevenson, Cape Town
Ndakavata pasi ndikamutswa nekuti anonditsigira, David Zwirner, London

2019
Portia Zvavahera – Gustav Klimt: A Dialogue, De 11 Lijnen, Oudenburg
Talitha Cumi, Stevenson, Johannesburg

2017
Take Me Deeper, Stevenson, Cape Town
I'm with You, Marc Foxx Gallery, Los Angeles

2016
What I See Beyond Feeling, Stevenson, Johannesburg

2015
I Can Feel It in My Eyes, Stevenson, Cape Town

2014
Wayfinding, Stevenson, Johannesburg
Mavambo Erwendo, Stevenson, Cape Town

2012
Duo: Virginia Chihota and Portia Zvavahera, Gallery Delta, Harare

2010
Under My Skin, National Gallery of Zimbabwe, Harare

SELECTED GROUP EXHIBITIONS

2024
Forbidden Territories: 100 Years of Surreal Landscapes, The Hepworth Wakefield
My Last Will, Casino Luxembourg – Forum d'art contemporain
Revered and Feared: Feminine Power in Art and Belief, CaixaForum Madrid and Barcelona

2023
My Last Will, Kunstsammlung Chemnitz
Making Their Mark, Shah Garg Foundation, New York
Brave New World – 16 Painters for the 21st Century, Museum de Fundatie, Zwolle
If You Look Hard Enough, You Can See Our Future: Contemporary South African Art from the Nando's Art Collection, African American Museum, Dallas, TX
The Artist List, Stevenson, Cape Town

2022
The Milk of Dreams, 59th Venice Biennale
Where do I begin, Stevenson, Cape Town
Vessels, David Zwirner, London
I See You, Tiwani Contemporary, Lagos

2021
The Power of My Hands, Musée d'Art Moderne de Paris
my whole body changed into something else, Stevenson, Cape Town

2020
Allied with Power: African and African Diaspora Art from the Jorge M. Pérez Collection, Pérez Art Museum, Miami, FL
Psychic Wounds: On Art & Trauma, The Warehouse, Dallas, TX
Witness: Afro Perspectives from the Jorge M. Pérez Collection, El Espacio 23, Miami, FL
This Corrosion, Modern Art, Helmet Row, London

2019
Future Genealogies: Tales from the Equatorial Line, 6th Lubumbashi Biennale
Moshekwa Langa, Viviane Sassen, and Portia Zvavahera, Andrew Kreps Gallery,New York
Crossing Boundaries, Gallery Delta, Harare
State Your Intentions: New Works in the WAM Collection, Weisman Art Museum, University of Minnesota, MN

2018
We don't need another hero, 10th Berlin Biennale
Five Bhobh – Painting at the End of an Era, Zeitz Museum of Contemporary Art Africa, Cape Town
Hacer Noche/Crossing Night, Centro Cultural Santo Domingo, Oaxaca
The Fabric of Felicity, Garage Museum of Contemporary Art, Moscow
The Assassination of Leon Trotsky, David Lewis Gallery, New York
9 More Weeks, Stevenson, Johannesburg
Talisman in the Age of Difference, Stephen Friedman Gallery, London
Both, and, Stevenson, Cape Town

2017
The Contested Body, Minneapolis Institute of Art, MN
A Painting Today, Stevenson, Cape Town
Identity, Gallery Delta, Harare

2016
Body Luggage: Migration of Gestures, Steirischer Herbst Festival, Graz
I Love You Sugar Kane, Institute of Contemporary Art Indian Ocean, Port Louis
The Quiet Violence of Dreams, Stevenson, Cape Town
Exchange, Galerie Hans Mayer, Düsseldorf
Gallery Delta Benefit/Collector's Exhibition, Gallery Delta, Harare
What About Us?, Gallery Delta, Harare

2015
African Odysseys, Le Brass, Brussels
Liberated Subjects: Present Tense, De 11 Lijnen, Oudenburg

2014
Shifting Africa: Artistic views from the Sub-Sahara, Kunsthalle Faust, Hannover
Shifting Africa, 4th Mediations Biennale Poznań
Dudziro: Interrogating the Visions of Religious Beliefs, National Gallery of Zimbabwe, Harare
Faces of Mankind, Gallery Delta, Harare
Flashback, Gallery Delta, Harare

2013
Dudziro: Interrogating the Visions of Religious Beliefs, Zimbabwean Pavilion, 55th Venice Biennale
Variations, Gallery Delta, Harare
You and I, Gallery Delta, Harare

2012
Idea of Self, National Gallery of Zimbabwe, Harare
The Annual Summer Exhibition 2012, Gallery Delta, Harare
Small works, Gallery Delta, Harare

2011
Zviro zviyedzwa, Dzimbanhete Arts Interactions, Harare
Beyond Borders, National Gallery of Zimbabwe, Harare
International Women's Day, National Gallery of Zimbabwe, Harare
Hope and Despair, National Gallery of Zimbabwe, Harare
Three Thoughts: Helen Lieros, Virginia Chihota and Portia Zvavahera, Gallery Delta, Harare
Art Zimbabwe Today, Gallery Delta, Harare
Colour Africa 2011, Gallery Delta, Harare
The Landscape in All Seasons, Gallery Delta, Harare
Past and Present, Gallery Delta, Harare
Still Life/Objects, Gallery Delta, Harare

2010
Another Perspective, Gallery 23, Amsterdam
35 Years, Gallery Delta, Harare
The Annual Summer Exhibition 2010, Gallery Delta, Harare
Live and Direct, National Gallery of Zimbabwe, Harare
Small Works 2010, Gallery Delta, Harare

2009
Ubuntu, National Gallery of Zimbabwe, Harare
Strength, National Art Gallery of Zimbabwe, Bulawayo
Unity, Gallery Delta, Harare
Expressions of Zimbabwe, University of Avignon
Tri-Lingual, Greatmore Studios, Cape Town
Structures, Gallery Delta, Harare
The Annual Summer Exhibition 2009, Gallery Delta, Harare
34 Years Plus – The Gallery Delta Benefit Exhibition, Gallery Delta, Harare

2008
Drawings and Graphics, Gallery Delta, Harare
Enriching Women, Gallery Delta, Harare
Post Election Selection, Gallery Delta, Harare

2007
Peace Through Unity in Diversity, Gallery Delta, Harare

2006
Persistence, National Art Gallery of Zimbabwe, Mutare

AWARDS

2014
FNB Art Prize, Joburg Art Fair

2013
Tollman Award for the Visual Arts

RESIDENCIES

2022
Guest Artists Space, Lagos

2019
Lubumbashi Biennale

2018
1 Shanthi Road Studio Gallery, Bangalore

2017
Gasworks, London

2012
History/Matters, Centre for Contemporary Art, Lagos

2009
Greatmore Studios, Cape Town

2008
National Gallery of Zimbabwe, Harare
Dzimbanhete Arts Interactions, Harare

SELECTED PUBLIC COLLECTIONS

Johannesburg Art Gallery
Minneapolis Institute of Art, MN
National Gallery of Zimbabwe, Harare
Pérez Art Museum Miami, FL
Tate, London
University of Chicago Booth School of Business, IL
Weisman Art Museum, University of Minnesota, MN

BIBLIOGRAPHY
MONOGRAPHS

2022
Portia Zvavahera, text by Meredith A Brown, interview by Allie Biswas, David Zwirner, London

2017
I'm with You, text by Nomaduma Rosa Masilela, Stevenson, Cape Town

2014
Wayfinding, interview by Lerato Bereng, Stevenson, Cape Town

SELECTED BOOKS AND EXHIBITION CATALOGUES

2023
Godfrey, Mark, and Katy Siegel (eds), *Making Their Mark: Art by Women in the Shah Garg Collection*, text by Allie Biswas, Gregory R Miller, New York
M+M (eds), *My Last Will*, Verlag der Buchhandlung Walther und Franz König, Cologne

2022
59th Venice Biennale: The Milk of Dreams, La Biennale di Venezia
Great Women Painters, texts by Alison M Gingeras, Phaidon Press, London

2021
Morrill, Rebecca, and Simon Hunegs (eds), *African Artists from 1882 to Now*, Phaidon Press, London
Delahunty, Gavin (ed.), *Psychic Wounds: On Art & Trauma*, texts by Carolyn Christov-Bakargiev,

Huey Copeland, Gavin Delahunty (et al.), MW Editions/The Warehouse, Dallas

2018
9 More Weeks, interview by Sinazo Chiya, Stevenson, Cape Town
Mutumba, Yvette, and Gabi Ngcobo, *We don't need another hero: 10th Berlin Biennale*, DISTANZ Verlag, Berlin

2013
Chikukwa, Raphael, *Dudziro*: *Interrogating the Visions of Religious Beliefs*, Edizioni Charta Srl, Milan

SELECTED ARTICLES AND REVIEWS

2023
Harris, Gareth, 'January Book Bag: from Californian counterculture to intimate artist portraits by the likes of Tacita Dean', *The Art Newspaper*, 10 Jan

2022
Gronlund, Melissa, 'Venice Biennale's main show "The Milk of Dreams" highlights great artists often overlooked', *The National News*, 28 Apr
Herriman, Kat, 'The Body Creates and Inspires at the 2022 Venice Biennale', *Cultured Mag*, 21 Apr

2021
Hine, Will, 'Portia Zvavahera's Spectral Dream Worlds Arrive in New York', *Ocula*, 18 Sep

2020
Bailey, Stephanie, 'Portia Zvavahera's Painted Dreams', *Ocula*, 22 Sep
Rea, Naomi, 'Studio Visit: Zimbabwean Artist Portia Zvavahera on Why She Had to Escape to the Mountains to Create Her New Show at David Zwirner', *Artnet News*, 31 Aug

2019
Joja, Athi Mongezeleli, 'Portia Zvavahera', *Artforum*, Sep
Elizabeth, Marcia, '"Talitha Cumi" by Portia Zvavahera: Painting figures of spiritual transcendence', *Bubblegum Club*, 30 May
Moloi, Nkgopoleng, 'Sacred shapes, transcendent paint: Portia Zvavahera's "Talitha Cumi"', *ArtThrob*, 30 May
Hlalethwa, Zaza, 'Portia Zvavahera: In the world – but not of it', *Mail and Guardian*, 24 May

2018
O'Toole, Sean, 'Portia Zvavahera', *Frieze*, 18 Jan

2017
Mabandu, Percy, 'Clawing at the sublime', *Sunday Times*, 15 Jan
Mathabathe, Gontse, 'Between love and dreams: Portia Zvavahera's What I See Beyond Feeling', *ArtThrob*, 23 Jan

2016
Mashabela, Khanya, 'Celebration and speculation: Koloane, Masamvu and Zvavahera', *ArtThrob*, 5 Sep
Sosibo, Kwanele, 'Zim artists see with spiritual eyes', *Mail and Guardian*, 30 Nov

2015
Blackman, Matthew, 'Portia Zvavahera: I Can Feel It in My Eyes', *Art Review*, Oct
Netsayi, 'Interview – Art: Portia Zvavahera', *Bomb*, Winter 2015/2016
Kuijers, Isabella, 'Dreams of summer and love', *ArtThrob*, 24 Aug
Fikeni, Lwandile, 'Of Love and Loss', *City Press*, 16 Aug
Jolly, Lucinda, 'Unique Afro-expressionist style', *Cape Times*, 6 Aug
Jamal, Ashraf, 'Twin exhibitions conjure the depth of feeling love and loss', *Business Day*, 31 Jul
Leiman, Layla, 'Portia Zvavahera Dreams of Exotic Blossoms of Love', *Between 10 and 5*, 31 Jul
Farago, Jason, 'Frieze New York review: Navigating the maze of art fair's eccentric fun', *The Guardian*, 14 May
Colvin, Rob, 'Painting According to Frieze New York', *Hyperallergic*, 15 May

2014
'2014 FNB art prize winner: Portia Zvavahera', *Elle Decoration*, 18 Aug
Mabandu, Percy, 'Wayfinding: Portia Zvavahera', *ArtThrob*, 1 Aug

2013
'Portia Zvavahera awarded the 2013 Tollman Award', *ArtThrob*, 27 Sep

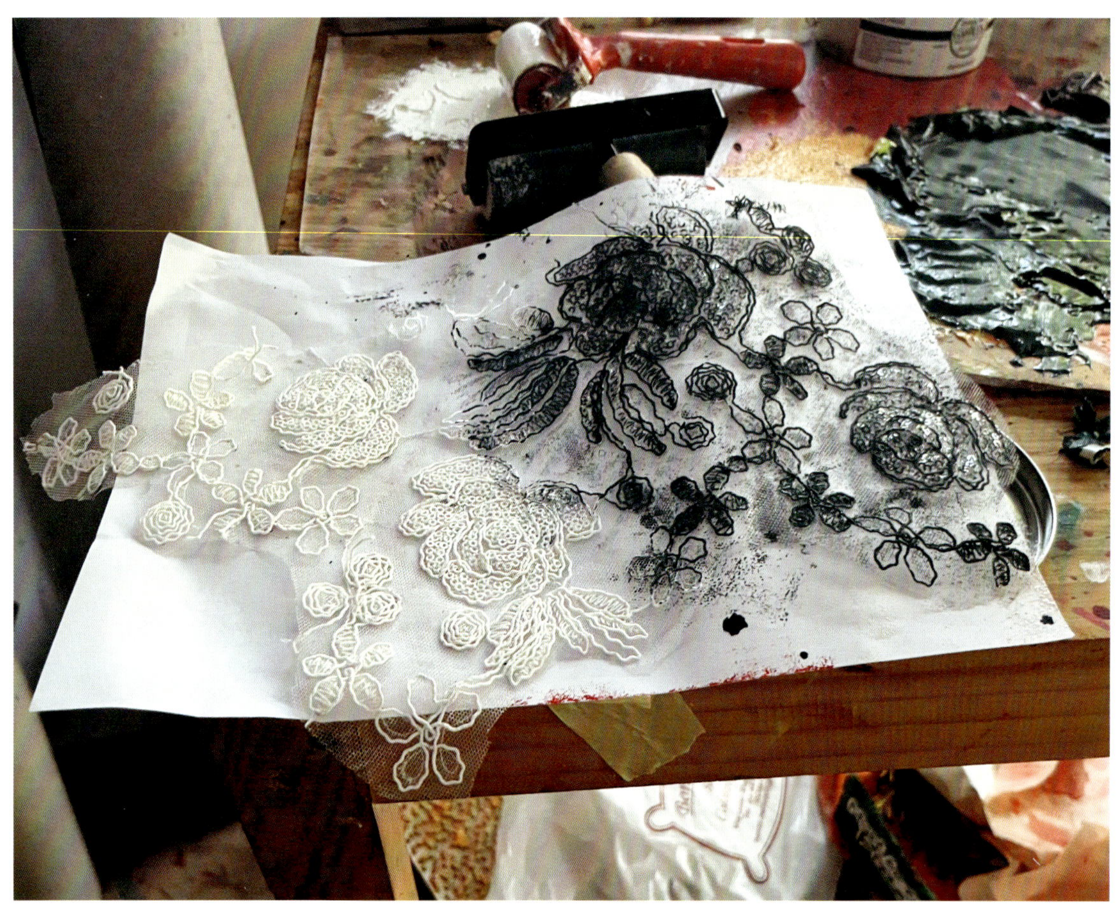

above and opposite:
Studio view, Harare, 2024
overleaf: ***Lifted Away***
2024 (detail)

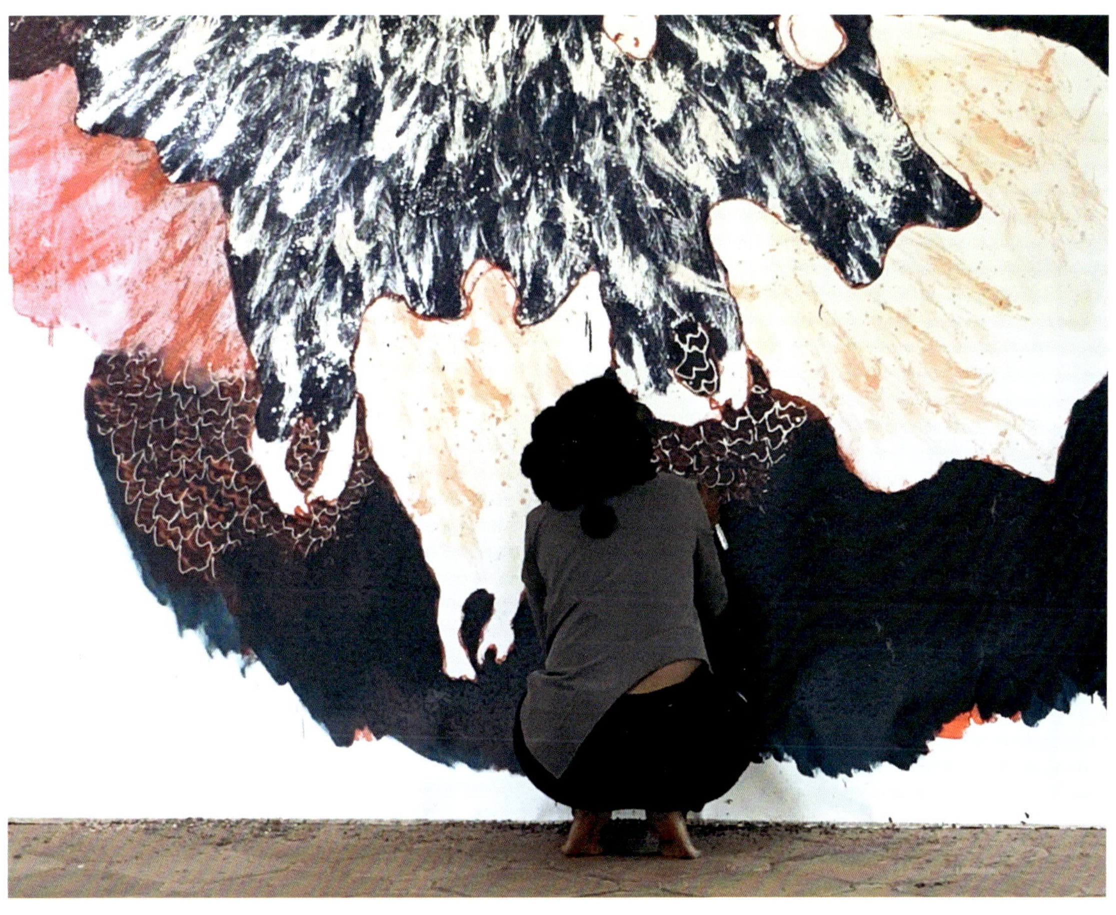

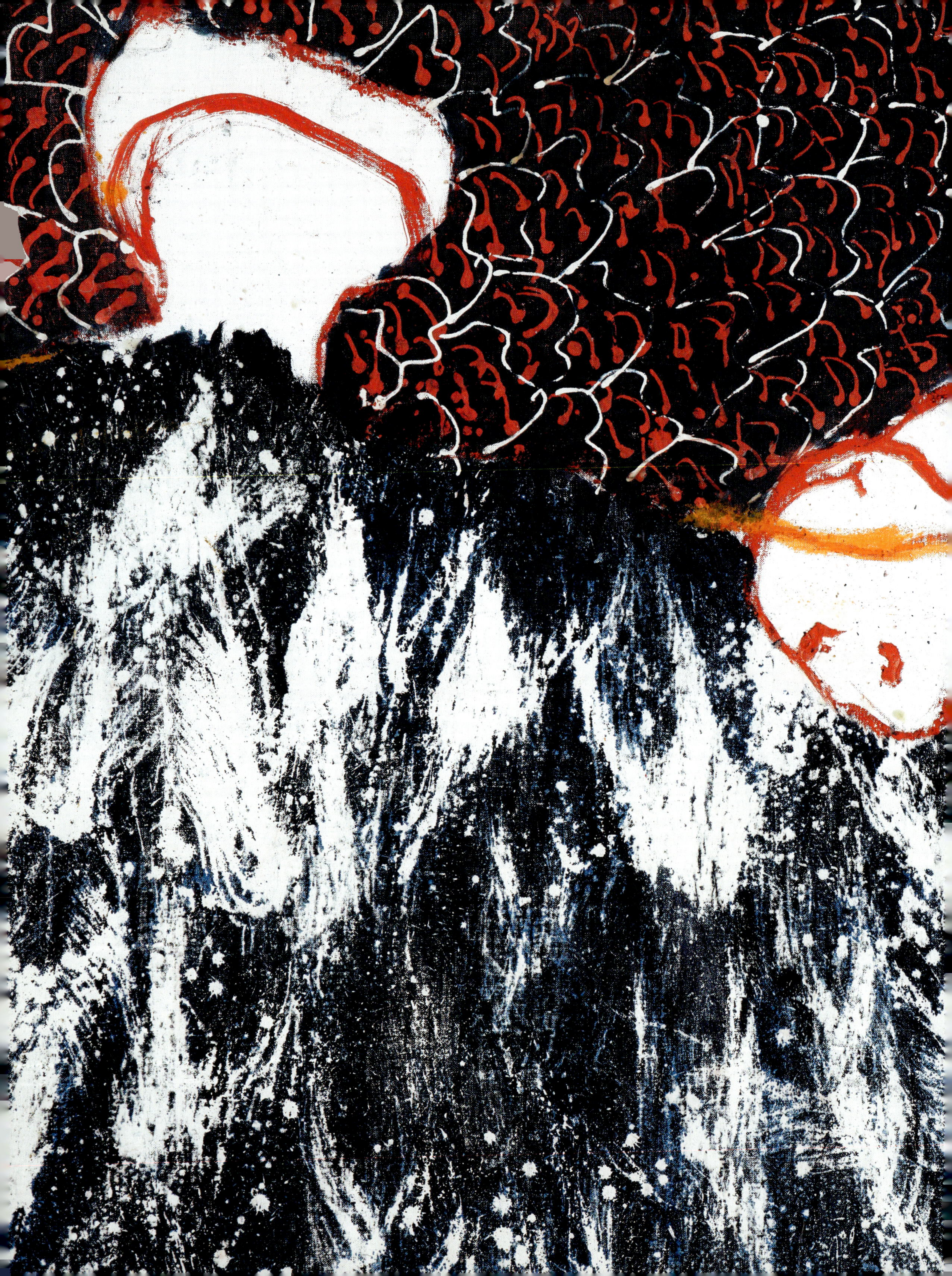

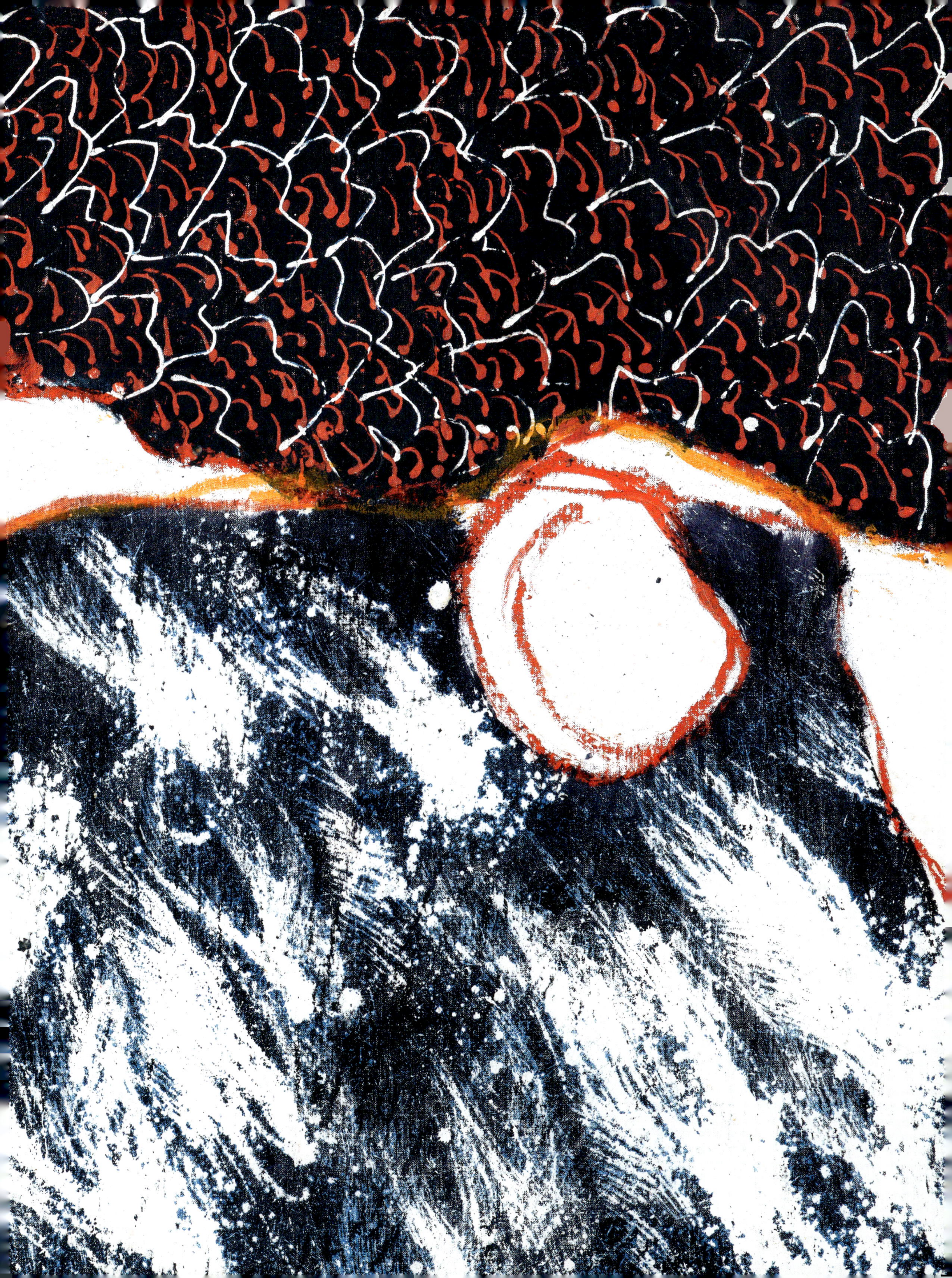

ACKNOWLEDGEMENTS

Fruitmarket
45 Market St.
Edinburgh, EH1 1DF
Tel: +44 (0)131 225 2383
www.fruitmarket.co.uk

The generosity of our supporters keeps our creative programme ambitious, free and accessible to all.

Programme Supporters:
Art Fund
Association for Cultural Enterprises
Bloomberg
Cordis Charitable Trust
Dr Guthrie's Association
EVOC (Edinburgh Voluntary Organisations' Council)
Garfield Weston Foundation
Henry Moore Foundation
Longrow Capital
Jane Hamlyn, Frith Street Gallery
Paul Hamlyn Foundation
Queensberry House Trust
Radcliffe Trust
RS Macdonald Charitable Trust
Thomas Dane Gallery
Vaughan Williams Foundation
White Cube
The Viewforth Trust
William Grant Foundation
William Syson Foundation
The Wolfson Foundation

Fruitmarket Council:
Richard Burns
Kave Sigaroudinia
Nick Thomas
Manuela Wirth

Programme Patrons:
Martin Adam and William Zachs
Elizabeth Cowling
Gail and Lindsay Gardiner
Lee Qian

Patrons:
Nan and Robin Arnott
Robin Bryson-Jack
Sophie Crichton Stuart
Tio Burnett Ainsworth
Catherine Holden
Florence and Richard Ingleby
Callum Innes
Werner Keschner and Catherine Muirden
Judy Riley
Karen Smith and Frank Krikhaar
Silvy Weatherall
Nicky Wilson

and all those who wish to remain anonymous

Fruitmarket Staff:
Fiona Bradley: Director
Ruth Bretherick: Research and Public Engagement Curator
Julia Carruthers: Visitor Experience Manager
Allison Everett: Buying and Retail Manager
Susan Gladwin: Print and Digital Designer
Kathleen Glancy: Development Manager (Trusts and Foundations)
Elizabeth McLean: Deputy Director
Davide Minuti: Exhibition Organiser
Tracy Morgan: Community Engagement Manager
Iain Morrison: Partnerships Curator
Amy Murray-O'Keeffe: Development Manager (Sponsorship and Individuals)
Matt Peet: AV and Digital Technician
Calum Rennie: Creative Learning Assistant
Zivile Siutilaite: Enterprise Coordinator
Armida Taylor: Head of Operations
Calum Thom: Gallery Manager
Louise Warmington: Head of Communications
Eleanor Williams: Administrator
Sam Woods: Curator
Colin MacFarlane: Senior Installation Technician Dino Forte, Danny Holcroft, Jonny Lyons, Duncan Marquiss, Campbell Sandilands, Graham Taylor: Installation Technicians
August Dawn, Evelyn Law, Kat Stanley: Duty Managers
Eleanor Affleck, Astrid Batts, Francesca Bruno, Sarah Calmus, Alyesha Choudhury, Andrew Gannon, Zoe Hay, Lindsay Hutchison, Jamal Abdul Jabbar, Gabriel Levine Brislin, Kate Livingstone, Benoît Loiret, Ines Mulford, Calum Rennie: Information Assistants
Martin Collins: Head Chef
Mehan McNab: Sous Chef
Thomas Castellani, Moya Cruden, Dimitrios Zacharopoulos: Chefs
Susan Clark: Kitchen Assistant
Craig Wheatley: Café Manager
Jaime Molina: Café Assistant Manager
Niamh Campbell, Matilda Kay, Lucy Kennedy, Keir Lynn, Esteban Mariño, Cabhan Marr, William Sherval, Junaina Valappil: Waiting Staff

Fruitmarket is a company limited by guarantee, registered in Scotland No. 87888 and registered as a Scottish charity No. SC 005576. VAT No. 398 2504 21

Registered Office:
45 Market St.,
Edinburgh, EH1 1DF

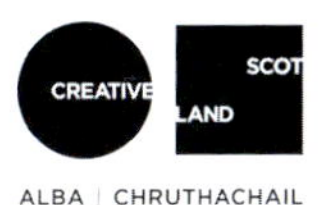

KETTLE'S YARD

Kettle's Yard
University of Cambridge
Castle St., Cambridge
CB3 0AQ
Tel: +44 (0)1223 748100
www.kettlesyard.cam.ac.uk

Kettle's Yard relies on the generosity of supporters to care for the collection and historic buildings, and to offer a full programme of activities, from exhibitions, learning activities and music, to publications and research. All gifts, large and small, help to safeguard the collection for future generations, and enable others to enjoy Kettle's Yard now and in the future

There are a variety of ways in which you can help support Kettle's Yard and also benefit as a UK or US taxpayer. For more information please visit www.kettlesyard.cam.ac.uk/join-support/

Kettle's Yard Portia Zvavahera Supporters Circle:
Carol Atack and Alex van Someren
Salim Currimjee
Emma Davis
Sabine Jaccaud
Katie Robyns
and those who wish to remain anonymous

Director's Circle:
Dr Carol Atack and Alex van Someren, Lily Bacon and Dr Andy Harter CBE, Sir Charles and Lady Chadwyck-Healey, John and Jennifer Crompton, Sarah and Gerard Griffin, Ruth Rattenbury, Samantha de Reus and Felix Zhang, Robert Sansom and Edith Eligator, Guy Vesey, Tamsin and Stewart Wilkinson and those who wish to remain anonymous.

Ede Circle:
Michael Allen OBE and Marjolein Wytzes, Stuart Ansell, Roger Bamber and Nicky Napier, Dr Sophie Bowness, Dr David Cleevely CBE and Rosalind Cleevely, Eve Corder, Nicholas Crompton, Jennifer Crouch, Dr Claire and Professor Martin Daunton, Emma Davis, Sean Gorvy, Tim Llewellyn OBE, Anne Lonsdale CBE, Nicki and Christie Marrian, James and Melanie McLaren, Suling Mead, Professor Keith Moffat, Marc and Rachel Polonsky, Jonathan and Nicole Scott, Professor Elizabeth Simpson OBE, Robin Vousden, Lord Wilson of Dinton and those who wish to remain anonymous

The Friends of Kettle's Yard

Corporate Supporters:
Anna's Flower Farm
A Practice for Everyday Life
City Asset Management
David Zwirner
Murray Edward's College
Resolute AV

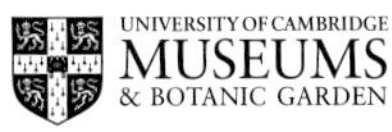

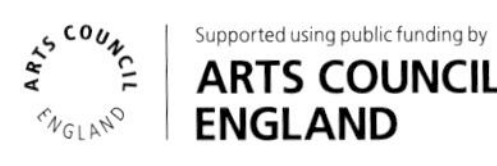

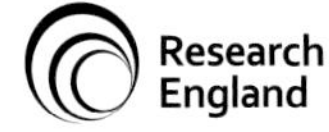

Chris Dean, Miriam Goddard, Yasemin Gyford, Antonia Leslie, Beth Hague, Rebecca Lindum Greene, My Linh Le, Katie Maynard, Shirley-Anne McAndrew, Elizabeth McDonald, Mac McNaughton, Adéla Minaříková, Alison McTaggart, Amie Monteclavo, Phil Neale, Aaron Ossia, Jack Pate, Sabrina Rippon, Sergio Santos, Hitomi Shinozaki, Andrew Smith, Kim Watson, Sid White-Jones: Visitor Assistants

Florence Austin, Liz Bouyea, Kiarash Khazaei: Retail Assistants

Photography by:
Anna Arca
Stephen Arnold
Gideon Gomo
Jack Hems
Anthea Pokroy
Mario Todeschini